PERFECTING THE AMERICAN STEAM LOCOMOTIVE

Railroads Past and Present
Edited by George M. Smerk

Perfecting the
American
Steam
Locomotive

J. Parker Lamb

INDIANA
University Press

Bloomington & Indianapolis

This book is a publication of

Indiana University Press
601 North Morton Street
Bloomington, Indiana 47404-3797 USA

http://iupress.indiana.edu

Telephone orders 800-842-6796
Fax orders 812-855-7931
Orders by e-mail iuporder@indiana.edu

The paper used in this publication meets the minimum requirements of American National Standard for Information Sciences—Permanence of Paper for Printed Library Materials, ANSI Z39.48-1984.

Library of Congress Cataloging-in-Publication Data

Lamb, J. Parker
Perfecting the American steam locomotive / J. Parker Lamb.
p. cm. — (Railroads past and present)
ISBN 0-253-34219-8 (cloth : alk. paper)
1. Steam locomotives—United States. I. Title. II. Series.
TJ603.4.A45 L36 2003
625.26'1'0973—dc 21 2002152284

1 2 3 4 5 08 07 06 05 04 03

Frontis: A steam locomotive at work presents a classic silhouette. Here is former Southern Pacific Mikado No. 786 near Burnet, Texas on a tourist train in 1991. J. Parker Lamb.

From my earliest years I was fascinated with machines and extremely curious about how they worked. My introduction to science and mathematics in high school afforded me an opportunity to begin to answer such questions, and ultimately led to a lifetime of engineering practice. Thus I wish to dedicate this book to the diligent high school and college teachers who facilitated my early intellectual development.

———————————————

CONTENTS

Preface
ix

Acknowledgments
xi

Introduction: Components of a Locomotive
1

1. The Steam Epoch Begins
5

2. American Designs Evolve
15

3. The Physics of Steam Power
33

4. The Second Generation
47

5. Motive Power Mavericks
69

6. Dawn of a New Era
83

7. Super Power Reigns
93

8. The Pinnacle of Design
131

9. Steam Technology's Final Thrusts
153

10. American Steam in Perspective
169

Appendix A:
Description of Steam Locomotive Components
175

Appendix B:
Service and Repair Facilities
185

References
189

Index
191

PREFACE

I was somewhat surprised when, during a chance meeting in 1999 with George M. Smerk and William D. Middleton, they mentioned the possibility of a book project for the Railroads Past and Present series of Indiana University Press. Even though I had not published in the area, I was asked to consider doing a book about the development of the steam locomotive, emphasizing the role of mechanical engineering in the evolution of this technology. Despite my initial misgivings that it would be difficult to add anything of significance to the extensive literature on this subject, I later agreed to prepare a proposal to the Press during my first year of retirement.

Unfortunately this phase of my life began with a period of recuperation from a heart attack. However, the extended period of inactivity created an excellent opportunity to begin background research on steam locomotives. Using first my own references and then borrowing from friends, and finally expanding my search to major libraries, I was soon deeply enmeshed in the fascinating history of the American steam locomotive. My initial concept envisioned a book highlighting the engineering achievements of the so-called super power era that began at the Lima Locomotive Works in 1922. However, it soon became evident that a more valuable contribution would cover the entire story, including both the beginning and the ending of the steam epoch in America. Therefore this volume begins with the Industrial Revolution and ends almost 250 years later with the unsuccessful attempts to build locomotives powered by steam turbines.

The primary audience for this book is a new generation of readers who have few, if any, personal experiences of the steam era. To this end I have introduced the subject at a descriptive level, and have included extensive tutorial material as well as a higher level of scientific detail than is usual for a general book. My reason for this was to allow readers to know exactly why certain design choices were made, as well as to emphasize scientific limits on the design process. I do not think, however, that a lack of background in technology will hamper anyone's overall understanding of the material.

Wherever possible I have highlighted those visionaries, designers, and builders who were the originators of significant innovations or improvements. This information enables readers to comprehend the extremely slow and somewhat chaotic process of technical evolution, including many experimental developments that were short lived or, at best, only marginally successful.

In addition to analyzing the design process and highlighting its major contributors, I have included extensive commentary on the corporate culture and operating patterns of both builders and railroads. Moreover, the text correlates the development of the steam locomotive with the parallel evolution of technical education that produced the inventive designers and builders who made that development possible. As a member of the American Society of Mechanical Engineers since 1953, I have noted this organization's critical role in the steam era, first as a protector of public safety, then as a facilitator of information exchange among a wide range of people such as academic researchers, designers, builders, and railroads, and finally as an archivist of its heritage.

ACKNOWLEDGMENTS

I am greatly indebted to those who have chronicled the steam locomotive with such breadth that hardly a gap exists. In this work I have relied on the thorough historical treatises of Professor John White, the comprehensive technical summaries of Alfred Bruce, Ralph Johnson, and Linn Westcott, the extremely detailed locomotive studies of Guy Dunscomb, Eric Hirsimaki, Gene Huddleston, Robert LeMassena, and Fred Westing, and finally the romantic prose of Lucius Beebe and David Morgan. It was Morgan's chronicles on steam that first made a deep impression on me as a teenager. As the longtime editor of *Trains* magazine, he also enlisted many of those just mentioned to write for this magazine, read by professional railroaders as well as avocational enthusiasts with a thirst for railroad history.

The broad coverage of this volume was made possible through the valuable assistance of an equally wide spectrum of historians, photographers, and photograph collectors. It is a pleasure to acknowledge their support. Those who provided specific locomotive data, or access to technical references, include Greg Ames (Barriger Library), Tom Balzen, John Corns, John Howell, Jim Fair, Ken Harrison, Robert Macdonald, Louis Marre, Jim Mischke, Mike Palmieri, David Price, Philip Schmidt, and Richard Tower. The author's meager collection of vintage steam photographs was expanded enormously through the generous cooperation of prominent photographers of the 1950s and 1960s, including Joe Collias, Stan Kistler, William Middleton, David Salter, Jim Shaughnessy, and Philip Weibler.

In addition a significant number of illustrations were contributed by a younger generation of collectors, including Ed Bowers, Eric Hirsimaki, Louis Saillard, and Jay Williams. From these collections we are able to appreciate again many classical images from early-twentieth-century photographers, including such names as Frank Ardrey, Gerald Best, A. E. Brown, Bruce Fales, Robert Foster, Preston George, and C. W. Witbeck. To complete the photographic coverage, I was fortunate to enlist the assistance of Ray George and Charles Marsh, along with Kevin Keefe and Rob McGonigal of Kalmbach Publishing, and Mark Reutter of the Railway & Locomotive Historical Society.

In this age of digital imaging, the preservation and use of antique photographs has become quite practical, and was of particular benefit in the present endeavor. I am deeply indebted to two experts, Tony Howe and Robert Macdonald, for their critically important efforts. Howe, an accomplished railroad painter, not only prepared the line art in digital form, but also scanned images from the David Price collection, whereas Macdonald, an expert on image rehabilitation, produced dozens of "like new" scenes from prints made between 1920 and 1950.

PERFECTING THE AMERICAN STEAM LOCOMOTIVE

Atlantic Coast Line engine
No. 1696, shown at Albany,
Georgia in 1946, illustrates
major components of an
American steam locomotive
circa 1925. David W. Salter.

INTRODUCTION

Components of a Locomotive

The role played by North American railroads in developing a transcontinental transportation network in the nineteenth century represents a glorious chapter in the history of human technical achievements. As succeeding generations of historians and rail enthusiasts have recounted the events of this important era, their interest has often been centered on the famous men who financed, owned, or built the early railroads, or the political leaders whose decisions were crucial to the legal framework of the railroad system. Others have documented in detail the design features and construction techniques for the machines that powered the railroads for over 120 years.

In contrast, much less attention has been focused on the large corps of technical talent that emerged during these early years and which constituted the brains behind the actual construction of the nation's rail system and its rolling stock. Two of the earliest branches of engineering were largely responsible for these achievements. The first, civil engineers, who can trace their heritage to the builders of the Egyptian pyramids, were necessary to plan and construct the rail routes over all types of terrain, including formidable natural barriers such as rivers, mountains, and deserts. A recent volume by William D. Middleton, *Landmarks on the Iron Road*, describes the spectacular achievements of this group.

The second branch was mechanical engineering, which emerged directly from the Industrial Revolution that began in England during the early part of the eighteenth century when machines were first designed and constructed to replace the physical effort of men and animals. The most significant machine of the Industrial Revolution was the stationary steam engine, which quickly found numerous applications in transportation propulsion. In this book we will review the evolution of the American steam locomotive, with emphasis on the period after 1920 when these machines reached their pinnacle of design and performance.

The discussion will present insights into the fundamental sciences underlying the design of steam locomotives, enabling us to "get into the heads" of the innovative mechanical engineers who produced these remarkable vehicles, and see clearly how they solved vexing design problems to meet the demands for low initial cost, ease of maintenance, and high fuel economy, as well as to accommodate limited mainline clearances, low track loading, and extensive grades or line curvature. Their collective innovation led to the world's most advanced steam locomotives, perhaps the grandest legacies of the Industrial Revolution.

Because some readers may not be familiar with these machines, we begin by describing the general features of a steam locomotive, using the accompanying photograph of Atlantic Coast Line engine No. 1696 for reference. Additional details are presented in appendix A, which includes illustrations and a description of components. Readers are urged to consult this section as they maneuver through the text. As suggested by the reference photograph, a locomotive consists essentially of two major assemblies, in which a cylindrical boiler sits atop a set of wheels, some of which are much larger than others. The purpose of the boiler is to *generate steam*. While the wheels support the weight, their primary role is to *convert the energy of steam* into rotation of the large driving wheels (or *drivers*).

At the rear of the boiler, its end enclosed by the crew cab, is the *firebox* (or furnace), in which a fuel is burned to produce hot gas. The boiler itself contains many small tubes through which the hot combustion gas flows, and around which there is water. Hot gas inside each passage heats each steel tube. In turn, the outer surfaces of the hot tubes heat the surrounding water, eventually causing small bubbles of steam vapor to form on the surface of the tube. These small bubbles percolate upward and coagulate into larger pockets of vapor. Eventually the vapor, being highly buoyant, will rise to the *steam dome*, the highest point in the boiler, seen in the photograph above the third set of drivers. The steam is now ready to pass through the throttle mechanism into the conversion component of the locomotive.

Meanwhile, after heating the water, the combustion gases exhaust from the tubes into a chamber at the front of the boiler (*smokebox*) and, merging with the exhaust steam from the power cylinders, escape through the stack into the atmosphere. The escaping exhaust steam also creates a strong draft that pulls the hot gas from the firebox through the boiler tubes. The larger housing on top of the boiler (above the first driver) is the *sand dome*. The two pipes running downward from this container allow sand to be sprayed onto the rails in front of the drivers. The dusting of sand increases friction on the drivers and prevents them from slipping when the rail is wet or the locomotive is pulling up a steep grade. The small housing above the firebox encloses the safety valves (*pop valves*) that will open if the boiler pressure rises to an unsafe level. The round object next to the pop valve is a steam-driven electric generator that supplies power for lights and other needs.

Below each side of the smokebox is a power cylinder containing a large piston that is driven by high-pressure steam from the boiler. The piston produces a reciprocating motion, which must be converted into the rotating motion of the drivers. This is accomplished by connecting the piston rod with a *crankpin* on the driver by means of the main driving rod (or *main rod*). As the illustration shows, the crankpins are located slightly off-center on each driver so that the reciprocating piston causes the driver to rotate. The front end of the main rod is connected to the piston rod by the *crosshead*. The main driver transmits force to the other drivers through *side rods*.

Controlling the flow of steam into, and away from, each cylinder is a reciprocating valve located in the upper portion of the power cylinder housing. The valve motion is modulated by a complicated set of mechanical links known collectively as the *valve gear*. These links are visible outside the first two drivers. The function of this linkage is to control the timing of steam admission into the power cylinder at the beginning of a stroke as well as its exhaust at the end of the stroke.

Although not apparent when observing a steam locomotive during operation, the strokes of the power pistons on each side of the locomotive are *not* synchronized. Thus, when one piston is at the end of its stroke, the other is in mid-stroke. This requires that the drivers on one side be "out of phase" from those on the opposite side by 90 degrees (one-quarter rotation). As can be easily recognized, if the strokes were simultaneous, there would be no force to move the drivers in the proper direction at the beginning or end of each stroke. As anyone who has ridden a steam locomotive will attest, these alternating piston strokes impart a significant (and periodic) sideways oscillation to the engine as it moves.

One of the most important visual features of a steam locomotive is the *wheel arrangement*, which largely determines its primary usage. Traditionally, passenger locomotives had large-diameter drivers that allowed high-speed operation. In contrast, engines used in mainline freight or yard-switching service generally rode on small-diameter drivers that produced more pulling force but at a slower speed than larger ones.

Table I-1
Summary of Wheel Arrangements

OOO	0-6-0	Six-wheel switcher
OOOO	0-8-0	Eight-wheel switcher
o OOO	2-6-0	Mogul
o OOO o	2-6-2	Prairie
o OOOO	2-8-0	Consolidation
o OOOO o	2-8-2	Mikado
o OOOO oo	2-8-4	Berkshire
o OOOOO	2-10-0	Decapod
o OOOOO o	2-10-2	Santa Fe
o OOOOO oo	2-10-4	Texas
oo OO	4-4-0	American
oo OO o	4-4-2	Atlantic
oo OOO	4-6-0	Ten wheeler
oo OOO o	4-6-2	Pacific
oo OOO oo	4-6-4	Hudson
oo OOOO	4-8-0	Twelve wheeler
oo OOOO o	4-8-2	Mountain
oo OOOO oo	4-8-4	Northern

The number of drivers and supporting wheels was also a function of the locomotive's usage. A set of small wheels in front of (or below) the power cylinders was known as the *leading truck,* whereas those behind the drivers formed the *trailing truck.* A two-wheel lead truck (often called a *pony truck*) was often used on freight locomotives, while a four-wheel arrangement was commonly applied to passenger power. Trailing trucks could also be either two- or four-wheel designs. In addition to carrying a portion of the engine weight, leading trucks also served an important function in steering the engine around curves at speed. Yard switchers generally had no other support wheels, in order to maximize the weight over the drivers and hence the engine's pulling power.

The crescent-shaped pieces appearing at the bottom of each driving wheel in the photograph are *counterweights* whose function is to balance the rotating forces produced by side rod connections on the upper side of the driver. It can be seen that the main driver counterweight is larger than the other two since it must counterbalance not only the side rod but also the main rod connection. Also notice the group of small dots on the lower side of the firebox. These represent rivets and staybolts that hold the firebox together and connect it to the boiler shell. There are many other such connections that do not appear because most of the boiler is covered with insulation beneath a sheet-metal jacket.

To classify the wheel arrangement of steam locomotives, a numerical system was devised in 1901 by the Englishman Frederic Methvane Whyte. In Europe it was customary to count axles, while the *Whyte System,* imported to the United States along with British railroad technology, counted the number of wheels. Thus we see that the engine shown here is a 4-6-2, since it includes a four-wheel leading truck, six driving wheels, and a two-wheel trailing truck. In many cases specific wheel arrangements were given names by the manufacturers. A listing of commonly used, rigid-frame wheel arrangements (and their names) is presented in Table I-1. More details on the origins of these names will be given in later sections, along with discussions of larger locomotives with articulated frames.

Another important feature of a steam locomotive was the trailing car (the *tender*) that carried water and fuel. Coal (or oil) was carried in a bunker adjacent to the cab, while water was in the lower and rearward section. Most tenders rode on a pair of four-wheel trucks, as shown, while larger ones used six-wheel trucks. Some tender designs incorporated a cylindrical tank for water, but the standard configuration was a rectangular "box" design as shown here. Switchers were often fitted with water tanks having sloping backs for better rearward visibility during switching duties.

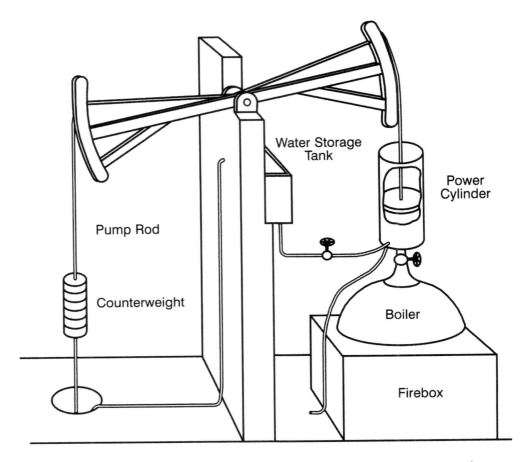

Schematic depiction of Newcomen's atmospheric engine used as a water pump in the eighteenth century. Adapted from A *Manual of the Steam Engine and Other Prime Movers*, Rankine.

CHAPTER 1

THE STEAM EPOCH
BEGINS

In the interest of completeness, some of the pioneering efforts during the early period of the Industrial Revolution will be considered. These rudimentary machines represented the highest level of technology of that era, and formed the basis for the American steam locomotive industry. However, it should be noted that early steam locomotives, although incorporating most of the elements described in the previous section, had very little physical similarity to those that eventually evolved in the United States.

The Industrial Revolution began in Great Britain, that country having the most advanced commerce and business in the eighteenth century. As Britain's industrial complexes grew ever larger, there was a critical need for power sources beyond the capabilities of men and animals, especially in mining, manufacturing, and transportation. Although numerous attempts had been made to produce a stationary engine, it fell to Thomas Newcomen, an ironworker with little formal education, and his assistant John Calley to produce in 1712 the first engine that successfully incorporated a power piston. Only a modest amount of power could be produced, since the piston motion was based on the difference between atmospheric pressure on one side and a steam-induced vacuum on the other.

Despite its low power, this engine was commercially successful as a water pump for coal mines and flooded areas behind seawalls. By the time of Newcomen's death in 1729, there were hundreds of these engines at work not only in England but also throughout Europe. The lack of power is not surprising in view of the absence of strong metals for use in boilers and power cylinders, as well as a lack of fabrication methods to produce close-fitting pistons (even if strong metals had been available). Newcomen's so-called *atmospheric engine* was of necessity quite large, since its piston force was equal to the area of the piston face multiplied by the small difference between the pressures on each side. Its single power cylinder sat approximately 34 feet above the base of the furnace (firebox), on top of which was the boiler that produced steam at a pressure near atmospheric.

With the piston at its highest position, a valve was opened to admit steam into the cylinder. As soon as the valve was closed, water (at ambient temperature) was sprayed into the cylinder, causing the steam to condense rapidly. Since, for a given amount of steam, the volume of liquid is much smaller than vapor, the condensed steam quickly drained to the bottom of the cylinder, thus producing a vacuum (or suction) on the lower piston surface. The higher pressure (atmospheric) on the upper face could then push the piston to the bottom of the cylinder, after which a counterweight on the pump rod returned the piston to its original position, thereby completing one cycle of reciprocation.

In operation each complete cycle required between 5 and 20 seconds (depending on piston size). Eventually the sequential operations of the engine were automated so that only one operator (a fireman) was needed. To perform mechanical work, such as pumping, the piston rod was attached to a pivoted *walking beam*, which actuated a pump rod extending into the volume being evacuated. Early machines had cylinder diameters of 52 inches and piston stroke lengths of 9 feet. The boiler was 18 feet in diameter and contained two flues. Within ten years of its commercial introduction, cylinder diameters had increased to 12 feet and the stroke to 10 feet. Between 1765 and 1774 John Smeaton devised a succession of improvements that brought the atmospheric engine to its highest level of development.

Credit for perfecting the early stationary steam engine is given to James Watt, a Scotsman trained at Glasgow and London as a mathematical instrument maker. While at the University of Glasgow in 1763, Watt was introduced to the Newcomen engine and began to study ways in which the concept might be further improved to provide greater power with faster operation.

With his scientific background, he eschewed the purely empirical approach used in developing previous engines, and began a series of experiments to determine the properties of steam as well as the amount of energy required to evaporate water. These studies led to a patent in 1769 for a much-improved atmospheric engine and later (1781) for a *double-acting engine* that used high-pressure steam on both sides of the power piston to double the power output. It also included a converter for turning reciprocating motion into rotary motion.

During his successful career as an engineer-inventor, Watt developed and patented many other engine-related devices such as pressure gauges, throttle valves, governors (speed regulators), and the steam hammer. For over 27 years he was a partner in Boulton & Watt, one of England's largest steam engine manufacturing firms, which by 1800 had constructed over 500 engines. After his death in 1819 at age 84, his title as the "father of the steam engine" was memorialized by a statue and a plaque at Westminster Abbey in London.

During the last decade of the eighteenth century there was much interest in using a steam engine to replace horses as the power source on existing tramways and railways. Richard Trevithick, an engine mechanic who had developed stationary engines with high boiler pressures and later worked for Boulton & Watt, became the leading proponent of using steam power for propulsion. In 1804 he constructed the first steam locomotive to pull a group of freight cars on a track, a 5-ton engine with four 56-inch, rod-connected drivers below a horizontal boiler, which was 6 feet in length and contained one U-shaped flue. Power was transmitted to the drivers by a series of gears, while a large flywheel stored rotary momentum of the mechanism.

While its 10-ton pulling power was satisfactory, the engine could not be used extensively because its weight caused widespread destruction of the cast-iron plates on which it ran. This was a problem with many early locomotives, and indeed was a harbinger of the entire history of steam locomotives, which were always destructive of their track. Unfortunately, Trevithick's business skills were much inferior to his design capabilities, and, unable to secure strong financial backing, he was forced to abandon his locomotive efforts in 1808. A major reason for this was that many of his ideas for locomotive design were stymied by patents already assigned to Boulton & Watt.

But just as Newcomen's design stimulated Watt's interest and later success, Trevithick's attempts, along with those of other locomotive developers, provided a platform for the eventual success of George Stephenson, another practical man with no formal education, but with great instincts as a mechanical designer, and later as a businessman. As an enginewright with a large coal company, he had observed the operation of an early locomotive called *Puffing Billy*, built in 1813 by Christopher Blackett and William Hedley. (This locomotive, the oldest still in existence, is in the Science Museum of London.) From his first exposure to this new type of power, Stephenson realized that a number of improvements were possible, and thus became interested in designing better locomotives for mine service. Starting in 1814 he soon completed 16 engines for various coal mines owned by his employer.

George's son Robert also exhibited a keen talent for technical work, and his father soon envisioned him as a worthy partner and successor. By age 19 Robert had completed his formal education at a leading private school. Soon he and his father began a successful collaboration that was formalized when the firm of Robert Stephenson & Company was organized in 1825 for the sole purpose of building steam locomotives, the first such company to exist. One of their initial ventures was the planning and surveying of England's first public rail line, the 25-mile-long Stockton & Darlington Railway, which opened in 1825.

The two also collaborated on the road's first locomotive, named *Locomotion*. Designed by George and built by Robert's company, it later pulled the first scheduled passenger train. Having a horizontal boiler like *Puffing Billy*, the *Locomotion* also used large, rod-controlled drivers connected to outside power cylinders. Both of these early engines proved that simple adhesion (friction between wheels and rails) was sufficient to pull a load. In contrast, earlier designs had employed rack rails and gear drives for adhesion since it was thought that smooth wheels would slip on smooth rails.

Early on, George and Robert realized that these longer runs, such as those of the S&D Railway, required a locomotive with a greater capability for generating steam, in order to avoid stops while pressure was rebuilt. This need for increased rates of steam production will resurface again and again in our review of locomotive evolution. It was one of the primary challenges to designers until the last two decades of steam engine production.

In 1827 George Stephenson designed his last engine. It was named the *Experiment*, since it incorporated a number of new features, including horizontal cylinders, a simple water preheater, and the use of small boiler tubes inside a large flue. Many of these ideas were so advanced that it would take decades for some of them to be fully perfected. After this design project, George increasingly turned his activities toward planning new railroad systems and serving as a national spokesman for railway improvements. As one of the first millionaires spawned by the Industrial Revolution, he spent his last years serving as an "elder statesman" on technical matters. Just as James Watt was considered the "father of the steam engine," George Stephenson carried the mantle of "father of the steam locomotive."

Meanwhile, Robert Stephenson was increasingly recognized as a leading designer and builder. In a competition sponsored by the Liverpool & Manchester Railway in 1829, his *Rocket* design was by far the most successful locomotive tested. With a horizontal 3-foot diameter boiler running at 50 pounds per square inch (psi), the engine had but one set of drivers (about 4 feet in diameter) plus a pair of trailing wheels. Although weighing less than 5 tons, it pulled 38 carriages (90 tons weight) at speeds of 12 to 16 mph and, without a load, could sprint as fast as 28 mph, which was a new land speed record.

The *Rocket*'s success was due largely to two new features. A *blast pipe* (exhaust nozzle) forced spent steam and flue gases out the stack with a high velocity, thereby improving the draft of air through the firebox. (This was an idea that had originated with Timothy Hackworth of the S&D Railway.) In addition Robert decided to use multiple tubes in the *Rocket*'s boiler to provide more evaporative surface, a concept developed independently and simultaneously by Marc Seguin of France.

Steam Locomotion Crosses the Atlantic

Although Robert Stephenson & Company continued building locomotives, its wealthy owner, like his father, eventually turned his interests to more global pursuits, first being elected to Parliament and later being knighted for his significant contributions to the industrial might of Great Britain. Robert also carries a historical connection with American railroading. In 1828 one of his engines was purchased by Horatio Allen, a prominent engineer from New York. The engine, named *America*, was shipped to the Delaware & Hudson Canal Company, but there are no records of where and when it operated.

Prior to buying the *America*, Allen had acquired three other engines for the D&H. These were constructed by Foster, Rastrick & Co. of Stourbridge, England in 1828. The first engine arrived in New York harbor in May 1829. Shipped by canal to Honesdale, Pennsylvania, the *Stourbridge Lion* was handled on its initial run by Allen himself, thus becoming the first steam locomotive to operate over an American railroad. Once again, the 7-ton engine weight proved to be too large for the track and trestles on the line, and it was relegated to stationary power service.

Credit for the first American-built locomotive goes to Colonel John Stevens, a distinguished engineer-inventor who, in the early 1800s, was the first major promoter of an American railway system. In 1826 he built a small demonstration locomotive at his own expense, and operated it around a circular track on his estate in Hoboken, New Jersey. Although he was unsuccessful in early attempts to gain widespread support for new railroad development, a few years after closing his demonstration line, Stevens and his sons, Edwin and Robert, founded and managed one of the nation's first railroads, the Camden & Amboy Railroad and Transportation Company (later part of the Pennsylvania Railroad).

The arrival of English locomotives also spurred a number of other American entrepreneurs into action. The first was Peter Cooper, a wealthy New York manufacturer and alderman who in 1829 built a one-ton, one-horsepower locomotive (*Tom Thumb*) to demonstrate the capabilities of steam power to the board of directors of the Baltimore & Ohio Railroad. It consisted of a vertical boiler mounted on a four-wheel car with a gear drive powering one axle. Its single cylinder was 3.5 inches in diameter with a piston stroke of 14 inches. On August 28, 1830 it pulled a carriage of passengers over B&O tracks in what was the first steam-powered passenger train on an American railroad. Although it later lost a race with a horse-drawn coach, the tiny engine had made a strong impression on the B&O brass, and thus paved the way for further development of steam power on one of America's first major railroads.

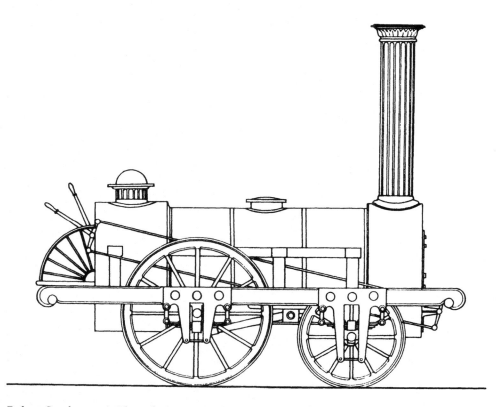

Robert Stephenson's *Planet* locomotive of 1830, a 2-2-0, was larger and much improved over his 1829 *Rocket* design, an 0-2-2. Adapted from *Pictorial History of Trains*, Hamilton.

Less than a year after *Tom Thumb*'s performance, the South Carolina Railroad began regular service with a four-wheel locomotive, *Best Friend of Charleston*, designed by E. L. Miller of Charleston and constructed by the West Point Foundry of New York City. This company also constructed the third and fourth American steam locomotives. The *West Point* was designed by Horatio Allen and built in 1830 for the South Carolina Railroad, while the *De Witt Clinton* was delivered to the Mohawk & Hudson River Railroad in 1831.

Soon both British and domestic locomotives were working on short railways up and down the eastern seaboard. Surprisingly, the total number of imported engines was only about 120, as the enterprising American mechanics and machinists quickly learned how to build these relatively simple machines. The decade of the 1830s witnessed the opening of a dozen small shops, mainly in the Northeast, for building this new generation of power that had captured the public's imagination and admiration. Suddenly, transportation by canals and roads was viewed as too slow. Thus both the commercial and public sectors of the nation became keenly interested in railroad development because it promised a faster mode of transportation. Indeed, the growth of early railroad mileage in the United States was nothing short of astounding. For example, in 1840, only 11 years after Robert Stephenson's *Rocket* design was unveiled, American rail mileage stood at 288, more than in all of Europe.

Among the first generation of early locomotive builders was Matthias William Baldwin, a former watchmaker turned machinist who had some experience in building stationary steam engines. In 1831 he was called upon to construct a small steam locomotive and carriages for public demonstration at the Philadelphia Museum. The successful performance of this model led to an order for a full-sized locomotive by the Philadelphia, Germantown & Norristown Railroad (later part of the Philadelphia & Reading Railway). Although Baldwin had recently observed the imported *John Bull* engine at work on the Camden & Amboy, he realized there was still much to learn about the manufacture of steam locomotives. Thus he made an agreement to assist the C&A, which had recently received a shipment of new (but disassembled) locomotives from English builders and needed someone to make them operational.

This valuable learning experience led in 1832 to construction of the first Baldwin locomotive, a four-wheel engine carrying a 30-inch diameter, horizontal boiler containing 72 copper tubes (1.5 inches in diameter). In appearance his 5-ton *Old Ironsides* was similar to Robert Stephenson's *Planet* of 1830, with 54-inch driving wheels and 45-inch front wheels. Cylinders were 9.5 inches in diameter, and the piston stroke was 19 inches. After entering service on the PG&N, the locomotive suffered from typical "prototype" problems that led to a strained relationship between builder and railroad, which did not think the engine's performance was commensurate with the contracted cost. After settling the dispute with a discounted price, a discouraged Baldwin remarked to one of his friends, "This is our last locomotive."

But of course that was not to be. Baldwin's disappointment soon turned to determination. And his enthusiasm soared during a visit from E. L. Miller of the South Carolina Railroad. As designer of the *Best Friend of Charleston*, Miller was able to give Baldwin some valuable advice about design improvements. Indeed, Miller soon ordered a new locomotive for his line, and it was delivered in February 1834. Using the four-wheel truck originated in 1832 by John B. Jervis, the new engine, named *E. L. Miller*, carried a 4-2-0 wheel arrangement and weighed over 7 tons. Its performance was much improved over Baldwin's initial design, and prepared the way for his lifelong devotion to the steam locomotive business that later bore his name. Indeed, the high quality of workmanship on Baldwin's initial machines quickly propelled his company into the leading position among builders, its prominence demonstrated by the production of 136 engines during the eight years following his disappointing experience with *Old Ironsides*.

Although later English and European designs were generally direct descendants of the early machines, the emergence of American builders highlighted significant differences in locomotive design philosophy between the two groups. The primary reasons for this were that (a) roadbed quality in Great Britain was much better than in the United States during these early times, (b) allowable clearances were much less in England, and (c) the average length of rail lines was many times greater in the United States. These requirements resulted in American locomotives being larger and more rugged than their English counterparts. A major difference in appearance was due to the American practice of mounting large headlights and "cowcatcher" frames (known more properly as the *pilot*) on the fronts of locomotives. Mechanically, many early English engines employed cylinders and valve gear situated inside the main frame, while this arrangement was seldom used in American locomotives after 1900.

In addition to Baldwin, two other pioneering builders of note were William Norris of Philadelphia and Thomas Rogers of Paterson, New Jersey. In 1831 Norris, the eldest of five brothers, teamed with S. H. Long, a former Army engineer, to organize the American Steam Carriage Company. In succeeding years, business fluctuations led to a number of reorganizations of the company, the last being as Richard Norris & Son in 1853. The plant was eventually bought by Baldwin in 1865, after constructing some 1200 locomotives.

A year after Norris started his company, Thomas Rogers opened a heavy machinery shop with backing from two New York financiers. The business continued to grow, even after Rogers's death in 1856 when it was renamed Rogers Locomotive & Machine Company. After the Norris shops closed in 1866, Rogers was a "solid second" in volume of production for over two decades. By 1890 its total production reached 4200, but it was later overtaken by a growing Schenectady Works for the number two spot. The company's last locomotive was produced in 1913, after which it became part of

American steam locomotive builders moved quickly to establish themselves in foreign markets. An example is this 4-2-0 engine built in 1840 by William Norris of Philadelphia for the Birmingham & Gloucester Railway in England. Note the slanted cylinders with outside drive gear, as well as the vertical firebox. Adapted from *Pictorial History of Trains*, Hamilton.

the American Locomotive Company conglomerate (usually known as Alco). Incidentally, three members of Rogers's engineering staff during the firm's last years went on to become technical leaders at other builders. Two of them moved over to Alco (J. B. Ennis, vice president for engineering, and Francis J. Cole, senior designer) and one went to Lima (W. L. Reid, vice president of manufacturing).

The next decade (1840s) saw three additional builders emerge. These were the Grant Works in Paterson, New Jersey, the Portland (Maine) Works, and the Taunton (Mass.) Works. Eventually there would be almost 150 firms from coast to coast involved in this business, but many were short lived, while others built only a few machines for local customers, or served a specialized market such as industrial engines or gear-drive locomotives. The national financial panic of 1857 wiped out a large percentage of the fledgling locomotive

Facing page, top: An 1883 rendering of Delaware & Hudson's *Stourbridge Lion*, America's first steam locomotive, reveals numerous mechanical details common to pioneering English designs, as well as the wooden rails on which they ran. At the rear of the boiler are the vertical power cylinders that drive walking beams, which in turn activate the rear drivers. Connecting rods then drive the front wheels. From *Delaware & Hudson*, Shaughnessy.

Facing page, bottom: The shop forces at Delaware & Hudson's Colonie shops in Albany, New York constructed a working replica of the company's famous *Stourbridge Lion* in 1933 for the Century of Progress Exposition in Chicago. The model now resides in the Smithsonian Museum. Jim Shaughnessy Collection.

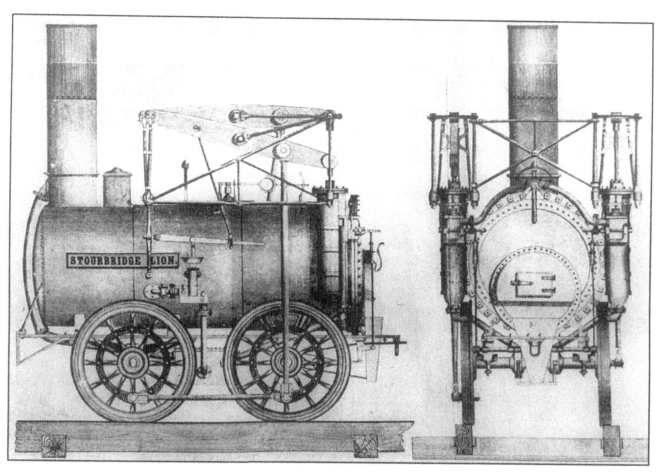

companies, as well as thousands of other businesses throughout the nation. Despite this, the decade of the 1860s saw over 4800 steam locomotives constructed in the United States. Of this total, one manufacturer was responsible for almost one-fourth. Baldwin's plant in Philadelphia had rapidly assumed a dominant position that it would maintain until the end of the steam era, 118 years after Matthias Baldwin constructed *Old Ironsides*.

In its earliest stages the American steam locomotive industry was scattered throughout 28 states stretching around the nation, from Maine to Alabama to California to Washington to Illinois. Only six states contained ten or more producers while 60 of the builders were concentrated in five states: Maryland, Massachusetts, New Jersey, New York, and Pennsylvania. Not surprisingly the Keystone State led the list with 27 entries, while the Empire State was second with 18. It is not difficult to understand this distribution, as these states were among the first to contain large commercial centers related to industrial concentrations in manufacturing, mineral extraction, metals production, and ocean-going shipping, all of which required a strong support base of heavy machinery designers and builders. For many companies the arrival of railway technology from Britain was merely one more opportunity to expand their markets.

In the 1880s, after 50 years of production, the character of the American locomotive industry began to change. Heretofore, the small locomotives could be readily assembled in modest buildings without the need for equipment with great lifting capacity. Indeed the

Three-foot-gauge, low-drivered 4-4-0 *Eureka* was built by Baldwin in 1875 as No. 4 for the Eureka & Palisade Railroad. The 22-ton wood burner still operates with its original boiler and tender. Rescued by a major film studio in 1939, it was rebuilt for movie work, but was then almost destroyed in a fire. Rescued again in 1986, it now operates regularly on tourist lines in the West. John Gruber.

Classic 4-4-0 configuration of the late nineteenth century is illustrated by Western & Atlantic No. 3, the *General*, which was rebuilt by the Louisville & Nashville in 1962 to commemorate the centennial of the "great railroad chase" in north Georgia during the Civil War. Steve Patterson, Ron Flanary Collection.

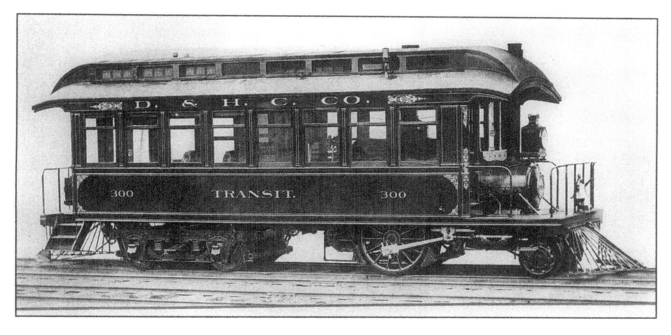

Civil engineering teams working on Delaware & Hudson's double-tracking project in the 1880s used this diminutive 2-2-4 with its enclosed cab as a "steam-powered van" to maneuver on the road. Built by Schenectady in 1899, No. 300's name is an advertisement for the roadbed engineer's profession. A *transit* is an accurately calibrated telescope used by engineers in land surveying. From *Delaware & Hudson*, Shaughnessy.

Rogers Works in Paterson, New Jersey was not even connected to a rail line. Finished locomotives were pulled by teams of draft horses through city streets to the nearest rail spur. But by the 1890s the situation had changed. Locomotives were now of such size and bulk that specialized, high-clearance shop buildings with overhead electric cranes were necessary. Thus the larger, more successful companies began to dominate the industry. This led to another watershed event during the early 1900s as a direct consequence of Baldwin's rapid growth.

In 1900 the Baldwin works produced 1147 engines, capturing 61 percent of the railroad market, 10 percent of the industrial market, and 29 percent of the export business. Not surprisingly, in response to this threat of monopoly, a rival company formed in 1901. The American Locomotive Company was the brainchild of New England financier Joseph Hoadley, who had purchased the Rhode Island Locomotive Works in 1898. Enlisting the assistance of two wealthy speculators, Pliny Fisk and Joseph Leiter, and using a holding company known as the International Power Company, the three men soon gained control of eight of the smaller locomotive builders and brought them under the Alco umbrella. Largest of the group were Brooks Works in Dunkirk, New York (near Buffalo) and Schenectady Works (near Albany). Others included in the initial merger included Cooke (Paterson, N.J.), Dickson (Scranton, Pa.), Manchester (N.H.), Pittsburgh, Rhode Island (Providence), and Richmond. Two more companies (Montreal and Rogers) were added to the conglomerate during the next three years, but it is clear in hindsight that the overall strategy of Alco's financial masterminds was to purchase and eventually close down smaller and less profitable shops so as to lessen competition for the larger ones. The closure of Rhode Island occurred in 1908, followed a year later by Dickson and in 1913 by Rogers and Manchester. In the meantime, facilities at Schenectady, Dunkirk, and Richmond were enlarged. The last closures began in 1926 with Cooke, followed by Richmond in 1927 and Dunkirk in 1928, leaving Alco's American business at Schenectady, with Montreal handling mainly Canadian orders.

The second decade of the twentieth century also saw the Lima Locomotive Works of Ohio rise to a prominent position as a producer of mainline locomotives. In 1878 Lima had begun producing both geared (Shay) and rod engines for lumber, mining, and industrial plant use, but in 1911 began to solicit business from major railroads. Its first orders for mainline power were five Pacifics for the Erie Railroad in 1911 and nine New York Central Mikados in 1914. That same year the company saw its production of rod locomotives surpass that of its Shay machines for the first time. Thus, during the decade preceding the stock market crash these three builders divided mainline power production (16,943 engines) in the following proportions: Alco 39.5 percent, Baldwin 49.7 percent, and Lima 10.8 percent. Virtually all of the later super power steam locomotives—representing the pinnacle of mechanical art—would be produced by these companies.

But there was an additional builder, serving only one railroad, that would emerge to make a significant contribution during the final period of steam power usage. Its history goes back to 1881 when the Roanoke Machine Works was chartered by the Virginia Company, a subsidiary of the Norfolk & Western Railway. It was thought that the company would be able to build engines for both its parent and other lines, but its independent business never developed because of competition with the larger builders. Thus by 1895 the Virginia Company was dissolved and RMW became a part of N&W.

CHAPTER 2

AMERICAN DESIGNS
EVOLVE

In the preceding discussion we have seen that most early locomotives had two axles, with either one or both supplying power. For example, George Stephenson's *Locomotion* was an 0-4-0, while Robert Stephenson's *Rocket* was an 0-2-2. Most of the early American-built engines were 0-4-0's (along with the imported *Stourbridge Lion*). Major exceptions were *Tom Thumb* and *Old Ironsides* (both 2-2-0). Some builders, such as Matthias Baldwin, soon realized that locomotives operated better on the relatively crude trackage of early American railways if they included a four-wheel leading truck. Thus Baldwin's second engine, the *E. L. Miller*, was a 4-2-0 model. However, this configuration was short lived, as the single driver was quickly found to provide inadequate pulling capability.

In 1836 Henry Campbell, chief engineer for the Philadelphia, Germantown & Norristown, patented a 4-4-0 locomotive as a way to "distribute the weight over rails more completely." Campbell contracted with a Philadelphia builder, James Brooks, to construct the first 4-4-0 in 1837. However, its performance was unsuccessful because its rigid axle mountings did not allow the eight wheels to conform to uneven track contours. The missing ingredient was, in modern terms, an independent suspension system. Fortunately, by 1838 Joseph Harrison Jr., another Philadelphia builder, patented a *weight equalization* method for locomotive wheels. It consisted of a series of interconnected, pivoted arms (*equalizer bars*) that allowed each driver to move up or down independently, and thus stay in contact with undulating trackage. The three-point suspension for the 4-4-0 included one point on each side between the two drivers and the third at the center of the leading truck. The new equalizers gave the locomotive an unusually effective tracking ability. Other favorable characteristics of the 4-4-0 design were a low center of gravity (due to a firebox between the drivers), an easily accessible valve gear (inside the frame but between the cylinders and drivers), and the flexibility to burn wood or coal.

By the 1840s the 4-4-0 design had become so widespread in usage that it came to be known as the *American Standard* type, later shortened to just *American*. It would be the main power source on American railroads for 60 years, a period that included the Civil War and completion of the nation's first transcontinental rail route. Indeed, in a reversal of the 1830s period, this wheel arrangement was exported to Britain in the 1870s and became a standard for them, as well as for major European railway systems.

Specifications for ordering early locomotives were extremely vague by modern standards, with much information based on a comparison with existing locomotives. As an example, the contract by the Rogers Works to construct some 4-4-0's for the Union Pacific

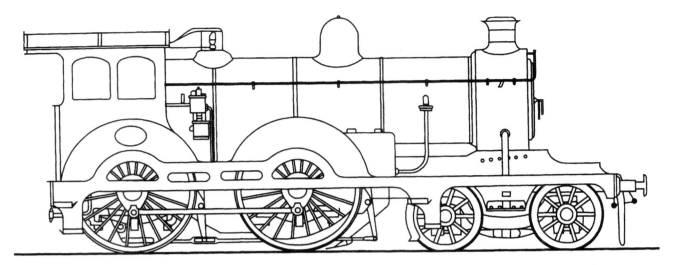

English locomotive designers followed the pioneering efforts of American builders in developing the 4-4-0 configuration. This is a compact 4-4-0 of the Claude Hamilton class, built in 1900 for the Great Eastern Railway. Note the usual English-style buffers in front, the absence of a pilot (cowcatcher), and the use of inside driving gear. Capped stacks and jacket-covered boiler piping were also characteristics of English designs. Adapted from *Pictorial History of Trains*, Hamilton.

The inspection engine was a standard component of mid-nineteenth-century railroading. By overlaying a small steam locomotive with a passenger car body, railroads could tour their lines with VIPs such as the road's executives, board of directors, potential shippers, and politicians. Delaware & Hudson's *Saratoga* was typical of these machines. Built as No. 4 (a standard engine) for the Cooperstown & Charlotte, it became the property of D&H after it absorbed the short line. The engine emerged from the D&H shops as an inspection locomotive in 1904. From *Delaware & Hudson*, Shaughnessy.

A comparison of firebox shapes used on American steam locomotives. Early engines used narrow fireboxes placed between the drivers, while camelback locomotives employed extra-wide Wooten furnaces that burned anthracite (hard) coal. The Belpaire configuration displayed a flat top that provided greater heating surface, whereas the most common design conformed to the boiler shape on its top surface but generally sat above the drivers or over trailing wheels so that it could be wide at the bottom. The firebox crown sheet is denoted in each drawing as CS. When the water level surrounding the furnace dropped below the top of the crown sheet, the structure could weaken and cause the boiler to explode. Adapted from *Steam Locomotives*, Westcott.

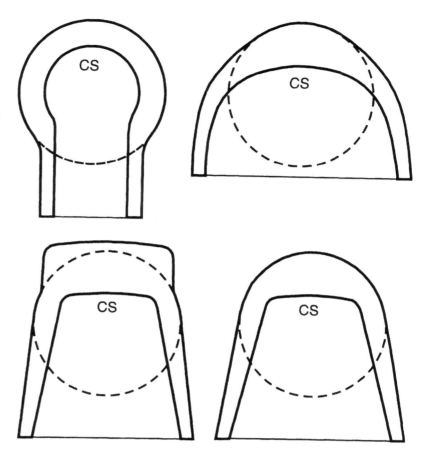

Freshly shopped Frisco 4-4-0 No. 216 (Alco Dickson, 1902) has just emerged from the road's Springfield, Missouri shops in 1923. Note the disk-type driver counterweights, which were used frequently around the turn of the century. Although many of Frisco's American types were operational into the 1930s after modernization with piston valves and superheaters, No. 216 did not receive such treatment and was scrapped in late 1929. Joe Collias Collection.

The narrow firebox on Atlantic Coast Line ten wheeler No. 7122, shown at Birmingham, Alabama in 1951, suggests a construction date near the beginning of the twentieth century. In fact, Baldwin turned out this engine in 1907 as No. 122 for the Atlanta, Birmingham & Atlantic. After bankruptcy, that road became Atlanta, Birmingham & Coast in 1926, and later rebuilt the locomotive with piston valves and a superheater in 1943. After AB&C was acquired by Atlantic Coast Line in 1946, all former AB&A locomotives were numbered in the 7000 series. J. Parker Lamb.

Slide-valve-equipped ten wheeler No. 501 (Alco, 1903), shown at Tennessee Central's Nashville shops during a major overhaul, displays details of its construction, including slots in the main frame that accommodate driving axles and bearings. Ed Bowers Collection.

Nashville, Chattanooga & St. Louis 2-8-0 No. 357 was built by Baldwin in 1900 but never upgraded. It carries the standard NC&StL capped stack (of English origin). Ed Bowers Collection.

Railway in 1876–78 specified driver diameter (54 inches), as well as size of engine bearings, valves, frame sections, cylinders (16-inch bore or diameter with a 22-inch stroke), and type of valve gear. However, there was no mention of engine weight, wheelbase, boiler and firebox data (such as size, steam pressure, plate thickness, rivet and staybolt diameters, heating surface, grate area), or tractive effort. Instead, reference was made to equivalence with a *main drawing* (presumably the company's standard design). Moreover, the contract made no mention of methods for constructing the boiler or the precision of machined parts. Nor was there any discussion of the metals to be used. Presumably, since only brass, copper, and iron (cast or wrought) were available, the use of certain metals for specific parts was clearly understood.

The next wheel arrangement to appear was the 4-6-0, which was slightly more powerful than the American type while retaining the four-wheel leading truck. First appearing in 1847, it was produced until the 1920s. Ironically, the two-wheel leading truck turned out to be difficult to design so as to provide the proper guiding capability on curved track. By 1860, when these two-wheel designs were finally perfected to a stage where they could be applied to locomotives, both the 2-6-0 and the 2-8-0 wheel arrangements had become common. The smaller Moguls were produced through 1910, while production of the more popular Consolidation types would last until the mid-1920s. Both types were used mainly in freight service.

Although locomotive designers during the first generation of American production realized quickly the importance of leading trucks, there was little concern for trailing wheels to carry larger fireboxes. Most engines through the 1880s carried fireboxes tucked between the last two sets of drivers, and thus their width was limited to about 42 inches with grate areas of approximately 17 square feet. However, by the turn of the century some locomotives included fireboxes that were raised above the drivers (especially the smaller drivers of freight engines), and thus their widths could be increased to 60 inches.

While the top of the boiler shell, as well as the crown sheet of the firebox inside the shell, was usually cylindrical in shape, a different design was introduced by Alfred Jules Belpaire in 1860. It was characterized by longitudinal bulges on each side near the top, resulting in a flat upper surface (see accompanying drawings). The reason for this unusual shape was

Delaware & Hudson camelback 4-4-0 No. 237 was constructed by Danforth & Cook in 1866, and rebuilt by D&H in 1898. Jim Shaughnessy Collection.

that it produced both increased structural integrity and a greater surface area for heat transfer. Unfortunately, due to the extra expense of fabricating this complex boiler shell, only two major railroads ever adopted the Belpaire furnace to any extent. Pennsy was by far the most extensive user, with Great Northern a distant second.

Another exception to the usual design was the Wooten firebox, introduced in 1877 specifically to burn anthracite (hard) coal that was mined principally in the Lackawanna Valley of northeastern Pennsylvania. Since the amount of heat liberated by hard coal was considerably less than from the same amount of bituminous (soft) coal, the firebox grate (bottom surface) for burning anthracite needed to be much larger than for a conventional firebox. Thus Wooten furnaces were generally around 90 inches in width. This led to a locomotive design that was distinctly different in appearance.

In most engines with Wooten fireboxes, the engineer's cab was moved to a position in front of the firebox, leaving the fireman in his usual location behind the firebox, laboring

Diminutive Delaware & Hudson camelback switcher No. 44 (class B4a) poses in the snow at Colonie shops in Albany, New York. A slide-valve engine with inside valve gear, it was constructed by Alco Dickson in 1903, and is attached to a typical slopeback switching tender, riding on arch bar trucks. From *Delaware & Hudson*, Shaughnessy.

beneath a short canopy. The resulting locomotive configurations, known as *camelbacks* or *Mother Hubbards*, were built in a wide range of wheel arrangements during the 1890–1910 period primarily for the Central Railroad of New Jersey, Delaware & Hudson, Delaware Lackawanna & Western, Erie, Lehigh Valley, and Philadelphia & Reading. Even two western lines (Union Pacific and Missouri, Kansas & Texas), which had access to low-grade coal supplies, bought a few of these locomotives.

One of the most complicated assemblies in a steam locomotive was the valve gear, a set of interconnected links that oscillated in a complex pattern so as to modulate a valve that admitted steam into the power cylinder and exhausted it at the proper intervals during the revolution of the drivers. Mechanics often referred to this linkage as "monkey motion" because of its gyrating movements.

There were six major designs for reciprocating valve gear employed on American locomotives. The Stephenson configuration came to America in 1850 and was widely used until around 1900. A later variation, the Joy design, saw little application. In both of these configurations, the links were attached to the main driver axle *inside* the locomotive main frame; so when repairs or adjustments were needed, workers usually gained access from beneath the locomotive. Eventually, this proved to be incompatible with American shop practice, and all later valve gears were attached to the outside of the driving gear.

By far the most popular valve gears were the Walschaerts and Baker designs. Belgian inventor Egide Walschaerts (1820–1901) patented his design in France in 1844. It was brought to America by the Mason Machine Works of Taunton, Massachusetts in 1876, but at first found little acceptance. However, between 1900 and 1905 it saw a resurgence in use and was quite popular until the end of the steam era. The advanced Baker gear was introduced around 1912 and had the unique advantage of avoiding sliding contacts, using only rotating elements connected with pins and bushings. Two other designs, Southern (1917) and Young (1920), were either too expensive or not sufficiently robust to be employed widely.

Along with the refinements in valve gears was an evolution of the valves themselves. Early locomotives used a *slide valve*, an inverted **U**-shaped block that slid back and forth across the intake and exhaust ports. The slide valve was also called a *D-valve*, since its external appearance suggested this shape. However, as boiler pressures increased, this design was less effective because of the difficulty in effecting a seal between two flat surfaces. Although an improved design was developed around 1866 by Thomas Davis, an engine mechanic, the *spool valve* (or *piston valve*) did not come into widespread use until 1902.

Details of Walschaerts valve gear on Southern Pacific 2-8-2 No. 786 (class Mk5; Alco, 1916). Attached to the alligator crosshead is main driving rod. Directly above this is the smaller eccentric rod that is connected to the reverse link (slotted and curved). From the crosshead, two rods connect upward to the piston rod, which is also connected to the reverse link by the radius rod. The horizontal rod at upper left is the reverse control. It lifts the reverse link to its top position in order to change direction of the locomotive. A mechanical lubricator pump, located above the crosshead, is driven by two small rods from the reverse link. J. Parker Lamb.

Missouri-Kansas-Texas 2-8-0 No. 664 (class K6c) was built for MK&T in 1894 but was rebuilt with superheater and piston valves by the railroad in the 1920s. Note that the inside valve gear was retained. Charles Felstead, J. Parker Lamb Collection.

Sketches of early slide valves (*right, top*) and modern piston valves (*right, bottom*). During each stroke of the power piston, the valve allows inlet steam into one of the passages at either end of the valve while simultaneously opening the other passage for exhaust steam, which later flows through the center of the valve. The slide valve (also called a *D-valve*) oscillated inside a rectangular chamber, whereas the piston (or spool) valve was contained within a circular cylinder and thus could operate at much greater steam pressures than the slide valve. Adapted from *Locomotive Valves and Valve Gears*, Yoder and Warren.

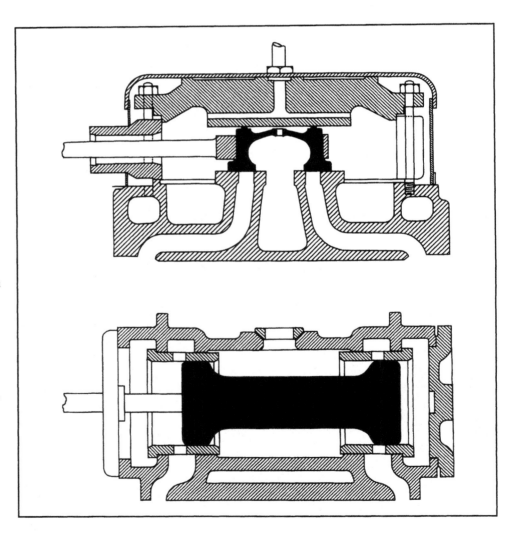

As its name implies, the sliding surface was cylindrical (similar to a power piston), but its cross-sectional contour was similar to a pair of slide valves placed back to back.

While differing in design details, the outside valve gears included common functional components. For example, all designs included an *eccentric crank* attached to the main crankpin. This transmitted the rotational position of the drivers to the other valve gear elements. The *eccentric rod* connected its crank to a pivoting element (*reverse link*), while the *radius rod* connected the pivot point directly to the piston rod. Further modulation of the valve position was required so that a *crosshead link* and *combination link* were also needed.

In the beginning, control of the valve gear was effected via a long rod (*reach rod*) from the cab to the radius rod. This connection allowed the engineer to change direction of travel. He controlled the reach rod with a lever called the *Johnson bar*. When the bar was fixed in a forward position the locomotive would move forward, while the opposite occurred if the bar was set in the rearward position. When the engine was operating at speed, it was common for the engineer to set the bar at an intermediate forward setting (called *cutoff*) that produced a shortened time of steam admission and thus allowed for more complete expansion in the cylinder. Usually a cutoff position of 70 to 90 percent of the full forward position was used for maximum performance.

For an emergency stop in the early days when brakes were either weak or nonexistent, many engineers would close the throttle and pull the Johnson bar backward so that steam paths in the valve chambers were reversed and thus the cylinders acted as a "steam brake." By 1913 an air-driven cylinder (*power reverse*) replaced the hand-operated Johnson bar. (Interested readers should consult appendix A for further details on valve gears.)

Occurring parallel to the development of first-generation, single-expansion engines were two other design concepts of note, which would eventually play an important role in the final glory of American steam locomotives. Both were originated by the Swiss-born designer Anatole Mallet (rhymes with "ballet"), who in 1874 patented a compound locomotive and, 14 years later, built the first articulated engine. The first concept relates to steam distribution, which is commonly classified as either *simple* or *compound*. In the simple design, steam is expanded once in a single power cylinder, and then exhausted, while in a compound design, the steam is first passed through a high-pressure cylinder, and then into a larger diameter low-pressure cylinder before being exhausted. The increased size is required to compensate for the lower average pressure, in recognition that the force on the piston face is equal to the steam pressure multiplied by the area of the face.

The main advantage of any compound design is that it improves power levels produced by the low-pressure portion of the steam expansion between boiler and atmospheric pressures. However, as with other such improvements, there was a price to pay in the added mechanical complexity, both initially and in maintenance. The general adoption of superheated steam by 1915 diminished the need to extract additional power from the low-pressure region of

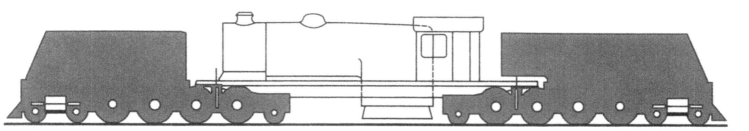

The Garratt type of articulated locomotive, licensed to the English builder Beyer, Peacock of Manchester, allowed both driving engines to pivot, and thus it could negotiate curved trackage easily. Fuel was carried over the rear engine (right) and water over the front. The wheel arrangement shown is a 4-8-2 + 2-8-4. Such symmetrical configurations gave Beyer-Garratt locomotives an inherent bi-directional capability. Copyright Kalmbach Publishing Company, used by permission.

expansion in a rigid-frame engine. However, a number of innovative designs were built before the compound technology was supplanted. These will be covered in chapter 5.

Mallet's concept of a jointed main frame with two sets of drivers was married to the idea of compounding from the beginning. In this design the rear driving gear, attached rigidly to the boiler, included high-pressure power cylinders, while the pivoted front drivers, which moved on a sliding surface beneath the boiler, used exhaust steam and thus needed larger cylinders. In addition to Mallet's design, four other European articulated locomotives were demonstrated in the 1880s, but the only other one to gain any long-term application was the Garratt design.

This configuration had the boiler-firebox-cab mounted on a platform that was supported on each end by a complete running gear (including leading and trailing trucks). Since each engine could pivot, Garratt locomotives were extremely agile on curves. The water tender was generally over the lead engine, while fuel was carried by the rear drivers, although their symmetrical layout facilitated bi-directional operation. The British locomotive builder Beyer, Peacock & Company of Manchester bought the license to build Garratts, and subsequently produced hundreds of Beyer-Garratts in a wide range of gauges and wheel arrangements. Although not popular in Great Britain, this design found widespread use in nations of the British Empire (Africa, Australia, and India).

The first American application of Mallet's design concept was an 0-6-6-0 built by Alco in 1904 for the B&O. Without leading or trailing trucks, these were powerful but slow-speed engines for hump yard and pusher service. Within five years a slightly larger 0-8-8-0 design was built for both B&O and Erie Railroads. The first mainline Mallets were 2-8-8-0's that were built until about 1915, at which time there were some 80 in service.

The Modern American Type

To a typical observer, the indelible image of the 4-4-0 locomotive is that depicted in dozens of Currier & Ives lithographs or shown in the dramatic Andrew Russell photograph depicting completion of the transcontinental railway at Promontory Point. These early representations show a gaudily decorated engine with a large, boxy headlight, an even larger diamond-shaped stack, and a cowcatcher pilot protruding 5 to 6 feet in front of the engine.

Indeed, this is a true depiction, but seldom do we consider what happened to the American type as time passed. Did it just gradually disappear around 1900? Or were there actually modernized 4-4-0's? Did they ever carry contemporary features such as piston valves

Katy 4-4-0 No. 309 (Baldwin, 1890) was rebuilt by the road in 1924 with a new boiler, superheater, and piston valves. Raymond B. George Collection.

Chicago & Illinois Midland's two 4-4-0's, constructed by Baldwin in 1927, were among the last built for domestic use. They operated in regular passenger service between Springfield and Peoria, Illinois until the mid-1950s. Number 502 is seen at Springfield in 1950. Charles T. Felstead, Louis R. Saillard Collection.

or even superheaters? Did any 4-4-0's operate after World War II? The answer to all but the first question is yes. The following discussion gives some of the details.

A perusal of post–World War II engine rosters reveals that a number of lines still operated American types as late as 1947–48. For example, the 1948 Missouri-Kansas-Texas roster contained ten 4-4-0's built by the railroad in 1925! Similarly, Frisco's 1948 roster includes six of these engines built by Pittsburgh Works in 1899, but rebuilt in 1928. Another southern road, Louisville & Nashville, bought 11 American engines from Northern Pacific in 1905–06 for branchline work. One of these logged over 2 million miles between 1882 and its retirement in 1926. L&N's last operating 4-4-0 was a Baldwin product (1916) that ran until 1947. Moreover, until 1953 Chicago & Illinois Midland operated its daily Springfield-Peoria passenger train behind one of the two modern Americans on its roster. These were Baldwin-built engines (1927) that included piston valves, superheaters, and Walschaerts valve gear, and were certainly among the last 4-4-0's constructed for domestic use.

In general, railroads found two major uses for aging 4-4-0's well into the pre–World War II period. Around major urban areas they were often used for commuter trains or, at the other extreme, on light-rail branches where neither speed was high nor tonnage large. Two major roads, one based in the east and the other a transcontinental headquartered in California, employed American types in large numbers and for a much longer period than virtually anyone else.

Southern Pacific (and its numerous subsidiaries) rostered a total of 710 American types during its early years. Eventually, there was a total of 40 subclasses of 4-4-0's in the road's E class. The oldest group was built in 1853–54 for the New Orleans, Opelousas & Great Western (Louisiana), while the last five entered service in 1924 on the San Antonio and Aransas Pass Railroad (Texas), absorbed by SP's Texas & New Orleans subsidiary in 1925. The newest, heaviest, and most modern 4-4-0's on the Pacific Lines were the 15 E27 engines built in 1911 for commuter service and scrapped in 1935–36. The last Americans on the Pacific lines were 30 E23's, built in 1900 and scrapped after 52 years of service. Similarly the final 4-4-0's on the Texas lines were two engines from class E40, built by Baldwin in 1922 for the SA&AP (above). These were scrapped in 1954.

On the other side of the nation, the Pennsylvania Railroad began building large 4-4-0's in 1895 with two sizes of drivers. Class L had 68-inchers, while the high-stepping class P ran on 80-inch wheels. Both classes carried 185 psi steam pressure and weighed 135,000 pounds (heavy for this period). When the PRR adopted a more rational engine classification system in 1897, classes L and P became classes D16 and D16a, respectively.

An unlikely trio of international technical talent came together to produce what would become the most highly developed 4-4-0 in the country that created it. The group was composed of French-born Frank D. Casanave, general superintendent of motive power, Swedish mechanical engineer Axel S. Vogt, and Theodore N. Ely, chief of motive power, who was

In 1953 Southern Pacific's last operating 4-4-0, No. 260 (class E40; Baldwin, 1922), chuffs northward through Texas ranch country near Gonzales with train No. 218, which consists of a lone Harriman-era RPO coach. Originally built for the San Antonio & Aransas Pass Railroad, it was scrapped a year after this classic photo. E. Brown, Louis R. Saillard Collection.

The low sun on a cool morning in Camden, New Jersey highlights details of perky D16sb No. 2082, waiting and ready to go to work with a Pennsy commuter train. Smokebox extension added during superheater installation in 1920 is clearly evident in this 1930 photo by pioneer eastern photographer Bruce D. Fales. Note also the unusual design of tender trucks. Jay Williams Collection.

also an authority in the field of architecture. Casanave supervised the design, whose details were refined by Vogt, while Ely, as overall supervisor, used his artistic talents to supply the external contours, and to design the paint scheme and striping of the finished product.

The first class P engine was No. 88, whose final engine weight was only 68 pounds off of the estimated value, a tribute to Vogt's careful attention to details. It also carried Ely's earlier design concept that placed the firebox above the main frame rather than dropping the furnace deep between the drivers. Its primary new feature was Pennsy's first application of the Belpaire firebox, which would become a Pennsylvania Railroad standard for over a half-century.

Subsequent firebox modifications produced class D16b for engines with the smaller drivers and classes D16c and D16d for those with 80-inchers. Naturally the smaller-drivered engines provide a slightly higher tractive effort (20,580 pounds) than the speedier group (17,500 pounds). In 1914 a D16b was modernized to a D16sb with piston valves and a Schmidt superheater. Although steam pressure was lowered from 185 to 175 psi, the total weight was increased from 97,100 to 98,500 pounds, giving a corresponding increase in tractive effort to 23,900 pounds.

The improved performance of the rebuilt engines led to production of additional D16sb's. Moreover, a few of the high-drivered models were modernized to D16sd's. Surprisingly, the Pennsy roster of July 1947 still included three of these modern American types. As with most railroads, the ubiquitous 4-4-0 was featured as PRR's primary passenger power for decades. Consequently, in usual Pennsy practice, it was produced in prodigious numbers until 1919, with a total of 429—four more than the later K4 Pacific.

One of the 4-4-0's most unusual legacies was its reliable tracking qualities, developed in the late 1830s after a weight equalization system was devised. In 1905, when PRR was developing an electric locomotive to power trains through its underground passage across the Hudson River into Penn Station, it tested a number of wheel arrangements, and found the 4-4-0 configuration was best in terms of stability and wear on the trackage. Thus its final design included a wheel arrangement that was equivalent to a pair of 72-inch-drivered 4-4-0's back to back, thereby forming a 2-B+B-2 running gear (using diesel and electric notation). These box-cab motors were designated class DD1 (since D represented a single American type). This experience merely confirmed the obvious conclusion that, as far as the roadbed is concerned, a good riding wheel arrangement is unaffected by its power source.

Averting Disaster

Another critical role of mechanical engineers during the early era of steam power was boiler safety. There was a distinct downside to the rapid development of the steam engine, and that was the proliferation of poorly constructed boilers. Between 1870 and 1910 there were over 10,000 explosions in the country, including some 1400 in the year 1910 alone. Following a lengthy study by the American Society of Mechanical Engineers, the ASME Boiler Codes of 1914–15 created a set of legally accepted requirements for constructing and testing pressurized boilers. Among these rules was a *safety factor of four* between the operating pressure and the bursting pressure of the boiler. As a direct consequence of the boiler codes, random explosions (due to poor construction) virtually disappeared.

To combat locomotive explosions, the Interstate Commerce Commission (ICC) instituted the first *Steam Locomotive Boiler Regulations* in 1911. Unfortunately, most early locomotive explosions resulted from crew error, generally by boiler water levels being allowed to drop too low. The firebox is virtually surrounded by water that prevents its structure from overheating. However, if the water level drops below the *crown sheet* (top) of the firebox, the internal structure is unprotected from the intense fire. Eventually the rear of the firebox would weaken and detach itself from the outer boiler shell. Once any small leak developed in the outer shell, high-pressure water inside would be exposed to atmospheric

On January 28, 1930 at
Arnold, Ohio the crown
sheet failed on New York
Central 2-8-2 No. 12. As was
common in such cases, the
explosion was due to a low
water level that was
undetected because of a
faulty sight glass. Although
the boiler was hurled 200
feet from the locomotive,
the running gear stayed on
the tracks. Railway &
Locomotive Historical
Society, Robert Reed
Collection.

pressure and would instantly flash into steam, producing a lethal cloud of scalding vapor. These explosions usually caused the rear of the boiler to rise, tear loose from the frame, and project itself end over end to a point well in front of the locomotive. In many instances the locomotive chassis would not even derail during an explosion since all the energy was directed upward.

By 1920 various appliances were available to both warn the crew of trouble and prevent an explosion scenario from developing. First, all engines were required to be equipped with two means of determining the water level, gauge cocks and sight glasses (often on both sides of the cab). Second, it became mandatory for there to be two means of supplying water to the boiler. This could be either by two injector pumps or one injector and one feedwater pump (used with the feedwater heater). In addition there were patented low-water alarms that emitted a shrill whistle in the cab to warn of unsafe conditions. Another device was a "soft plug" made of brass surrounded by a soft metal alloy. If temperatures reached unsafe levels, a precursor of danger, the soft metal would melt, causing the brass plug to drop and creating a deliberate leak that would drown the fire with jets of water. Usually two or three of these plugs were placed along the top of the crown sheet. Because some explosions were the result of equipment failure, they continued to occur, although rarely, until the last decade of steam power use. Indeed, the last boiler explosion on an American common carrier was on a compound articulated locomotive in December 1955 on the Norfolk & Western Railway, west of Roanoke.

Mechanical Art and Early Locomotives

The earlier discussion of the Industrial Revolution showed clearly that technical progress in the eighteenth century was implemented largely by practical people who had little or no scientific background. Thus these early steam locomotives (wherever built) should be considered as products of mechanical *art* rather than mechanical *engineering*. The primary cause of this situation was the embryonic state of applicable sciences such as the physics of heat, chemistry of combustion, and microstructure of metals. Moreover, methods of predicting important size and performance information had yet to be developed.

Thus virtually all knowledge about designing and constructing steam locomotives was based on empiricism (trial and error), with each designer-builder experimenting independently until he achieved a workable machine. It also meant that one gained expertise in mechanical art by becoming an apprentice to someone who was successful. American publications of the 1880s included detailed discussions of locomotive construction and maintenance so that an apprentice was involved in both self-study and shop experience. Characteristic of these publications were the numerous "rules of thumb" based on past

A 1937 snapshot shows Katy machinist J. O. Birger Johnson in the driver storage yard at Bellmead shops near Waco, Texas. Note that the drivers have been stored without flanged tires, which will be added after any machine-shop work is done on the driver itself. The crankpin below Johnson's left hand is seen to be 90 degrees out of phase with the corresponding one opposite. Raymond B. George Collection.

Katy's Bellmead shops (near Waco, Texas) were opened in 1923, and functioned as a major rebuilding facility until its closure in the early 1950s when MKT phased out its steam power. As this photo shows, the 475-foot-long erecting bay could hold up to 15 engines. Most of the locomotives in this photo are 4-6-0 and 2-8-0 types that were the mainstay of the road's motive power during the first few years after the shop was opened. The 180-ton overhead crane had little trouble lifting these small engines but later had to move 165-ton Mikados, the road's largest power. Note the insulation blocks (lagging) on boiler in the foreground. J. Parker Lamb Collection.

Working out its last operating days in 1951 as a yard switcher in Meridian, Mississippi, IC 2-8-0 No. 742 (Rogers, 1903) displays the result of modifying slide-valve steam chests to accommodate piston valves and superheated steam. Illinois Central carried out such improvements in the 1930s at its vast Paducah, Kentucky shops. J. Parker Lamb.

experiences. In the absence of scientific methods these were the only guides to locomotive design until the first decades of the twentieth century.

A personal experience will illustrate the education of steam locomotive mechanics and design engineers during this period. While searching for early references on American locomotive development, I located the personal railroad library of a deceased employee of the Missouri-Kansas-Texas Railroad. Mr. J. O. Birger Johnson, known widely by his initials (JOB) or by his nickname "Swede," was born in April 1911 near Austin, Texas. After completing high school he hired on to the Katy Railroad in May 1933 as an apprentice mechanic at the Ray Shop in Denison, Texas. Two years later he moved to the locomotive backshop at Bellmead (Waco), Texas where he remained, except for a brief wartime stint at Denison, until his retirement in 1975. He remained a devoted "railfan-historian" until his death in 1997 at age 86.

The Bellmead shop, constructed in 1923, was a typical high-bay (four story) structure some 475 feet long that held up to 15 locomotives. The shop, serviced by an overhead electric crane with a 180-ton capacity, handled major steam locomotive rebuilding projects before the switch to diesels began in 1947. In particular, this shop was a major player in Katy president Matthew Sloan's aggressive 1940 rebuilding program in which almost every engine received power reverse gear, boiler-firebox improvements, and conversion from coal to oil burning.

Thus Swede's 42 years of experience included some 14 years of work on the seven types of steam locomotives that the Katy Railroad operated, most of them being Pacific and Mikado types. Undoubtedly, with the Katy's later purchases of 23 diesel models, it had been necessary for him to study manuals for these locomotives, but in his private collection of railroad material were four steam locomotive books that he had used during his early years as an apprentice and eventually as a journeyman mechanic. These were *Catechism of the Locomotive* (1879) by Matthias Forney, a famous engine designer, *Standard Cyclopedia of Steam Engineering* (1908), *Locomotive Valves and Valve Gears* (1917), and *The Locomotive Up to Date* (1923). Written for the novice mechanic or designer, they summarized the state of steam locomotive technology during the first two decades of the twentieth century. How he came into possession of these is a mystery. They could have been handed down from retired mechanics, or he could have bought them during his early years as an apprentice. However, it is obvious that he used them frequently, as they contain copious notes in the margins as well as pieces of yellowed paper where he had jotted additional instructions to himself, especially in the book on valve gears. Setting the valve gear correctly for a rebuilt engine was one of the most daunting tasks of the steam era. A team of mechanics was required to assemble a dozen heavy links and align them in a specific way within an eighth of an inch. Moreover, the position of the valve gear on one side had to be correlated closely with that on the opposite side.

It is clear from early British writings that even the most learned men understood the limitations of their scientific capabilities. For example, Professor William J. M. Rankine of the University of Glasgow, a pioneer in steam engine thermodynamics, included this passage in his 1885 book, *A Manual of the Steam Engine and other Prime Movers*: "In the history of mechanical art two modes of progress may be distinguished—the empirical and the scientific. Not the practical and the theoretic[al], for that distinction is fallacious; all real progress in mechanical art, whether theoretic or not, must be practical. The true distinction is this: that the empirical mode of progress is purely and simply practical; the scientific mode of progress is at once practical and theoretic" (p. 100)

The preceding observations on technical progress suggest a natural correlation between the evolution of American engineering education and the development of the steam locomotive. The nation had no formal schools of engineering until 1817 when the U.S. Military Academy established such a curriculum, based on the successful programs of the Ecole Polytechnic system in France. The first civilian engineering degree was established in 1825 at Rensselaer Polytechnic Institute in Troy, New York, while the first American locomotives were produced in the 1830s. With the rapid emergence of a corps of formally educated mechanical engineers, 50 of the most prominent members of this group met in New York City in 1880 to form the American Society of Mechanical Engineers (ASME). (Americans again followed their British counterparts, who had formed the Institution of Chartered Mechanical Engineers in 1847.) From beginning steps such as these came the pool of technical talent that would eventually serve as the intellectual base for American steam locomotive development over the next half-century.

An insightful comment on the influence of early mechanical engineering on locomotive development in the late nineteenth century is found in the 1977 book *Pictorial History of Trains* (see list of references). The author, David S. Hamilton, notes that "these men [British designers] were mainly of the trial and error school. Having little theoretical inclination, they preferred to progress by intuition and experiment rather than by abstract thought. In general, this approach became the hallmark of British locomotive engineers and helped to ensure, firstly, that British locomotives were reliable and well tested but, secondly, that after about 1875, most major advances in steam locomotive design were made by Continental Europeans or by Americans" (p. 34).

Another comment reveals the unabashed pride of early American locomotive designers and builders. It comes from an 1883 book entitled *Modern American Locomotive Engines; Their Design, Construction, and Management*, written by Emory Edwards, a mechanical engineer. The title page calls the book *A Practical Work for Practical Men*. Concluding his chapter on the history of the nation's locomotive development are these words: "other builders entered the field, each and all improving their existing types, until we have the American locomotive of today—one of the most perfect pieces of mechanism wrought out by the hand and mind of man." (The "American" locomotive referred to is the 4-4-0.)

From our contemporary view it may seem somewhat humorous that early steam locomotives, even though crudely designed and built, often carried grandiose names. But we must remember that each of these vehicles was a handmade original, representing the leading edge of accomplishment for that era. Thus the awarding of special names in this era expressed the same type of pride in technical progress as was manifested later in the nineteenth century in the naming of oceangoing vessels and cross-country passenger trains, and in the twentieth-century naming of early airplanes and then spacecraft that, for the first time in history, escaped Earth's gravity. Each of these represented a new (and usually faster) mode of transportation, and their ensemble reminds us forcefully that technical evolution is a continuum.

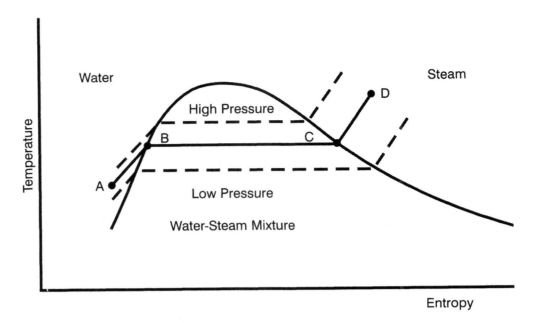

Temperature-entropy diagram showing the thermodynamic process of producing steam. Pressure is constant along line A-B-C-D.

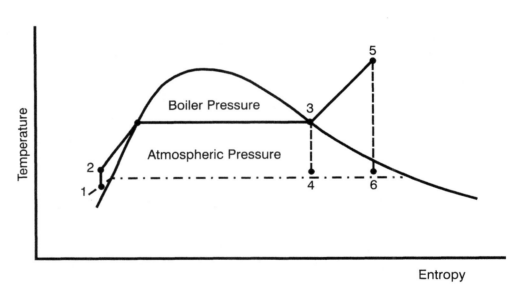

Temperature-entropy diagram of the Rankine cycle for a steam engine, showing energy levels at various points in the cycle. Boiler pressure exits along line 2-3-5.

CHAPTER 3

THE PHYSICS OF
STEAM POWER

To better understand how steam locomotives are designed, we must look at the branch of physics known as thermodynamics, which traces its roots to the seventeenth century, long before the Industrial Revolution. It was during this era that pioneering thinkers were developing the physical concepts and laws that would be the basis of all early engineering fields, and especially of mechanical engineering. However, as often happens with new technology, the *invention* stage of steam locomotive development (emphasizing mechanical art) proceeded steadily throughout the nineteenth century while the *theoretical* understanding progressed somewhat slower.

One of the most fundamental concepts is credited to the French military engineer Nicholas L. S. Carnot, who in 1824 published a paper entitled "Reflexions on the Motive Power of Fire [Heat], and on Machines Fitted to Develop That Power." Carnot conceptualized an ideal engine that had no losses due to friction or heat transfer. He anticipated that the performance of such a "perfect" machine would provide an upper limit on the performance of any real engine that would later exist. In succeeding years his first concepts were improved, but his general framework was eventually accepted as the proper way to describe the ideal limits for all heat engines. His theories also provided a simple method for comparing the performance of any engine, no matter what its source of heat.

Thermodynamic Concepts

Carnot's conceptual engine was composed of four basic processes that formed a thermodynamic cycle. A *working fluid* would traverse these processes in the following order. The fluid is first compressed, thereby gaining mechanical energy. Then heat is added to give it a high level of thermal energy. This energetic fluid then passes through a conversion unit, transforming the fluid energy into mechanical work. At this point in the cycle, the spent fluid traverses a final process, where it loses most of its thermal energy and returns to its original state. It could thus re-enter the compressor and begin the entire cycle once again. It is clear that, for a steam engine, the working fluid is water, and the conversion process is implemented via a steam-driven piston.

Despite its abstractions and idealizations, Carnot's early work inspired many others to move toward more realistic concepts for heat engines. One of these was Scottish engineering professor William J. M. Rankine, who in 1853 devised a specific thermodynamic cycle for the steam engine. Six years later he would write the first textbook on thermodynamics. The Rankine cycle contained much more detail about the four basic thermodynamic processes mentioned by Carnot, and permitted improved prediction of engine performance. A closer examination of the Rankine cycle will lead us to a greater understanding of how and why continuous improvements were made in steam locomotive design, especially during the 25-year period beginning in the early 1920s.

In order to present a thermodynamic description of the production of steam, we will use the accompanying drawing, which depicts in a schematic form the variation of pressure, temperature, and entropy for water. While the first two parameters are familiar from everyday experience, the parameter known as entropy is quite abstract and not directly measurable. However, this feature will not hamper our understanding. It is needed only to recognize that, when heat is added to a substance, its entropy generally increases, while the reverse is true when heat is lost.

The first drawing illustrates energy levels associated with a change of *phase*. It is common knowledge that, with sufficient cooling, water will change from a liquid phase to a solid phase (ice). Similarly, heating water causes it to enter the gaseous (vapor) phase. We see in the drawing a dome-shaped demarcation line with only water to the left and only steam to the right. Beneath the dome is a region in which there is a mixture of vapor and liquid water. Three typical lines of constant pressure are shown, each having a slight **S** shape. We now focus our attention on the transition from liquid to vapor as indicated by line A–B–C–D. Imagine that we can follow the history of a small packet of water that has been drawn into the lower part of the boiler. At point A the water begins to receive heat and its temperature rises until it reaches point B, known as the *saturated liquid* line. As we add additional heat beyond B, we see that the temperature remains constant while the added heat energy goes into converting some of the liquid water into vapor.

As we move to the right along segment B–C (increased heating), more and more vapor is created. Eventually the mixture of liquid and vapor reaches point C, the *saturated vapor* line, denoting that all liquid has evaporated. Saturated vapor is usually denoted as *dry steam*. To the left of point C the steam is considered *wet*. Additional heating of dry steam produces a superheated vapor, in which the temperature rises once again until it reaches point D.

Using the same temperature-entropy diagram as before, the second drawing displays the complete Rankine cycle. It shows an *open* cycle in which exhaust from the power pistons is discarded to the ambient. In contrast, a *closed* cycle allows the spent steam to be condensed and recirculated. The latter type of cycle is used in modern electric generating plants powered by steam turbines.

Consider an engine operating between atmospheric conditions and a boiler pressure of approximately 200 psi. Water enters the boiler feed pump at point 1, and then enters the boiler as a pressurized liquid at point 2 where heating occurs as described previously. Two possible end-points for the heating are shown. Point 3 is saturated steam and point 5 is superheated steam, while the vertical lines below points 3 and 5 indicate the approximate thermodynamic path of the steam as it passes through the power cylinders. As the incoming steam pushes the piston toward the opposite end of the cylinder, its pressure and temperature drop rapidly toward atmospheric conditions. The exhaust steam passes into the smokebox at points 4 or 6.

The difference between operating power pistons with saturated or superheated steam can have significant practical implications. The first is *power*. The relative lengths of the piston expansion lines, 3–4 (saturated) and 5–6 (superheated), are also an indication of the relative amount of mechanical work (and power) done by the power piston. This is a reflection of the fact that the total energy contained in a given amount of superheated steam is much larger than in the same amount of saturated vapor at the same boiler pressure.

The second effect of superheat is *moisture*. We see that both end points, 4 and 6, are left of the saturated vapor line, but since 6 is nearer the saturated limit it represents a dryer

THE PHYSICS OF STEAM POWER

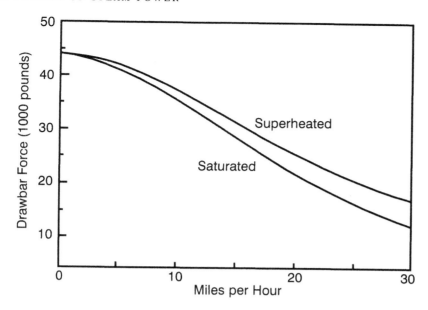

Variation of drawbar force for engines using saturated and superheated steam at same boiler pressure. Superheated steam contains much more thermal energy than saturated vapor. This enhanced energy is then converted to increased mechanical work by the piston-cylinder. Superheaters became widespread around 1915–17. Adapted from *The Steam Locomotive*, Johnson.

steam than does point 4. Along path 3–4 the steam expansion is completely within the wet steam region, and thus we would find considerable condensation on the cylinder walls. Over time this would lead to surface degradation (due to corrosion and pitting) that would damage the seal between the piston and cylinder wall. On the other hand, path 5–6 is within the wet steam zone only during the last part of the expansion and thus would produce much less damage. These performance advantages led to widespread adoption of superheaters by 1910, and by 1915 even switchers included this appliance.

We now consider the efficiency of the steam engine. Based on Rankine's early work, the thermal efficiency of any heat engine cycle can be defined as

$$\text{thermal efficiency} = \frac{\text{net work produced by working fluid}}{\text{total heat input to working fluid}}$$

Since thermodynamics recognizes heat and work as merely different forms of energy, we can express both of these quantities in the same physical units (such as feet or pounds). Thus the efficiency is merely a decimal fraction. This notion is expressed another way by rearranging the above equation to the form

$$\text{net work produced} = \text{total heat input} \times \text{thermal efficiency}$$

From this we see that the efficiency merely expresses the proportion of heat (entering the working fluid) that can be delivered as useful work. For a steam locomotive the thermal efficiency is a primary indicator of how much fuel must be burned to produce a given tractive effort or horsepower. This idea will be pursued much further in later discussion, as it is a fundamental factor in the quest for designing high performance locomotives. We also recognize that the Rankine cycle thermal efficiency is but one of many such efficiencies that determine the overall efficiency of an entire locomotive.

Table 3-1
Rankine Cycle Performance Parameters

Boiler Pressure	Saturated Steam		Superheated Steam		Temp increase
	Efficiency	Quality	Efficiency	Quality	
105 psi	10.3%	0.91	11.6%	0.99	200°F
285 psi	16.0%	0.85	18.0%	0.98	300°F

Notes: Boiler pressure measured above atmospheric pressure.
Steam quality at exhaust state (10 psi above atmospheric).
Superheat temperature is the increase above saturation temperature.

We note in passing that during the early period of American locomotive development, the emphasis was on constructing engines that were sturdy and reliable. The main goal was to build a locomotive that would pull cars at a reasonable speed. With cheap coal, or even wood, as a fuel, the thermal efficiency of the cycle was not considered (or even known about) by anyone except designers. When improvements were made, they were usually aimed at increasing tractive effort (pulling force) or strengthening the running gear.

A manual calculation of the thermal efficiency of a Rankine cycle can be carried out rapidly, using tabulated properties of steam at any temperature or pressure. As a by-product of these cycle computations, we can also determine a numerical value for the *wetness* of the exhaust steam. Known as *quality*, this numerical value represents the proportion of vapor in a liquid-vapor mixture. Thus a quality of 1.0 means dry steam (saturated vapor), while a quality of 0.6 represents 60 percent vapor.

Table 3-1 displays the results of cycle computations for engines with two boiler pressures. In each case, performance with both saturated and superheated steam is presented. For each regime we present the Rankine cycle efficiency as well as the exit steam quality. Note that we have adjusted the amount of superheat for each boiler pressure so as to produce exhaust steam with less than 3 percent moisture (quality greater than 0.97). This is the most desirable operating condition since, for early designs, it was quite wasteful to send superheated steam up the stack. However, in more modern designs there was need for extra exhaust steam to operate various appliances. This led to engines that did in fact have superheated steam leaving the power cylinders.

We immediately see that a higher boiler pressure leads to a much better efficiency, while superheating has little influence on efficiency. But the most surprising aspect of these results may be that, on an absolute basis, the thermal efficiencies for early locomotives were quite low. For example, contemporary steam power plants for electrical production use pressures of 5500 psi and temperatures of over 1000°F, conditions that produce much higher thermal efficiencies.

In order to gain more perspective on the low efficiencies in Table 3-1, we turn to the ideal Carnot cycle for comparison. We ask, "How does the Rankine cycle efficiency compare with the Carnot cycle efficiency for the same conditions?" In other words, how far from perfection were the energy conversion processes in early steam locomotives? Carnot's analysis showed that the efficiency of a perfect cycle is dependent only on the ratio of the lowest and highest temperatures in the cycle. Table 3-2 presents the ratio of Rankine to Carnot efficiencies for the data in Table 3-1. The results are enlightening. For the 285 psi boiler pressure, we see that the 16 percent thermal efficiency (using saturated steam) is actually 42 percent of that for a perfect machine. These ratios thus suggest a greater capability than do the cycle efficiencies alone. Incidentally, the lower ratios for superheated steam are merely an artifact due to the much higher peak temperatures in these cycles that result in higher Carnot efficiencies.

Table 3-2
Ratio of Rankine to Carnot Efficiencies

Boiler Pressure	Saturated Steam	Superheated Steam
105	0.32	0.26
285	0.42	0.33

A view inside the smokebox of Southern Pacific Mk5 Mikado No. 786 reveals the front flue sheet, with small holes for evaporator tubes as well as large holes for superheater flues and tubes. At the top is box-shaped feedwater heater (Worthington model SA), while directly behind this is the superheater header, from which two curved pipes connect with the valve chests above each cylinder. Because this locomotive was built (1916) without a feedwater heater, the exhaust steam transfer pipes were attached to the front of the cylinder saddle during this retrofit. It is seen that exhaust steam is led into the feedwater box from the left side, while the heated water exhausts to the right. Photo at Austin, Texas in 1990 during rebuilding of this locomotive after 34 years of storage. J. Parker Lamb.

In seeking additional ways to improve thermal efficiency of the Rankine cycle, we again examine the definition, which states that efficiency is the ratio of *work output* to *heat input*. While we have seen that superheated steam increases work output and thus efficiency, we also note that by decreasing the amount of heat added to the water (inside the boiler) while keeping the output work constant, the efficiency would further increase. By 1910, steam engine designers realized that the engine's exhaust (composed of steam from the cylinders and combustion gas from the firebox) was being pumped out the stack while still at a temperature considerably above the surroundings. In a stroke of innovative reasoning, they concluded that a portion of this *waste heat* could be captured to preheat the water before it entered the boiler, thus reducing the heat needed from the firebox. At the same time, the steam going into the cylinders would remain unchanged and thus the work output would not decrease.

When adapted to a locomotive, such preheaters are normally called *feedwater heaters* and can be of various types, as will be noted later. Modifying the results of Table 3-1 to include feedwater heating to 150°F before the boiler heating begins, we find that the cycle efficiency is raised by 0.7 percent in the 105 psi boiler and by 1 percent in the 285 psi boiler. While these are not spectacular increases, the more important result is that the heat input is reduced by 5 to 6 percent, representing similar decreases in fuel and water needed. In later years, results such as this were generalized into a guide for designers, specifically that, for each 10 degrees of feedwater heating, there would be a 1 percent decrease in fuel costs. This allowed designers to determine the economics of specifying feedwater heaters for new locomotives based on lower fuel costs.

For decades Pennsy yards relied on a fleet of almost 500 sturdy B-class 0-6-0 switchers, such as No. 8026 posed at Columbus, Ohio in 1947. A smokebox extension was added during superheater installation when the engine was modernized into the B28 class. Note also that the inside valve gear was retained, but the rebuilt engine was connected to a larger tender, originally for a mainline engine. Paul Eilenberger, Jay Williams Collection.

Illinois Central 0-8-0 switcher (Baldwin, 1927) works Carbondale, Illinois yard in 1959. Note extended coal bunker on tender, which allowed locomotive to work 24 hours before refueling. J. Parker Lamb.

Katy 0-8-0 No. 49 (class C1a; Lima, 1920), one of the road's most modern locomotives, is typical of heavy 0-8-0's used during the last decades of steam. J. Parker Lamb Collection.

With over 440 Moguls on its roster, including 10 of the most powerful ever built, Southern Pacific was a major user of the 2-6-0 wheel arrangement. Here is an M10 class machine (Baldwin, 1912) working at Lafayette, Louisiana in 1950. Note high-visibility tank-type tender for yard service. W. H. B. Jones, David S. Price Collection.

A

B

C

D

We can summarize the major conclusions from these Rankine cycle calculations as follows:

a. Higher boiler pressures give higher thermal efficiencies.
b. Superheated steam is more desirable than saturated vapor because it produces greater power for a given boiler pressure and also results in less condensation and corrosion inside power cylinders.
c. Preheating the boiler feedwater results in improved efficiency.
d. Higher thermal efficiency leads to improved fuel economy.

We conclude by noting that these characteristics of engine performance, and many others, were discovered over a 70-year period starting in 1830 through the process of building locomotives, testing their performance, then re-building and re-testing. Indeed it was not until accurate steam tables were developed that cycle performance could be quantified in advance. Although Professor Rankine analyzed his steam engine cycle with crude tables in 1859, reasonable accuracy was not available until around 1909.

As we have noted, early locomotives were built with narrow fireboxes fitted between the rear drivers. In later designs wider fireboxes were situated above the rear wheels. Passenger engines gradually evolved from 4-4-0's to 4-6-0's, while freight power grew from 2-6-0's to 2-8-0's and, on a few roads, even to 2-10-0's. We see that the evolutionary improvement in performance was manifested by increasing the number of drivers, and thereby the *tractive effort* (similar to drawbar pull). Clearly each pair of additional drivers increased the frictional surface area in contact with the rails, and thus the ability of the locomotive to pull more.

However, early builders also learned about another important principle in their attempts to put more drivers in contact with the rail. It was found that the engine weight supported by the drivers should be about four times its tractive effort. This was known as the *factor of adhesion*. If its value dropped below four, designers found, the engine would slip easily. Slipping was an indication that there was insufficient friction between the drivers and the rail. One can explain this reasoning by considering a block of steel resting on a flat plate of steel (both surfaces smooth and polished). In order to cause the block to slide, one must

---

Facing page, **A**: Oil-burning ten wheeler No. 384 of Missouri Pacific Texas–based subsidiary International–Great Northern (class TN63; Baldwin, 1906) was typical power for light trains during the first generation of steam locomotive development. W. H. B Jones, David S. Price Collection.

Facing page, **B**: Illinois Central Consolidation-type No. 959 was constructed by Baldwin in 1909 using Common Standard designs developed during the Harriman era. Vanderbilt tenders were rarely used on the IC but came to the line because of the practice of allocating similar locomotives to Harriman-affiliated lines from coast to coast (including Union Pacific, Southern Pacific, and Erie). C. W. Witbeck, J. Parker Lamb Collection.

Facing page, **C**: The Decapod type represented the maximum pulling capability in the first generation of rigid-frame engines. Gulf, Mobile & Ohio predecessor Gulf, Mobile & Northern acquired 10 of these in 1921–22 after a Russian order from Baldwin was cancelled because of the Bolshevik revolution. Impressed with the 2-10-0's lugging ability, the GM&N opted to order an additional 16 from Baldwin between 1923 and 1927. Number 263 (1926), equipped with smokebox-mounted Coffin feedwater heater, is at Jackson, Mississippi in 1937. John B. Allen, Louis R. Saillard Collection.

Facing page, **D**: Pennsy developed the Decapod type to its highest level, with nearly 600 engines in the I1 class. During their final years most were relegated to yard and transfer service and seldom worked on mainline trains. Here is No. 4306 at Columbus, Ohio, working out its last months of service in 1956. J. Parker Lamb.

push with a force slightly greater than one-fourth the weight of the block. The fraction 1/4 is known as the *coefficient of static friction* and depends upon the surface materials and their smoothness. Note that the factor of adhesion is merely the inverse of the coefficient of friction but expresses the same idea, namely that one must keep the tractive effort and the engine weight (on drivers) in the correct proportion in order to minimize slipping on dry rail. If there is too much tractive effort for the engine weight, then the factor of adhesion will be too low and the engine's drivers would likely slip when starting a heavy train.

Mechanical Work vs. Power

We now discuss another important aspect of locomotive design, the heat source. Unlike today's ubiquitous internal combustion engines (automotive and diesel), the steam engine is an *external combustion* power source. By that we mean that combustion does not occur within the power cylinders but in a furnace (firebox) external to the boiler tubes where steam is created.

As trains grew heavier, there was also a need for more speed. Consequently most of these *first-generation* locomotives encountered another shortcoming. After starting a train, they could keep it moving at a slow to moderate speed along a level main line, but would slow or stall, due to an inadequate steam supply, upon encountering a grade or attempting to accelerate. This required a delay while steam pressure was rebuilt or necessitated a helper engine.

In the late nineteenth century, there was general recognition that a locomotive's pulling force was influenced by boiler pressure, cylinder dimensions, and driver diameter, but there was little understanding of their relationship. However, during the first decades of the twentieth century, analytical capabilities had progressed to the point where engine performance could be characterized in a more reliable fashion using one basic parameter known as *tractive effort* (more correctly, rated tractive effort). By determining the mechanical work done by the power pistons to move a locomotive through one rotation of its drivers, we obtain a formula with only two empirical factors. Thus, in 1924 the Mechanical Division of the Association of American Railroads adopted the following equation for calculating starting tractive effort.

$$\text{starting tractive effort} = (0.92) \times (0.92\ P) \times (C^2 S)\ /\ D$$

where P is boiler pressure, C and S are the cylinder diameter and stroke, respectively, and D is driver diameter. All lengths are in inches and pressure is in psi. The first factor, 0.92, refers to the mechanical efficiency of the engine when starting, and assumes that the locomotive has friction bearings. This effect will be discussed in chapter 7. The second factor, 0.92, indicates that during steam expansion in the cylinders the mean effective pressure acting on the pistons is less than the boiler pressure. In common practice, the two numerical values were multiplied to obtain 0.85 as the empirical factor. We note also that the factor $(C^2 S)$ is directly related to the volume of each cylinder.

It is clear from the above formula why driver diameters were quite different for freight and passenger locomotives. Since starting tractive effort is inversely related to driver size, freight locomotives, designed for heavy trains, needed smaller drivers than passenger engines, while the latter needed larger drivers for greater speed. We also note that tractive effort is a computed parameter and, while approximately the same as the locomotive's starting drawbar pull, is not equivalent. Indeed the actual force is always less than the rated tractive effort. However, the latter was always reported with other engine specifications and became the most convenient way to compare engine performance at low speed.

We now need to introduce some additional thermodynamics terminology. In physics the basic measure of heat (using the English system) is the *British thermal unit* (Btu), while the corresponding unit of mechanical work is the *foot-pound* (amount of work required to lift a one-pound weight a distance of one foot). Meticulous measurements have determined that 778.16 foot-pounds of work equals one Btu. This is known as the *mechanical equivalent of heat*, and confirms that mechanical work and heat are merely two forms of energy.

Cycle computations discussed previously provide values of work done and heat added per pound (mass) of steam. However, in order to estimate performance of an actual locomotive we must include the pounds of steam produced by the boiler per unit of time. This is the steam production rate (often called the *steaming rate*). With this background we can write the dimensional expression for *cycle power* as

$$\text{cycle power} = \frac{\text{work done}}{\text{time}} = \frac{\text{work done}}{\text{mass of steam}} \times \frac{\text{mass of steam}}{\text{time}}$$

This statement defines *power as the rate of work*, and also shows that power produced by a steam engine (of any kind) is equal to the work done by the working fluid (calculated from Rankine cycle) multiplied by the rate of steam produced in the boiler. In the English system, power is measured in *horsepower*. One horsepower is equivalent to 550 foot-pounds/sec (or 2545.5 Btu/hr). Both the name and its value were the result of James Watt's pioneering experiments.

Horsepower is but one of many whimsical names in the English system of measurement. The more modern, and strictly scientific, alternative is the metric system, which is much easier to understand and use but has none of the colorful reminders of past eras.

As noted, early fireboxes were limited to the width of the locomotive main frame but were later widened. As was learned in the 1910s, the real measures of firebox size are the grate area (bottom of firebox) and the volume. The first parameter determines the surface covered by combustion, while a large volume allows the fire to be hotter and thus maximizes the amount of hot gas flowing through the boiler tubes and superheater flues. In turn, the amount of water evaporated is directly related to the outside surface area of all boiler tubes (since that is where boiling occurs). From these facts we conclude that even if the cycle efficiency is high, the power will be limited if the firebox is too small. It was this realization that led designers to consider locomotives with larger fireboxes supported by trailing trucks. Eventually these longer furnaces also produced a need for mechanical stokers to spray crushed coal into the firebox at much greater rates than any fireman was able to sustain.

During the production of first-generation locomotives, builders seldom listed any horsepower values—for at least three reasons. First, the mainline pulling capability of an engine was not yet recognized to be significantly different from that when starting. In addition, locomotive horsepower, unlike construction data, does not have a fixed value but varies with speed. Moreover, there are multiple definitions of horsepower. Earlier, for example, we noted how one goes about computing *cycle horsepower* from cycle analysis and steaming rate. Another is the *boiler horsepower* that is estimated by the empirical equation

boiler horsepower (maximum) = (1/6) grate area (square feet) × boiler pressure (psi)

The power produced by the cylinders is also known as the *indicated horsepower*, so named from the use of an *indicator card* that displayed the variation of steam pressure inside the cylinder during a power stroke. By tapping a small hole into each end of the cylinder (either the *head* face or the *crank* face), the instantaneous value of pressure could be measured. Simultaneously, the motion of the piston could be determined by measuring the travel of the piston rod (outside the cylinder). Superimposing these measurements onto a single page (the *card*) produces the indicator diagrams shown in the accompanying sketch. Since all steam engines are double acting, there are two variations (mirror images), one for each side of the piston, during one revolution of the drivers.

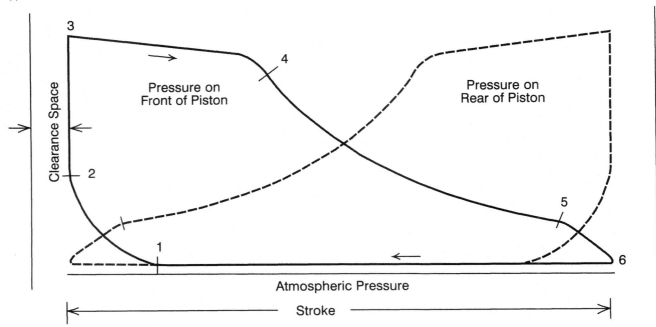

Variation of steam pressure within a power cylinder, showing the symmetrical changes that occur on opposite sides of the piston. Early in the twentieth century these distributions were recorded mechanically on an indicator card, which allowed designers to determine the exact amount of power developed by the cylinders under all operating conditions. Adapted from *The Steam Locomotive*, Johnson.

These indicator diagrams provide the most easily understood display of the various events during one cycle of reciprocation. For example, at point 1, as the piston approaches the end of its exhaust stroke, it begins to compress the residual steam in the cylinder. At point 2 the admission valve opens, allowing high-pressure steam into the cylinder, and driving up the cylinder pressure rapidly. The piston reverses direction at point 3 and begins its power stroke, with steam admission continuing. The pressure shows a slight decrease due to the increased volume created by the piston travel. The inlet valve is closed at point 4 (cutoff) and the vapor is allowed to expand, pushing the piston toward the opposite end of the cylinder. The exhaust port is opened at point 5 and the spent steam begins to flow out of the cylinder. The power stroke ends at point 6, and the exhaust portion of the reciprocation cycle begins. The sketch shows that the same events occur on the opposite face of the piston, but the timing is exactly reversed.

To determine the indicated horsepower, one must refer to thermodynamic equations that show the work done by the power piston is proportional to the *area* enclosed within the indicator diagram. Although theoretical methods are now available to calculate this work, in the early days a mechanical calculator (called a planimeter) was traced around the circumference of the actual indicator card, and produced a value for the enclosed area. By scaling the physical area (so that it has the dimensions, foot-pounds per square inch), multiplying by the area of the cylinder bore, the driver rpm, and the number of strokes per driver revolution (two on each side of the engine), one can arrive at a value of foot-pounds/sec, or horsepower.

Indicator cards also led to another commonly used term by designers, the *mean effective pressure* inside the cylinder (denoted as MEP). This term arises from the recognition that the actual area of the pressure trace (thus the work done by the piston) can be represented by an equivalent rectangular area, computed by multiplying the piston stroke by some constant (or mean) pressure. Symbolically we have

$$\text{actual area (from card)} = (N) \times \text{boiler pressure} \times \text{stroke} = \text{MEP} \times \text{stroke}$$

where N is a decimal fraction. Therefore we define the mean pressure as

$$\text{mean effective pressure} = \frac{\text{area inside indicator card}}{\text{stroke}} = (N) \times \text{boiler pressure}$$

By analyzing the pressure variations on indicator cards for many types of locomotives, it was found that the value of N was almost a constant at low speed. Thus designers could discuss cylinder horsepower and other performance parameters in terms of mean effective pressure. With higher reciprocation rates, the value of N was found to decrease because the cutoff position (point 4 on indicator card sketch) was required to move closer to the front of the cylinder.

Other horsepower values in common use were the *brake horsepower* and the *drawbar horsepower*. The brake (or rail) horsepower equals the cylinder horsepower minus the power required to rotate the drivers (overcome bearing friction) and move the valve gear. Typically this is the power measured by a stationary dynamometer that allows only the drivers and valve gear to move. It indicates how much power is available to propel the engine, tender, and train (plus all resistances due to track, wind, etc.).

The advantage of a stationary laboratory dynamometer was that it allowed locomotive speed and power to be controlled much more closely than while pulling a train. Only three such facilities were ever constructed in the United States. These were at Purdue University in Indiana, the University of Illinois, and in the Pennsylvania Railroad's Juniata shops at Altoona, Pennsylvania. Of these only the latter facility was operated continuously until the end of the steam era.

Finally, the drawbar power is determined with a dynamometer car located between the engine and the train. Such rolling measurement laboratories appeared around 1900 and carried a concentration of equipment for measuring almost two dozen performance variables on a continuous basis. The first dynamometer cars used the deflection of a large compression spring for determining drawbar force, while more modern designs employed a hydraulic system that required only a pressure measurement of the compressed hydraulic fluid.

To measure drawbar horsepower we must measure the variation of drawbar force as speed increases. Thus we can write that

$$\text{drawbar horsepower} = \frac{\text{drawbar force (pounds)} \times \text{speed (mph)}}{375}$$

where the number 375 is merely a conversion factor needed to make the dimensions consistent.

Later discussion will illustrate that drawbar force decreases as speed increases. Therefore, the product of these two values will always produce a maximum value. In general, freight locomotives generated maximum power at speeds between 30 and 40 mph, whereas

Delaware & Hudson dynamometer car No. 1, constructed by the railroad in 1905, rides on unusually long trucks and has a cupola for observation of the locomotive and train. In operation the test car was placed between the locomotive and train, and used calibrated springs to measure drawbar pull, along with many other performance parameters. A newly developed booster engine on the rear tender truck behind camelback 2-8-0 No. 901 is the reason for the 1923 test runs when this photo was taken. From *Delaware & Hudson*, Shaughnessy.

passenger power usually peaked at 65 to 75 mph. Examples of these variations will be presented in chapter 9.

As was noted earlier, there were many rules of thumb used during the early years of locomotive construction. A prime example was the publication in 1897 by the American Railway Master Mechanics Association (ARMMA) of a compilation of suggested ratios for sizing grate area, heating surface, and cylinders. While the approach was sound, the overall utility was minimal because there was simply not enough understanding of the way in which various design parameters interacted.

The general idea behind their approach was to take data from the best performing engines and create ratios of key specifications (such as the ratio of grate area to firebox volume, or boiler pressure to cylinder volume). Indeed, this general process was formalized many years later as a standard engineering design tool known as *physical modeling using similarity concepts*. The first step toward understanding the interaction of locomotive design parameters occurred in 1912 when Professor William F. M. Goss of the University of Illinois conducted evaporation tests in Coatesville, Pennsylvania on a heavily instrumented boiler. Although this test boiler was somewhat smaller than those in locomotive use, the data were considered to be an accurate representation of the evaporation processes. The major conclusion from these tests was that the water surrounding the firebox produced steam at six times the rate of that surrounding the boiler tubes. This was a significant finding and began the process of developing a science-based design methodology for steam locomotives.

Two years later Francis J. Cole of Alco carried out a detailed analysis of these tests and recast the results using the ARMMA idea of ratios. His report, *Tables of Locomotive Ratios*, became the primary design guide for steam locomotives and remained so until the super power era (1933), when some modifications were required. Using the Cole ratios, a designer could start with a desired performance (tractive effort or maximum horsepower) and, with a minimum amount of effort, end up with sizes for cylinders, boiler pressure, heating surface, and grate area. Finally there had emerged a more scientific basis for steam locomotive design.

CHAPTER 4

THE SECOND
GENERATION

In reviewing the evolution of American steam locomotives it is instructive to recall those wheel arrangements that were most popular. Considering only those engines used on American railroads, it is not surprising to find the 4-4-0 leading with 25,000, while the 2-8-0 was second at 21,000. In contrast, the two most popular second-generation engines were the 2-8-2 (19,500) and the 4-6-2 (6000). As is well known, the latter two types of locomotives were used on virtually every railroad and appeared in a wide range of sizes. Their popularity was a reflection of their versatility. They had the tractive effort to start heavy trains and the steaming capacity to provide sufficient horsepower to crest mainline grades at speed. Indeed, 2-8-2's could handle passenger trains if necessary, and a few roads used 4-6-2's in freight service on lines with flat profiles. Incidentally, the production numbers for other second-generation engines, the 4-4-2, 4-8-2, and 2-10-2, were almost the same, about 2000 each.

It is also no surprise that the introduction of trailing wheels (attached rigidly to the frame) did not coincide with improved fireboxes. In 1893 Baldwin produced a 2-4-2 (*Columbia* type) for the World's Columbian Exposition in Chicago and in 1895 delivered a batch of 4-4-2's to the Atlantic Coast Line (hence the name *Atlantic*). The first Atlantic type, with an enlarged firebox and a movable trailing truck, was delivered by Alco in 1900 to the Chicago & North Western. Both the builder and the railroad wanted to call it the *North Western* type, but the Atlantic name stuck.

Most Atlantic types were produced during the 1900–06 period and clearly demonstrated the importance of steaming rate to sustaining high speeds on the main line, but eventually long strings of all-steel passenger cars overwhelmed their pulling capability. The zenith of this configuration occurred three decades after its introduction, when the Milwaukee Road bought four streamlined, shovel-nosed models for Hiawatha service between Chicago and the Twin Cities. Conceived by the road's chief designer, C. H. Bilty, and built by Alco in 1935 with contemporary technology, the oil-burning *Hiawatha* types, as the Milwaukee Road named them, had ample grate area, a 300 psi boiler pressure, and 84-inch drivers. They routinely met, or bettered, a schedule that called for short sprints of 102 mph with a train of six to nine lightweight cars. Eventually, however, they suffered a common end for Atlantic types. They were replaced on the Hiawatha by 4-6-4's in 1938, but remained in service until late 1951.

The first decade of the twentieth century would see production begin on three other second-generation machines. The next new design appeared in 1902 when Missouri Pacific began receiving an order of 4-6-2's from the Brooks Works, while Alco (Schenectady)

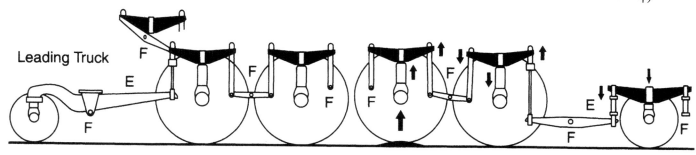

Leading Truck

was delivering similar models to the Chesapeake & Ohio. But the MP connection gave it the *Pacific* name. This reliable machine, whose precursor was a narrow-firebox model delivered to Milwaukee Road in 1896, would have a production run lasting until 1930. Well-known Pacifics included B&O's P7 class, Southern Railway's green and gold Ps4 (heavy USRA), and Pennsy's K4 with its distinctive Belpaire firebox. These are discussed in the following section.

Somewhat surprisingly, the next model to appear was not a beefed-up 2-8-0 but a stretched 2-10-0. Santa Fe needed more horsepower for its challenging profiles in the Far West and, in 1903, received from Baldwin the first of 250 engines with a 2-10-2-wheel arrangement. Naturally, they were called *Santa Fe* types. Only a year after these engines went into service, the first American 2-8-2's were delivered to Northern Pacific. While most engines of this type had driver diameters of 61 to 53 inches, Great Northern's O8 class was built in 1932 with 69-inch drivers that gave it more speed. Among the largest 2-8-2's were New York Central's H10 class, which will be discussed in chapter 6. Incidentally, the name *Mikado* for the 2-8-2 wheel arrangement came about after Baldwin shipped a group of such machines to Japan in 1906. (*The Mikado* was the name of Gilbert and Sullivan's enormously popular 1885 comic opera, set in Japan.) Even though these were not second-generation engines, the name stuck, although during World War II roads such as the Central of Georgia, Lehigh Valley, and Union Pacific called them *MacArthur* types.

The final model of second-generation, rigid-frame locomotives to appear was the 4-8-2 (*Mountain* type), delivered to C&O by Alco in 1911. Their initial usage was for heavy passenger trains between Charlottesville and Clifton Forge, where they were able to replace double-headed Pacifics. On many roads the 4-8-2 was also used for high-speed freight service. Both Illinois Central and Frisco used their company shops to rebuild lower-speed 2-10-2's into higher-horsepower 4-8-2's with 70-inch drivers, while the 50 engines of New York Central's L4 class (known as *Mohawks*), built by Lima in 1942–43 with 72-inch drivers, could take full advantage of the NYC's "water level" profiles.

Equalization rigging for a typical 2-8-2 locomotive shows independent suspension systems for front and rear sections of the main frame. Each section includes two driver axles and a supplementary axle. Points fixed to the frame are designated by F, while the pivoting equalizer bars are shown as E. Note the cross equalization of wheels on one side with those on opposite side. Adapted from *Steam Locomotives*, Westcott.

Facing page, top: Apex of the Atlantic: Milwaukee Road's C. H. Bilty designed an oil-burning 4-4-2 for the Hiawatha trains that pushed mid-1930s technology to its limits. With its 7-foot drivers and a large steaming capacity, the four streamlined locomotives built by Alco between 1935 and 1939 were the most advanced model of this wheel arrangement. Eric Hirsimaki Collection.

Facing page, middle: Louisville & Nashville light Pacific (class K2a) No. 172 was constructed by the road's South Louisville shops in 1907. High-mounted headlight and large trailing wheels with inside bearings were common features of early L&N engines. Shown at Mobile, Alabama in 1951. J. Parker Lamb.

Facing page, bottom: Frisco No. 1057 (Alco, 1912) represents a typical light Pacific, although it was unusual for one to have the elaborate striping pattern used by the SL-SF. Shown at St. Louis in 1939. Robert J. Foster, Joe Collias Collection.

Illinois Central 2-10-2 No. 2713 (Lima, 1920) eases out of the Louisville, Kentucky roundhouse and onto the turntable in 1957. Designated as the Central type, these heavy haulers were used on the hilly, coal-producing Kentucky Division between Louisville and Paducah. J. Parker Lamb.

The use of Belpaire fireboxes on American locomotives was confined largely to two major roads, Pennsylvania in the east and Great Northern in the west. Baldwin-built Mikado No. 3233, shown at Grand Forks, North Dakota in 1954, is an example of the later road's motive power in the second generation. Paul Eilenberger, Louis R. Saillard Collection.

Approaching the end of its operating days, a veteran Mikado can still strike an attractive pose on a summer afternoon in 1951. Built by Baldwin in 1912 as Erie No. 3036, it became Southern Railway No. 6637 (class Ms7) in 1942, and then went to short line Tennessee, Alabama & Georgia as No. 350 after the war. J. Parker Lamb.

With steaming rates increasing due to larger fireboxes carried by trailing trucks, designers soon realized that there was sufficient power available at low speed to add a small booster engine to drive the trailing axle. This idea was first conceived by Howard L. Ingersoll, a member of the New York Central's progressive mechanical department. In attempting to enhance the starting tractive effort of the road's K11 Pacifics to handle heavier trains, he devised a small, fully enclosed, two-cylinder steam engine that drove a pinion (small gear), which was connected via an intermediate gear (idler) to the trailing axle. As soon as the train speed reached 10 or 15 mph, the booster was cut off, the idler gear retracted, and the locomotive began operating in its usual mode. The additional starting tractive effort was usually between 10,000 and 15,000 pounds. Franklin Supply Company bought the production rights to these booster engines, and they were used until the end of the steam era to assist high-speed locomotives in starting heavy trains.

In 1906 the first Mallet with a large firebox appeared when Baldwin delivered a prototype 2-6-6-2 to the Great Northern Railroad. Its tractive effort was 59,500 pounds, and its job was to replace Consolidation types on Cascade grades and curves. GN's favorable response to its performance was reflected in the production models that featured a larger boiler diameter (from 7 feet to 8 feet), larger cylinders and grate area, and a 20 percent increase in tractive effort (to 71,600 pounds). Weighing in at some 355,000 pounds, these were the heaviest American locomotives built to that date.

The second-production articulated compound was also a 2-6-6-2. In 1911 Alco produced 25 class H2 engines for the Chesapeake & Ohio. Following GN's practice, the C&O engines were a replacement for double-headed 2-8-0's on the mountainous Hinton Division. By 1923 the road rostered 120 similar engines in the H2, H3, H4, and H6 classes (H5's were USRA designs of the World War I era). Even at the end of the steam era (four years after World War II ended), the C&O remained loyal to its coal-traffic base and ordered ten H6 engines. These became the last domestic locomotives built by the Baldwin Works.

One of the most common Harriman Standard designs was the Mikado, of which the two shown here are typical. Southern Pacific No. 786 was built in 1916 by Alco Brooks for the Houston & Texas Central (later part of the Texas & New Orleans), while Illinois Central No. 1274 was constructed by Lima to the same standard plans in the same year. The SP locomotive, except for the addition of a superheater in 1941, is virtually the same as when built, whereas the IC engine was substantially modified by the road's Paducah shops, which rebuilt hundreds of older locomotives during the latter half of the 1930s. The most obvious change was replacement of the small sand dome with a larger and more easily fabricated boxy shape, but there was also the addition of larger cylinders and a higher boiler pressure. The IC engine was recorded in 1951 at Meridian, Mississippi, while No. 786 was photographed 38 years later after being rebuilt near Austin, Texas for tourist service. J. Parker Lamb.

Lanky 4-8-2 No. 186 was one of three on the Western Railway of Alabama. It was part of a fleet constructed by Alco in 1924–28 for the Florida East Coast, which later sold them to a number of roads, including Western Pacific, Cotton Belt, Atlanta, Birmingham & Coast (later ACL), and National Railways of Mexico. J. Parker Lamb.

In 1936 Frisco's Springfield, Missouri shops, using boilers from its drag-era 2-10-2's, constructed ten modern 4-8-2's fitted with Scullin disk drivers. Number 4306 is shown at St. Louis in 1940. Robert J. Foster, Joe Collias Collection.

A low winter sun highlights the running gear of IC 4-8-2 No. 2527 heading from Centralia to Carbondale, Illinois in 1959. Built by the road's Paducah shops in 1939, modern Mountain types such as this were IC's premier tonnage engines in the final decades of steam power. J. Parker Lamb.

Pennsy's M1 class 4-8-2's were the backbone of its freight operations until the onslaught of World War II traffic brought the J1-class 2-10-4's onto the road. Here is grimy M1b No. 6796 (Lima, 1930) at Bradford Junction, Ohio in 1947 ready for the next coal train. Clyde E. Helms, Jay Williams Collection.

Pennsy's M1b 4-8-2's represented the road's last developmental step with this wheel arrangement. Here No. 6739 pulls a coal train into Enola yard in 1954. Note that the headlight and generator have been relocated from their original positions. Jay Williams Collection.

A 1922 Lima photo provides details of a two-cylinder booster engine applied to a trailing truck. The small cylinders are situated parallel to the tracks and drive a shaft that is parallel to the truck axle. The two shafts are connected with gears that can be disengaged at speeds up to 15–20 mph. Eric Hirsimaki Collection.

One of the significant features of these and most later Mallet compounds was that the engineer could start his train with the engine operating in a "simple" mode (i.e., high-pressure steam to all cylinders). Once the train was moving, the engineer closed a diverter valve and allowed the locomotive to revert to compound operation. This feature led to the most powerful of the ponderous compounds, Virginian Railway's ten 2-10-10-2's. Built by Alco in 1918, they rode on 56-inch drivers and developed a whopping 176,000 pounds of tractive effort when starting as a simple engine.

The idea of a completely simple, articulated engine materialized in 1912, only a year after C&O received its first H2 compounds, when the Pennsylvania Railroad received a 2-8-8-2 from Alco. Seven years later PRR's Juniata shops in Altoona built the first of its HC1-class 2-8-8-0's, which provided a starting tractive effort of 135,000 pounds. Chesapeake & Ohio received 25 simple 2-8-8-2's from Alco in 1924 and another 20 from Baldwin in 1926. The road would have preferred compounds, but its old tunnels lacked the clearance for the large low-pressure cylinders. With their 57-inch drivers, these were purely drag engines. Indeed, virtually all articulated engines of this early period were used mainly in slow-speed service, as pushers or helpers. Their usual role was to provide tractive effort in hilly terrain, not to speed along on the flat profiles. Eventually, over 3000 articulated locomotives would be built in the United States, with the majority being Mallet compounds.

Right and facing page:
The meaning of articulation: Articulated locomotives allowed designers to add more drivers (for greater power) without extending the rigid wheelbase of the locomotive. Two Norfolk & Western engines, Class A No. 1221 at Roanoke, Virginia and Y6b Mallet compound No. 2176, provide graphic illustrations of the flexibility of these behemoths. For example, the Mallet is on a curve as well as a section of undulating trackage at Grundy, Virginia. Nevertheless the ponderous beast is flexible enough to handle it with ease. Phillip A. Weibler.

The desire to move from compounds to simple, articulated locomotives was mainly a matter of efficiency (fuel economy). The massive front cylinders of the Mallets were very heavy and thus required robust side rodding that made balancing difficult, while their use of low-pressure steam made them less efficient. A simple engine required much smaller cylinders, pistons, and other moving parts on the lead engine. However, in the beginning, all articulateds were confined to low-speed service because there was little understanding of ways to control the lateral motion of the front engine, caused by dynamic loads from the alternating piston strokes. Moreover, in common with early two-wheel leading trucks, the front engine did not provide enough guiding force when the locomotive was negotiating a curve at speed. By the end of the 1930s both the lateral motion and guidance problems would be solved, and articulateds would become high-speed mainline machines.

Although the first two decades of the twentieth century had seen the emergence of more powerful engines with improved steaming rates, the third decade dawned with a clouded future for American railroads. Unpopular control by the U.S. Railroad Administration ended on March 1, 1920 and with it went the forced standardization of motive power. A recent book by E. L. Huddleston, *Uncle Sam's Locomotives*, covers this unique period in American railroad history. While USRA designs were adequate for many roads, their technology represented the status quo, and some of the larger, more progressive lines were eager

Most roads of the South found that engines from USRA designs of the World War I period were rugged and reliable. Thus they continued to order derivatives for many years afterward. Southern Railway heavy Mikado No. 4817 (Alco Richmond, 1923), shown in 1951 at the Meridian, Mississippi roundhouse, was typical of the engines that were the backbone of Southern's freight service, except in mountainous lines or routes with light roadbeds. This engine is fitted with a large Worthington model BL feedwater heater above the last driver. J. Parker Lamb.

Frisco's heavy Mikado No. 4137 (Baldwin, 1925), shown at St. Louis in 1949, is based on a USRA design but has a number of additional features such as tender booster, top-mounted air tanks, and 12-wheel tender. Robert J. Foster photo, Joe Collias Collection.

Baltimore & Ohio Mikado No. 4405 (class Q4; Baldwin, 1921) was assigned to helper service during its final months of operation. Here we see the USRA-type engine tucked behind the lead diesel units on an eastbound train from Dayton to Washington Court House, Ohio in 1956. Note the cab extension, which provides an extra seat for the head brakeman (behind the fireman). J. Parker Lamb.

Frisco's 4-8-2 No. 1517 (Baldwin, 1923) is posed in a classic "rods down" position at St. Louis in 1938. These engines were the road's premier passenger power until the acquisition of diesels. A sister engine (No. 1522) was restored for contemporary operation. Robert J. Foster, Joe Collias Collection.

for the next performance breakthrough. Among these was the New York Central, which had leaned heavily on Alco, an on-line industry, for its motive power.

A few years before the USRA era, there was a seemingly unrelated event in Ohio, home of the Lima Locomotive Corporation, which had fallen on hard times during 1915. Early the next year its midwestern owners sold out to a group of eastern financiers, led by super-salesman Joel Coffin and attorney Samuel G. Allen, who were managing partners in a number of locomotive appliance companies, including Franklin Railway Supply Company and American Arch Company. Within two months Coffin and associates had snagged a $3 million order from, who else, the New York Central, for 70 Mikados and 15 switchers. In April 1916 a new corporation was created, Lima Locomotive Works, and a new group of technical leaders was soon recruited, primarily from Alco. Thus was born a partnership of former Alco technical talent working for a small Ohio company on NYC motive power. From this unlikely group would emerge the next "performance breakthrough" in American steam locomotives.

Pacific: Queen of a Golden Age

A locomotive with the 4-6-2 wheel arrangement first appeared in a George Strong–designed, experimental camelback built in 1886 for the Lehigh Valley Railroad. Known more for its two marine-style furnaces than for the number of wheels on which it rode, it was soon rebuilt as a 4-6-0 and eventually destroyed in a collision. A narrow-firebox 4-6-2 was built for the Chicago, Milwaukee & St. Paul a year after the Valley engine and gave a sterling account of itself in high-speed (60 mph) passenger service. It too was later converted to a ten wheeler.

But the first *serious* engines of this wheel arrangement for an American railroad were delivered by Brooks to the Missouri Pacific in 1902, and the name *Pacific* was born. Generally overlooked were 13 Baldwin-built narrow-gauge (3.5 feet) 4-6-2's with wide fireboxes sent to New Zealand Railways a year earlier. The 1902 delivery to MP was followed closely by Pacifics to C&O (1902) and Santa Fe (1903). During the following two years, Pacific-type engines also went to B&O, Erie, Frisco, L&N, NYC, Milwaukee Road, SP, and UP. Indeed, an ICC census in 1911 showed 2240 Pacifics were in operation as compared to just 670 Mikados.

It is no accident that the blossoming of passenger service on American railroads during the first three decades of the twentieth century occurred parallel to the development of the Pacific as the premier passenger locomotive. For example, between 1900 and 1920, passenger miles on American railroads increased from 15 billion to 47.5 billion, a threefold traffic increase that was credited largely to longer trains powered by 4-6-2's, especially during the second decade of this period. How do we know this? There was an "ordering bulge," encompassing an astounding 2536 Pacifics, during a scant seven years starting in 1911. When this number is added to the 1911 census figures, it reveals that 80 percent of the 6000 American-built Pacifics had been delivered before 1920.

Not surprising, then, is the pervasiveness of the 4-6-2's contribution to the nation's rail service. In terms of geography, it operated in every mainland state, while the named trains it headed formed a pantheon of early American premier travel. An alphabetical sampler includes drumheads such as Alton Limited, Broadway Limited, Capitol Limited, Crescent Limited, Crusader, 400, George Washington, Mercury, Olympian, Panama Limited, Pan American, Sunshine Special, Texas Special, and Twentieth Century Limited.

Its longevity of service was a reflection of the Pacific's versatility, reliability, and capability for being modernized. Year after year 4-6-2's gave steady and outstanding performances such as those of Erie's big K5's, which routinely covered the 830 miles between Jersey City and Marion, Ohio without change. Moreover, reliable L&N Pacifics handling the crack South Wind were given the road's only 12-wheel tenders in order to run nonstop for the 205 miles between Nashville and Birmingham. Although 4-6-2's on many major passenger routes

Baltimore & Ohio Pacific No. 5216 (class P5a; Baldwin, 1919) waits at Washington Union Station with the northbound Capitol Limited in the late 1930s. B&O Railroad, James Mischke Collection.

To head up its Firefly train between Kansas City and Tulsa, Frisco covered the light 4-6-2 No. 1026 (Baldwin, 1919) in an attractive shroud. Here train No. 118 pulls past the depot at Sapulpa, Oklahoma in 1946. Joe Collias.

were supplanted on heavier trains by Mountain and Hudson types after 1930, there were a number of roads, both large and small, that transitioned directly from Pacifics to passenger diesels. Examples include Alton, Chicago & Eastern Illinois, Monon, Erie, Kansas City Southern, Katy, L&N, Reading, and Southern.

But the most staunch Pacific user (until after World War II) and the road that owned the largest fleet did not embrace the 4-6-2 until almost 1917. Although the Pennsylvania Railroad bought its first experimental 4-6-2 engine in 1906 and began using its K2 design in 1910, it was not until the Pennsy's chief mechanical engineer J. T. Wallis directed the development of the K4 model that its roster of 4-6-2 engines began to soar in size. During the decade starting in 1917, PRR produced a whopping 425 copies of the K4 design that served as the backbone of its passenger power pool until the road bought 52 duplex T1's in 1944–46 (see chapter 9). Even as late as July 1947 the roster of K4's had shrunk by only *three* engines.

From visual evidence of boiler and driver sizes, most observers will conclude that the Belpaire-boilered K4 was merely an elongation of the road's highly successful E6-class Atlantics. In actuality however, most of the K4's mechanical features were matured on two early experimental Pacifics (with rounded boiler tops) produced by Alco. These in turn had much in common with Schenectady's famous No. 50000, the nation's first *heavy* Pacific, designed by Francis Cole and built in 1911. This pioneer machine was a forerunner of the later super power era, with 79-inch drivers, cast-steel cylinders, superheater, and a large grate (60 square feet). Eventually sold to Erie after a demonstration tour, she gained a new number (No. 2509, class K3) and the nickname *Big Liz*. She provided outstanding service until the scrapper came calling in 1950.

In comparison with many other designs of the period, the Pennsy K4 proved itself in the beginning without such amenities as a mechanical stoker, power reverse, superheater, or trailing truck booster. In other words, the early K4's were all about *brute strength*, both from the crew and the 80-inch-drivered machine with a generous steaming capacity. With subsequent and inevitable modernization they became the most powerful Pacifics in history. There were also the unforgettable daily scenes in downtown Chicago stations around 1918 when three, four, or even more sections of PRR's Broadway Limited and NYC's Twentieth Century Limited were lined up for departure with gleaming Pacifics in the lead of every train. A short time later the two trains sprinted eastward beside each other on parallel tracks after leaving suburban Inglewood station. This was the brightest period of limelight for these high-wheeled machines.

Pennsy K4s Pacific No. 5485 (Juniata, 1927) is ready to depart St. Louis with The American in 1937. In true PRR tradition, the locomotive carries the train name on a cast plaque under the Keystone number plate. Robert J. Foster, Jay Williams Collection.

Caught at speed in a classic wedge shot, K4s No. 5421 tears up the track near Columbus, Ohio with Pennsy's Fast Mail in 1937. Jay Williams Collection.

With a long heavyweight train the Pennsy found it necessary to use a pair of K4 engines during the years before and during World War II. Here is the Liberty Limited at Englewood, Illinois in 1941, headed by K4s No. 5352. Jay Williams Collection.

Atlantic Coast Line liked its light USRA Pacifics (of World War I vintage) so much that it later ordered 165 low-drivered, dual-purpose 4-6-2's (class P5b) from Baldwin between 1922 and 1926. Here is No. 1655 leaving St. Petersburg with a freight in the 1950s. George W. Pettengill Jr., C. K. Marsh Jr. Collection.

For locomotive historians, however, what may be the most puzzling question is why Pennsy's final order for 100 Pacifics in 1927–28 occurred at all. In making this massive expenditure, the road seemed to ignore not only the possible future expansion of its electrified territory but also the new steam locomotive technology being developed beyond the doors of its shops at Altoona (i.e., the super power Hudson type). Thus, a proud and stubborn Pennsy was boxing itself into two decades of double-headed passenger trains that other roads were dispatching behind a single Hudson or Northern locomotive. Such was the price it paid for strict adherence to the motive power philosophy (circa 1867) espoused by then master of machinery Alexander J. Cassatt, and continued by General William W. Atterbury, general superintendent of motive power. Their dictum was "build a locomotive fleet using only a few proven, standard designs." While great for the bottom line, such practices often stifled innovation, and encouraged incremental improvements to solve immediate shortcomings rather than revolutionary changes that might have been effective for a much longer time.

Another source of later Pacifics was the standardized designs of the U.S. Railroad Administration between 1917 and 1920. Of the 1830 engines constructed, 81 were *light* Pacifics and 20 others were *heavy* models. Collectively they represented only slightly more than 5 percent of the total, since motive power needs for freight were of more strategic importance than for passengers. And as we have noted, there was already a good supply of this wheel arrangement. For many wealthy and progressive roads, the USRA designs were treated with some disdain as being pedestrian. On the other hand, many lines that initially chafed under the revolutionary concept of "one size fits all" later duplicated and improved these designs once government control ended.

The region that generally found the most to like about USRA engines was the South, where much of the freight traffic was composed of lightweight agricultural products since there were relatively few large industrial complexes in this region. USRA 4-6-2's found one of their most unexpected roles on a southern line whose name was "Atlantic" but which operated as a "Pacific" railroad. The Atlantic Coast Line was allocated over half (45 of 81) of the USRA light 4-6-2's, and after World War I it bought 25 more to complete its P5a class. Shortly thereafter it asked Baldwin to build what it called a *dual-service* Pacific by increasing the boiler pressure from 200 to 210 psi and decreasing the driver diameter from 73 to 69

inches. The result was an astounding 165 locomotives of the P5b class. The 235 engines of the P5 class were the mainstays of a roster that also included 83 pre-USRA designs, giving 4-6-2's a dominant position (25 percent) in the ACL locomotive roster.

Needless to say, 4-6-2's monopolized the road's web of Florida lines as well as its double-tracked, water-level main lines whose traffic was dominated by passengers and perishables. Thus a typical Coast Line 4-6-2 would regularly haul an expedited reefer train one day and lead the Havana Special the next. And when tonnage increased the road merely added another Pacific on the front end. After World War II the ACL gained 13 older Pacifics from its takeover of the Atlanta, Birmingham & Coast Railroad in 1946. Most of these were former Florida East Coast Railway engines, but one was, of all things, a former Great Northern engine that sported a Belpaire firebox.

Another railroad where USRA Pacifics rose to prominence was the Southern Railway System, whose passenger power carried a green color scheme with gold striping and white trim. In 1923–24 Schenectady built the first 21 heavy USRA 4-6-2's of the Ps4 class. Their

Atlantic Coast Line's profiles along the East coast and in Florida allowed its 165 class P5b Pacifics, such as No. 1730, to work both freight and passenger trains with equal facility. ACL's use of the Pacific as a dual-purpose locomotive was unique in the United States. David Price Collection.

Southern Railway's Ps4 heavy Pacific No. 6691 (Alco Richmond, 1926) was based on a USRA design. Shown at the Birmingham, Alabama station in 1947, it was assigned to subsidiary Alabama Great Southern Railroad. J. E. Jones, Frank E. Ardrey Collection.

The Wimble smoke duct mounted on Southern Ps4 No. 6482 (Alco Richmond, 1926) is a clear sign that this engine was assigned to the famous Rat Hole Division (Cincinnati to Chattanooga), named for its numerous tunnels. Shown at Cincinnati in 1937. Louis R. Saillard Collection.

Pacific No. 1380 (class Ps4; Alco Richmond, 1923) was streamlined in 1941 for service on Southern's streamlined Tennesseean between Washington and Memphis. C. W. Witbeck, Frank E. Ardrey Collection.

Pacific No. 5301 (class P7d) leads Baltimore & Ohio's Cincinnatian northward from Dayton, Ohio in 1955. Built by Baldwin in 1927, it was one of a group rebuilt and streamlined in 1946. It lasted until the end of B&O steam. J. Parker Lamb.

outstanding performance between Washington and Atlanta resulted in an additional 15 engines in 1924, while two years later 23 more were delivered, the first to receive the green and gold paint scheme. While on vacation in England in 1925, SR president Fairfax Harrison came to admire the light green engines of that country's Southern Railway and decided to order the Richmond Works to apply a similar paint job on the Ps4's then under construction.

The decision was a public relations bonanza for his line in particular and the railroad industry in general. The Ps4's appearance was also enhanced by Southern's practice of assigning its senior crews to certain engines, allowing them to install optional equipment on *their* locomotives. Thus operating crews and shop forces worked together to turn the clock back to the highly decorated 4-4-0's of the 1850s, adding such trim items as brass candlesticks flanking the headlights, stars on cylinder heads, brass rings on stacks, and eagles on smokebox doors. No wonder so many "Yankee" railfans were captivated by the sight of these engines on their daily visits to Washington, D.C. and Cincinnati. The final five Ps4's were delivered by Baldwin in 1928, giving the road a total of 64 copies of this handsomely proportioned and strikingly painted Pacific, which epitomizes the legacy of the versatile 4-6-2 wheel arrangement. Fortunately, one of these locomotives, Southern No. 1401, is permanently enshrined in the nation's display case, the Museum of American History at the Smithsonian Institution.

No discussion of the Pacific would be complete without mention of the B&O's President-class engines, 20 heavy 4-6-2's (class P7) built by Baldwin in 1927 with a slight resemblance to the USRA configuration. Originally outfitted in olive green with red and gold striping, they carried the names of the first twenty chief executives. By 1943 all had been repainted into B&O's last passenger scheme of royal blue and had lost their names. The twenty-first President Pacific was built in 1928 by B&O's Mt. Clare shops as a test bed (class

Baltimore & Ohio's only
P7e Pacific, No. 5315
(Baldwin, 1929) was
modernized in 1949 during
one of the last B&O engine
rebuilding projects. Shown
at Dayton, Ohio in
December 1955. J. Parker
Lamb.

P9) for the Caprotti valve gear and an Emerson-type water tube firebox (see chapter 9).
Both of these were eventually removed (the valve gear after a year and the firebox some
17 years later).

In 1937 the road's Royal Blue was given a streamlined consist, while P7 No. 5304 received a bullet-nosed shroud to match (class P7a). However, as soon as ElectoMotive cab
units were delivered in 1939, the 4-6-2 reverted to its original unstreamlined exterior. A 1944
rebuilding of six engines produced an almost new locomotive, both mechanically and in
appearance. New cast-steel main frames with integral cylinders were utilized along with
feedwater heaters, shielded air pumps on the pilot beam, and a sleek, fully jacketed boiler
with a centered headlight on the smokebox. These P7c machines were almost unrecognizable as traditional B&O locomotives.

Four other Presidents were also rebuilt as P7d's in 1946 for the streamlined Cincinnatian.
Along with the new shrouds, Nos. 5301–5304 received roller bearings throughout. Timken
had offered these to the industry in 1930, but the normally progressive B&O had taken 16
years to embrace them (see chapter 8). Five years after World War II ended and 10 years
after passenger diesels were introduced, the nation's oldest railroad was still tinkering with
its 1927 Pacifics. The road finally installed roller bearings on two additional Presidents
(P7e's) and added a skirt along the running board. Such modernization was no doubt
welcomed by crews, but it would last only six or seven years.

CHAPTER 5

MOTIVE POWER MAVERICKS

As we have seen, American engine designers and builders were known as both innovative and diligent, always seeking to make improvements in locomotive performance even though they were aware of their limited understanding of the real causes for performance failures. We have also seen that their constant experimentation, although mostly unsuccessful, opened the door to later improvements. In this chapter we review a group of the promising design concepts that were carved out of steel for public demonstration. Some were successful and lasted for a while until supplanted by new technology. Others failed to live up to their expectations and quickly disappeared. Their failure was often due to an overlooked or unknown aspect of the physics of locomotion.

In an earlier section we mentioned briefly the concept of compound engines that expanded steam in two cylinders rather than one. When this concept came to America in the 1880s it was directed first toward improving rigid-frame (first-generation) engines. However, this proposal immediately provoked a heated debate among railroad mechanical departments. Some saw significant economic advantages for engines that used steam twice, while others said the added mechanical complexity wasn't worth the fuel savings. The Baldwin Works came down on the pro side and, using its considerable industrial prowess, promoted and produced these designs for nearly four decades.

One of the first attempts to build a high-speed simple articulated occurred in 1930 when the Baltimore & Ohio constructed two experimental 2-6-6-2's, one of which contained a water tube firebox. In 1932, George Emerson, B&O's chief of motive power, had this engine remodeled into a 4-4-6-2 for possible passenger service. Denoted as class KK1, No. 7400 carried 70-inch drivers and generated 250 psi steam. Unfortunately, its operational success was limited both by its unusual boiler and a lack of tracking ability by the lead engine, and the locomotive was returned to its original wheel arrangement in 1933. This company photograph is one of the few visual records of a rare locomotive whose life span was only a year. Baltimore & Ohio, James Mischke Collection.

Switcher on steroids: Switching locomotives operated at low speeds in yard and industrial settings and thus did not need leading trucks. In the modern era most shifter designs were 0-8-0's, although a few roads added tender boosters to increase tractive power and others used 0-10-0's for hump pushers. In 1936 the Union Railroad of Pittsburgh, a U.S. Steel line, received five of the largest switcher-type engines ever built. Needing enough power to move loaded iron ore and coal drags of up to 80 cars from a connection with the Bessemer & Lake Erie to the steel mills, the road opted for a unique 0-10-2 configuration, augmented with a tender booster. The result was a drag engine with a starting tractive effort of 90,900 pounds, equivalent to an articulated. Eric Hirsimaki Collection.

Early Compound Designs

We will examine four major configurations for compound, rigid-frame locomotives that represent an interesting chapter in American locomotive evolution. The simplest was Mallet's original design, called a *cross compound,* which carried a high-pressure cylinder on the left side and a larger (by 2.5 times) cylinder on the other side that was powered by the exhaust. Those who watched and heard a cross-compound locomotive at work were often heard to remark that it was "a lopsided, off-beat sounding creature."

The next compound design in the United States was developed by Samuel M. Vauclain, who had begun his railroad career as an apprentice mechanic with the Pennsylvania Railroad's shop in Altoona. He joined Baldwin in 1883, was promoted to general superintendent of the works in 1886, and made a partner in 1896. Upon formation of the corporation in 1911, he was made a vice president, becoming senior vice president in 1917 and president in 1919.

Almost every railroad that bought Baldwin locomotives participated in the compound era. Brand-new Norfolk & Western ten wheeler No. 72 (circa 1900) displays its brightly jacketed Vauclain stacked cylinders, and their associated dual crosshead, along with a Belpaire firebox. Baldwin photograph, Kalmback Publishing Co.

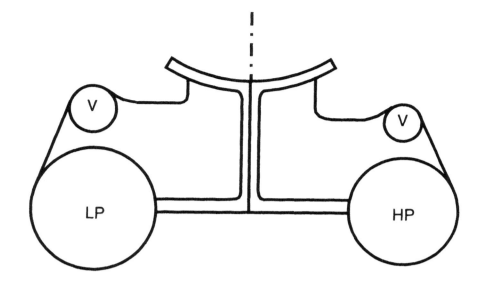

Arrangement of cylinders and valves for a cross-compound locomotive. View is toward the front of the engine. The smaller, high-pressure (HP) cylinder and its valve (V) are on right.

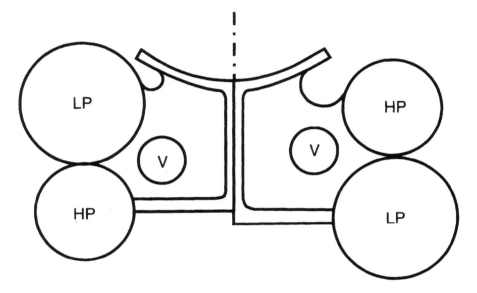

Arrangement of cylinders in a Vauclain compound, in which high-pressure and low-pressure cylinders are stacked atop one another. The most common configuration is shown at right. For engines with small drivers, it was necessary to move the large, low-pressure cylinder to the upper position, as shown on left.

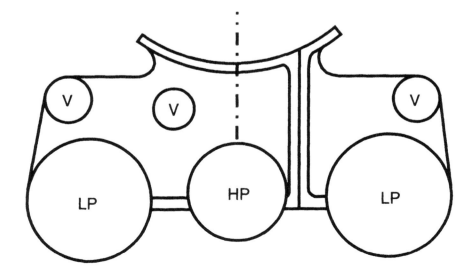

Arrangement of cylinders for a three-cylinder, balanced-compound design. The center (high-pressure) cylinder drives a cranked axle (inside the main frame), whereas the two outside, low-pressure cylinders are sized so that their operating pressure will produce balanced loads between the two sets of driving gear (inside and outside). Adapted from *The Steam Locomotive in America*, Bruce.

Soon after arriving at Baldwin, he patented a four-cylinder configuration (*Vauclain compound*) in which both low- and high-pressure cylinders were located on each side, *one above the other*. In most cases the smaller-diameter chamber was placed above the low-pressure one. The two piston rods were attached to a common crosshead that was connected to the main driving rod. For an engine with a small driver diameter and less ground clearance, it was necessary to place the smaller cylinder in the lower position (an "upside down" compound). The first Vauclain compound was a beautiful blue 4-4-0 for the B&O, delivered in October 1889. In mid-1897 a Baldwin-built camelback Atlantic set speed records on the Camden–Atlantic City run of the Philadelphia & Reading. Over a period of 52 days, it averaged 69 mph on a 55-mile stretch.

By 1891 Baldwin had sold scores of its Vauclain compounds, but the company, and especially "Mr. Sam," wanted to convince railroad people throughout the nation that these locomotives could be used in dual service, both passenger-express and expedited freight service. So in October 1891, a new ten wheeler, numbered 82 and resplendent in deep olive green with gold leaf striping, was rolled out for a public display. Soon it hit the road for what turned into a five-year barnstorming tour, running on the B&O, on the Pennsy to Chicago, the Burlington out of Chicago, the N&W and Southern Railway in Virginia, and even some tests on the Reading and B&O using fuel oil. Doubtless this "fancy green nomad" helped Baldwin bolster its sales figures, with an eventual total of over 2000 compound locomotives, around 70 percent of which used the Vauclain design. Many of these went overseas to virtually every national railway system in existence.

In 1902 the Baldwin Works celebrated its seventieth anniversary as Vauclain unveiled his new *balanced-compound* design, embodied in a 4-6-0—locomotive number 20,000 to carry the Baldwin builder's plate. The engine was part of an order for the Plant System in Florida (a predecessor of the Atlantic Coast Line). The word "balanced" refers to the arrangement of the four piston strokes. The two high-pressure cylinders were inside the frame and drove the first axle that was built with two "cranks" (similar to those on an automobile crankshaft). The two low-pressure, outside cylinders drove crankpins on the first drivers in the usual manner (with outside crankpins out of phase by 90 degrees). But, in addition, the strokes from the inside pistons were out of phase by 180 degrees from those on the outside of the same drivers. The result of this mechanical timing was that virtually all of the rotational forces on the drivers were balanced out. Thus the driving-wheel counterweights could be very small and there was almost no pounding of the rails.

But Vauclain's design wasn't the only balanced compound to appear. In 1904 the de Glehn configuration debuted in the United States when the Pennsylvania Railroad ordered a demonstration 4-6-0 from a plant in Belfort, France. Although its performance was satisfactory, it was, in common with most other European-built engines, too light to haul American-length trains. Ironically, only three years later Baldwin constructed 20 de Glehn 4-6-0's for the Paris-Orleans Railway using construction drawings furnished by the railroad. These were of course expressed in metric system dimensions, a first for the works.

Alco joined the balanced-compound field in 1904 when it unveiled Francis J. Cole's design of an Atlantic-type locomotive for the New York Central & Hudson River. His configuration differed in detail from Vauclain's, with high-pressure (inside cylinders) shoved forward onto the pilot beam. They drove a cranked front axle, while the low-pressure cylinders were connected to the second axle in the traditional manner. A similar engine went to the Pennsylvania a year later, but the Cole design saw little application.

The final type of rigid-frame, dual-expansion engine was the *tandem compound*. In this design, both the low- and high-pressure cylinders were on the outside of the frame and were placed *one behind the other*. This arrangement had the advantage of producing more power with much simpler mechanisms (thus less maintenance costs). Although Brooks Works designer John Player produced the first workable model of a 2-8-0 for the Great Northern in 1892, it was left to a Santa Fe designer (with the same name but unrelated) to push this design toward the mainstream. In the late 1890s, the Topeka shops built a 4-6-0 express engine and several 2-8-o's for testing. These engines proved to be very efficient, and when the road turned to Baldwin for an entirely new type of locomotive, it specified tandems. Between 1903 and 1917 Baldwin turned out 160 such engines with the 2-10-2 wheel arrangement (Santa Fe type).

The end of the compound era for rigid-frame locomotives came around 1914 when Baldwin built a group of four-cylinder Pacifics for the Santa Fe Railroad. Writing in the September 1951 issue of *Trains* magazine, David P. Morgan noted: "The bullet that slew it [the compound] was a gadget called the superheater. At one stroke it gave simple engines compound economies without compound maintenance costs. Better yet, superheaters could easily be fitted onto existing engines. In essence, the compound was a dead number when the doughboys sailed for France." The result was that most rigid-frame compounds were soon scrapped or rebuilt as simple engines with superheaters.

Delaware & Hudson's Philosophy

Although Morgan was correct in assessing the national trend, there were at least two important railroad figures who would *not* let the compound idea die. Besides Vauclain there was Leonor Fresnel Loree who, after serving as president of the B&O between 1901 and 1906, became president of the Delaware & Hudson in 1907. Although Loree had shown an affinity for using Mallet articulateds on both the B&O's Sand Patch grade and the D&H's Ararat Summit, what set him apart from the industry was his redesign of the D&H's camelback Consolidations with their wide fireboxes.

During the 25 years between the two world wars, Delaware & Hudson converted many camelback engines into conventional configurations. Mechanically the process transformed engines using saturated steam and slide valves into ones using higher-pressure, superheated steam in piston valves. These two photos illustrate the transformation of ten wheeler No. 556, built by Alco in 1907 (*top*). We see that the modernized engine, completed in 1927 (*bottom*), is fitted with outside ash pans for its Wooten firebox, along with a leading truck using outboard bearings. In a cosmetic move, all piping was hidden beneath a shiny nickel-plated jacket, satisfying D&H President Loree's desire that his engines exhibit the "clean, English-like" appearance. From *Delaware & Hudson*, Shaughnessy.

Experimental Delaware &
Hudson Consolidation No.
1400, the *Horatio Allen,*
posed for this portrait soon
after delivery in 1924. This
unusual 2-8-0 contained a
water tube firebox, cross-
compound cylinders, and a
tender booster engine,
which exhausted through
the top of the water tank.
The compound steam
delivery also necessitated
use of the unconventional
valve gear configuration
seen here. From *Delaware
& Hudson,* Shaughnessy.

Under Loree, D&H's able mechanical department at its Albany headquarters, along
with its superb shop facilities at nearby Colonie, pursued a different path from the national
trend toward second-generation engines with trailing wheels and more drivers. As an anthracite hauler with short routes in mountainous territory, D&H saw drawbar pull, not
speed, as its primary need. And, like nearby coal lines such as Lehigh & Hudson River,
Lehigh & New England, and Reading, it found that the tried-and-true 2-8-0 configuration
would serve very well, thank you. Indeed, during the two decades between the two world
wars (1918–40), D&H built 14 Consolidations and three Pacifics in its Colonie shops.

However, by 1924 it began a general overhaul of its ancient camelback 2-8-0's, which used
saturated steam and incorporated Stephenson valve gear connected to slide valves. Over 100
engines (of various wheel arrangements) were thoroughly rebuilt between 1924 and 1936,
including a few 2-8-0's that were converted to 0-8-0 switchers. The 35 rebuilt Consolidations
emerged from Colonie shops with their mid-boiler cabs replaced by small, conventional
enclosures perched on the rear of the Wooten fireboxes. Moreover, the D&H designers
covered most of the pumps and piping with boiler jackets and shrouds. Higher boiler pressures and modern valve gear boosted tractive efforts from 38,000 to 51,000 pounds.

The second of D&H's trio of experimental 2-8-0's was No. 1401, the *John B. Jervis,* seen here
in 1927 with it original boiler shroud, which was later extended up to the bell. Clearly
evident is the large low-pressure cylinder, which is fed by the exhaust from the opposite side
through the large pipe in front of the stack. Circular shapes at the ends of the firebox
shrouds are the ends of high-pressure steam drums (400 psi) in the water tube boiler. The
tender rides on a three-axle lead truck and a two-axle booster truck. From *Delaware &
Hudson,* Shaughnessy.

Since tonnage ratings were of primary importance, D&H designers began using Franklin booster engines, developed by the New York Central in 1919 for trailing axles. Instead, they applied the boosters to the first axle of the rear tender truck, using a short side rod to connect the second axle so as to put four additional drive wheels in contact with the rail. First installed on an older camelback 2-8-0 for testing, the tender booster produced a 50 percent increase in the engine's tonnage rating, making it better for both mainline grades and hump yard service. Of all the D&H innovations, the tender booster saw the widest application.

But Loree still wasn't fully satisfied that the rebuilt 2-8-0's were the ultimate mountain engine for the D&H. Calling in an old colleague from his B&O days, Loree asked John Muhlfeld (now a consultant) to develop a new design that would improve fuel efficiency on the road's 2-8-0's. Soon he settled on a high-pressure marine-type steam generator, called a *water tube* firebox in contrast with the conventional *staybolted* design, as well as a Mallet cross-compound steam delivery system.

Working with its exclusive builder, nearby Alco in Schenectady, the railroad displayed the first of its new super Consolidations on December 14, 1924. Named *Horatio Allen* in honor of the man who first ran D&H's *Stourbridge Lion* in 1829, No. 1400 displayed a unique top-heavy appearance that included a myriad of pipes and tanks around the large boiler and firebox. In front, a pair of spoked lead-truck wheels were situated far from the cylinders. Muhlfield noted that the water tube firebox contained 37 percent of the evaporative surface, as opposed to the usual 27 to 30 percent, and that the boiler produced steam at 350 psi. However, most of those who heard Muhlfeld's remarks at the rollout ceremonies probably chuckled quietly when he said, "There is nothing unusual about the *Horatio Allen*."

The 1400's unique appearance was matched by its impressive performance on the road, pulling the same tonnage on 8 tons of coal that two conventional 2-8-0's would have hauled using 12 tons. Thus, after two severe winters of service without problems, Alco delivered a near duplicate (No. 1401) named *John B. Jervis*, with a boiler pressure of 400 psi and slightly smaller cylinders. The final member of the trio was No. 1402, built in 1930. The *James Archbald* carried 500 psi steam under a voluminous boiler shroud that covered all the previously exposed plumbing. It also used 63-inch drivers rather than the usual 57 inchers.

Although the three 2-8-0's had performed beyond expectations, Loree and Muhlfeld had one more demonstrator to produce. The largest and most elaborate of the D&H's experiments left Alco in 1933 carrying the name of the man behind these locomotive ventures. The *L. F. Loree* was a triple-expansion 4-8-0 carrying 500 psi steam that fed two pair of opposed, external cylinders, all of which drove a common axle. A high-pressure cylinder was mounted beneath the cab (engineer's side), and it exhausted to an intermediate pressure that powered a companion cylinder under the fireman's feet. In turn the two front cylinders were both fed from exhaust of the intermediate cylinder. The valves were cam-driven

The final experimental locomotive for the D&H was constructed by Alco in 1933, and was the nation's sole domestic delivery during that lean year. Named for President L. F. Loree, No. 1403 was a triple-expansion 4-8-0 that generated 500 psi steam in its water tube firebox. This was sent first to the cylinder beneath the engineer's seat (shown here) and then exhausted to a companion cylinder on the opposite side of the cab. The exhaust from this cylinder was directed to the two low-pressure cylinders in the front. The long control rod between the main driver and the rear cylinder provides the necessary mechanical connection to the Dabeg poppet valve control cams. For this engine a Bethlehem booster engine on the rear truck drove three axles, giving this small but complex locomotive the same starting drawbar force as a Mallet articulated (108,000 pounds). From *Delaware & Hudson*, Shaughnessy.

poppet types. When starting as a simple engine, with tender booster cut in, the *Loree* generated 108,000 pounds of tractive effort, over twice as much as the rebuilt conventional 2-8-0's. We note in passing that these four experimentals were among the final American steam locomotives to carry names.

As often happens with experimental machines, by the time the technology is available to produce them, the window of opportunity for their commercialization and utilization has closed. And so it was with these four interesting locomotive designs. They were high-quality machinery in both design and construction, but the D&H by this time was changing from a coal drag route to a fast-freight, bridge line with Canada. Two years after Loree retired from the D&H in 1938 due to poor health, Alco was delivering super power locomotives with high drivers and four-wheel trailing trucks.

Vauclain's Grand Experiment

Even as the allure of compound engines began to fade around 1920, none other than Baldwin president Samuel Vauclain led his company in a bold move to keep alive the cause of compound steam delivery. A year after Loree started building his experimental 2-8-0's, Baldwin decided to make another public relations statement with a new locomotive model that would tour the nation celebrating the company's production of engine number 60,000. Surprisingly, Vauclain decided to use the gigantic 4-10-2 (*Southern Pacific* type) as his "base engine design," even though the original models of this wheel arrangement were Alco products. Schenectady had sent 10 of these to the Union Pacific in 1925 and 49 more to the Southern Pacific in 1926–27.

Since the UP bought the first examples of this wheel arrangement, some have called them *Overland* types, but Southern Pacific was the more common name for these uncommon locomotives. All were three-cylinder compounds, with one cylinder between the frame. They also used 12-wheel Vanderbilt tenders, which Vauclain decided to retain. As his engineering team came together on the design, they decided that the high-pressure, center cylinder would power the second pair of drivers via a cranked axle, while the two outside cylinders would drive the third pair. All three cylinders would be the same size in order to better balance the loads.

To supply the necessary steaming capacity the designers decided to use a 350 psi boiler pressure, which was beyond the capability of a conventional staybolted design. In lieu of a trailing truck booster, they allowed a "simple start," as did most compounds of this era. And so, like Muhlfeld of the D&H, Vauclain decided on a water tube firebox. Learning of the Brotan design used on the Austrian State Railways, Mr. Sam sent an engineer over for discussions with the developer. This was a fortunate move, as the European design had some flaws that the Baldwin engineers were able to correct. Although it was common for long-wheelbase engines to have some flangeless drivers (for negotiating curves), the Baldwin designers kept flanges on all drivers but mounted the lead axle on a lateral motion pedestal that allowed it to move sideways, and thus permit the 4-10-2 to maneuver around a 17-degree curve if necessary.

On a March day in 1926, engine No. 60000 emerged from the Eddystone (Pa.) shop clad in an exhibition finish of royal purple with gold leaf striping. As soon as it finished a few test runs with freight trains near Philadelphia, Vauclain sent the engine to the Pennsy test lab in Altoona, where its performance amazed longtime test engineers. The big engine's output had never been equaled in their facility. Using cutoff settings of 50 to 90 percent on the high-pressure cylinders and 20 to 70 percent on the low-pressure ones, the engineers found the indicated horsepower ranged from 1500 to a peak of 4515, the first time any engine had reached the plant's capacity. In addition there was a noticeable absence of vibrations owing to the new type of load balancing between the power cylinders.

(*Top*) Builder's portrait of 4-10-2 No. 60000 reveals the large water tube firebox and a jacket virtually devoid of piping. The lack of clear view beneath the boiler (just above the first driver) is a reminder of the valve gear, crossheads, and other machinery associated with the high-pressure cylinder. (*Bottom*) Once inside the Franklin Museum, No. 60000 was made visitor friendly to better entertain those curious about how a steam locomotive works. Just behind the flag (in foreground) is the high-pressure cylinder below the boiler and its associated valve. Both are identified by name. *Top*: Baldwin photograph, Kalmbach Publishing Co.; *Bottom*: Kalmbach Publishing Co.

Then it was on to the Pennsy main line for runs between Enola and West Morrisville, where the 4-10-2 competed with the PRR's largest freight engines. The big brute proved it could lug a 7000-ton train up a 26-mile grade, while using less coal than comparative power. The national tour began, as had others, on the B&O. But this time the engine was assigned to mountainous lines, where it performed extremely well during biting winter weather, surpassing the road's S1 class 2-10-2's by 27 percent in average speed. Next it worked westward to Chicago on Erie rails, where it set performance marks that would later be challenged by the road's 2-8-4's.

While No. 60000 was in the Windy City, over 20,000 spectators streamed past to observe and admire this huge embodiment of power. Later it competed against Burlington's 2-10-2's on Southern Illinois coal trains, where its performance and potential savings were extremely impressive. Moving over to the Santa Fe at Fort Madison, Iowa, it underwent a series of track tests. These proved that such a large balanced-compound locomotive produced much lower stresses within the rails when compared with conventional engines of similar weight. Next there were some dynamometer tests on the Santa Fe between Clovis and Belen, New Mexico, where the 60000 was compared with AT&SF's 3800-series 2-10-2's. Again the 4-10-2 displayed savings of 20 to 25 percent in fuel and water.

Then it was scheduled for a long stint on the Southern Pacific. First, the engine was hauled to the Sacramento shops for conversion to oil burning. There was also a thorough checkup, since the engine had run 75,000 miles after leaving the works. After the driver tires were turned and new packings were put on pistons, the engine was ready for a touch-up paint job and another public display. During the midst of these ceremonies an Interstate Commerce Commission inspector, not knowing of the special firebox design, climbed into the cab, spotted the steam pressure gauge at 350 psi, and immediately put a red tag on the cab handrails, meaning that the locomotive was embargoed. Baldwin soon cleared the matter with ICC's Washington offices, and No. 60000 was ready to work SP routes.

Emphasis was on the challenging line between Roseville and Sparks, Nevada, where the 4-10-2 was tested with a dynamometer car in both passenger and freight service. On eastbound freights the trains were 3100 tons from Roseville to Colfax, and then 2100 tons over the summit and into Sparks, while westbound tonnage was 5000 to Truckee, where it was reduced to 2000 over the summit. By January 1928 (and nearly two years of service) the engine arrived for a three-day exhibit in Portland, and then moved to GN's Everett shops before starting the long trek eastward. It worked on oil to Minot, North Dakota, where it was reconverted to coal before making two round trips to the Twin Cities.

A final run on the Chicago, Burlington & Quincy into Chicago completed its demonstration runs. From there it ran light over the Pennsy to Philadelphia. With glowing test reports throughout its tour, Baldwin expected some inquiries from American railroads, and it got them. Anticipating some orders, the works proceeded to order materials for the heavyweight pipes and drums used in the water tube firebox, and even worked out some preliminary designs for roads such as Atlantic Coast Line, B&O, Boston & Maine, Burlington, Central of Georgia, Pennsylvania, and Southern Pacific.

What happened next was a bit of a surprise for the world's largest locomotive builder. In modern parlance, we would say that No. 60000 was OBE (overtaken by events). There were two major reasons for the resounding silence when it came to orders for this type of locomotive. The first was related to the general resistance of most motive power people (and some rail executives) to radical change. The high-pressure firebox horrified many who had no real understanding that while water tube fireboxes were new to railroading, they were not experimental devices, having been used on large ships and in stationary power plants for a number of years.

The second major concern continued to be that old bugaboo mentioned at the beginning. Savings in fuel were often balanced (or even overshadowed) by the extra mechanical complexity. For example, mechanical people were worried that cleaning scale from all the intricate piping would be slow and costly. But there was also another factor. In addition to having concerns about design features, some progressive railroads were looking closely at locomotive developments under way at the two other builders. While Sam Vauclain's "pride and joy" was gallivanting around the nation, design engineers at both Lima and Alco had been concentrating on something more revolutionary than a three-cylinder compound. We will find out more about their activities in the next chapter.

What happened to the 60000, you ask? Well, it is still around for us to admire. In 1933, the Franklin Institute of Philadelphia planned a move to a new building that would house an extensive display on the evolution of rail transportation. Hearing of this, Mr. Sam decided to donate the idle 4-10-2 to the museum. So the engine was trucked gingerly through mid-city traffic and inserted into a large opening in the nearly complete building, where it remains.

Misguided Applications of Mechanical Art

The foregoing experiments on rigid-frame engines were paralleled during the 1910s by a half-dozen railroads, and at least one builder, who pushed the Mallet articulated concept beyond its practical limits. There was a flurry of activity in 1910–11. First, the Erie took a conventional 2-8-0, lengthened its boiler, and had Baldwin build a 2-6-0 low-pressure running gear to put underneath it. The resulting 2-6-8-0 was much less expensive than a new Mallet compound, but alas, it didn't last very long. The rear part was later converted into an 0-8-0 switcher. B&O tried exactly the same thing in 1911. A Belpaire-boilered 2-8-0 was linked to a Baldwin-built front running gear to produce another 2-6-8-0. Its fate was the same as that of the Erie's homebuilt engine, except the rear part was rebuilt as a 2-8-0.

During the same period, two western lines got into the act. In 1910, Santa Fe's Topeka shops chopped up a pair of 2-6-2's to make a 2-6-6-2 with a flexible joint in the boiler. At first this seemed like a good idea, so the road ordered a few more from Baldwin. However, after a few years of service, the impracticality of a jointed boiler was evident. Again the rear locomotives were returned to the 2-6-2 wheel arrangement. The same fate befell Topeka's efforts to create 10 rigid-boiler 2-10-10-2's from 20 Texas types. Eventually the transformation was undone and the 20 single-expansion engines re-emerged.

Chicago Great Western's Oelwein, Iowa shops tried out a slightly different idea in 1910. Although it produced three Mallet 2-6-6-2's the same way Santa Fe had done, it used the front part of the boiler for a "super sized" feedwater heater. The combination of this extra preheating and the compound delivery produced a starting tractive effort some 57 percent higher than that of a single Prairie type, even though there was no increase in the steaming capacity of the base 2-6-2 boilers.

However, by far the most audacious attempt to stretch the Mallet articulated concept occurred in 1913 when the Erie Railroad mechanical department decided to order a *triplex* compound from Baldwin. The idea was to put what was called a "tractor engine" beneath the tender of a 2-8-8-0 to produce a 2-8-8-8-4 wheel arrangement. Although operated as a compound, it contained six cylinders of identical size. In operation, each of the high-pressure, center cylinders exhausted to a pair of the low-pressure cylinders. Exhaust from the third set of drivers exited from an exhaust stack at the rear of the tender.

In its first test, the prototype named *Matt Shay* lugged a 250-car train (17,900 tons and 1.6 miles long) up a slight grade (0.09 percent) and around a five-degree curve. But soon it became clear that this mammoth machine, with its impressive 160,000-pound starting tractive effort, had such a low steaming rate that it could not attain a speed of more than 10 to 15 mph, and even that would not last very long. Despite its shortcomings Erie received two more triplexes in 1916, assigning the three to pusher service around Susquehanna. The Virginian Railway also received one of these locomotives in 1916, and its experience paralleled that of the Erie. By 1920 this locomotive had been rebuilt by Baldwin into a 2-8-8-0. A trailing truck was added in 1942, and this remnant machine was not scrapped until 1953.

Two from one: In 1916 the Virginian Railway "dipped its toe into the water" of the triplex compound when it received a 2-8-8-8-4 from Baldwin for extensive testing on its mountain grades out of Elmore, West Virginia. Designed with only 75 square feet of grate (about half of what the road's later 2-6-6-6's would have), a low steam production rate quickly sealed its fate. In response, the frugal VGN mechanical department sent the monster back to Philadelphia where it was rebuilt into a 2-8-8-0 Mallet and a conventional Mikado (also with a grate area of 75 square feet). The articulated acquired a trailing truck in 1942, and both locomotives worked until 1953. Railway & Locomotive Historical Society, Frank M. Swengel Collection.

Even the tender driving gear was salvaged and became part of a conventional 2-8-2 that also lasted until 1953.

The Southern Railway's mechanical department, never known for any significant loco-motive experimentation, latched on to the tender-tractor idea in 1915 and mounted the tender of a standard Mikado over a 2-8-0 running gear. A few others were built in 1916 and 1917. These unusual compounds, products of Spencer shops in North Carolina, proved capable of pulling almost 30 percent more tonnage than the Mike alone over the moun-tainous Asheville Division line that included the famed Saluda grade. Building on this success, in 1918 an S-class 2-10-2 was augmented with a brand-new 2-6-2 running gear be-neath its tender that increased tractive effort from 71,000 to 89,000. But the fates of these experimental locomotives were the same as the others. By 1926 all had been rebuilt as conventional engines.

The first tractor engine on the Southern Railway was constructed at Spencer shops in 1915 and attached to the tender of light Mikado No. 4537 (Baldwin, 1912). The augmented engine was tested extensively between Spartanburg, South Carolina and Asheville, North Carolina on a line that included Saluda hill. However, the experiment proved to be only modestly successful and the tender-tractor was removed in 1924. Baldwin Locomotive Works, Louis R. Saillard Collection.

With our present understanding, we can see clearly why these experimental articulated engines had virtually no chance of succeeding. The most important failure of the railroad mechanical staffs was not recognizing that merely putting more driving wheels on the rails was insufficient to guarantee improved performance on the main line. For example, it seems almost laughable that the Erie and Virginian triplexes would be designed with grate areas of only 75 square feet. This area was slightly smaller than Baldwin had put into the 2-6-6-2's it built for GN in 1906, and about the same size of Milwaukee's streamlined Atlantics of 1935. This lack of familiarity with earlier designs meant that neither the total evaporative surface nor the firebox volume would permit the necessary steam generation rate.

Although Baldwin's name was attached to most of these experimental articulateds, one cannot lay complete blame on the builders for these blunders in design. Baldwin, in particular, made its money as the world's largest *builder* of locomotives. In general, it contracted to construct an engine to the specifications developed by client lines. These contracts usually did not include any performance analysis or guarantees. Indeed, there is considerable evidence to suggest that, of the three major builders, Baldwin had less concern for, or more trust in, its clients' designs than did its competitors.

Lima's official portrait of H10 No. 132 delivered to NYC's Michigan Central in 1923. Note that a long-distance tender was not deemed necessary at this time. Later MC numbers were moved to the 2000 series. Eric Hirsimaki Collection.

CHAPTER 6

DAWN OF A NEW ERA

The newly reorganized Lima Works received a modest share of the 1830 USRA locomotives that were ordered, constructing 160 machines (8.3 percent). It also expanded production facilities between 1918 and 1920 in anticipation of a sales boom that never materialized. However, with business picking up in 1922, Lima was able to afford more plant expansions that gave it first-class boiler and erecting shops. This time, it was a fortuitous event, as we shall see.

During the Lima reorganization of 1915–16, one of the most significant hires from Alco was William E. Woodard (1873–1942), who became principal mechanical engineer, with Herbert L. Snyder, another erstwhile Alco man, as his assistant. Within two years another reorganization of the executive suite would bring Woodard the title of vice president for engineering. A Cornell University graduate, Woodard was a small, intense man whose intellectual demeanor was amplified by his silver-rimmed glasses. He brought to Lima a wealth of design experience that included stints at Baldwin as well as earlier builders Dickson and Schenectady. In particular he was a protégé of Alco's senior designer, Francis J. Cole.

As Lima's design guru, he set about to investigate the fundamental ways in which motive power could be improved. A staunch easterner, he did not relocate to Ohio, but worked out of Lima's New York City offices where he could also participate in the other Coffin-Allen locomotive enterprises mentioned earlier. What he and his engineering staff found was that wartime traffic, along with rapid growth of the nation, had strangled the rail network, with much of the blame placed on locomotives that could not move long trains fast enough. Moreover, neither railroad mechanical officers nor major builders had stepped forward after the war with any new concepts. Virtually everyone was content with incremental changes to existing designs, such as Alco's emphasis into the mid-1920s on three-cylinder engines and the addition of more drivers to stretch 4-8-2's into 4-10-2's or even 4-12-2's.

Lima Leads the Way

Soon after its formation, the Lima engineering group (Woodard and his associates Snyder, George Basford, a consulting engineer, and W. H. Winterrowd, a former chief mechanical officer for Canadian Pacific) found one railroad that prided itself on developing new power. It had been a pioneer in testing each class of its locomotives (both inside special laboratories and on the road) so that subsequent designs could be improved. That railroad was the New York Central, with which both Woodard and Snyder had worked closely during their tenure with Alco.

In the early 1920s the NYC was focusing its efforts toward improvements to the road's two workhorses, the H7 Mikados and the L1 Mohawks (4-8-2). Soon Lima had taken the lead in reworking the smaller of the two engines, while Alco, NYC's major supplier of power, worked on the L1 design. The first hints from Lima's brain trust about their thinking came from a technical paper coauthored by Snyder and Woodard and presented by Snyder at a meeting of the American Society of Mechanical Engineers in May 1921. The paper, entitled "The Necessity for Improvements in Design of Present Day Locomotives," emphasized that engines had reached their physical limitations due to clearances and weight restrictions, and that only internal changes such as large and efficient fireboxes, and appliances such as superheaters and feedwater heaters, represented possible improvements.

Later that summer, Lima and New York Central agreed on a redesign of the H7 Mikado, with the company funding a prototype engine that the NYC agreed to test. Clearly, if Lima wanted to capture future sales, it had to produce a "showstopper." It has been speculated that Lima agreed to cover the initial cost if the engine could be used as a demonstrator on other roads and thus gain a wider audience rather than becoming an NYC locomotive immediately after delivery. On the other hand, it agreed to allow the engine to be lettered for the Michigan Central, an NYC subsidiary.

Construction of the improved 2-8-2, designated the H10 class, began in late 1921, and it left the plant in early June 1922 as MC No. 8000. One of Woodard's goals was to demonstrate how the performance of an existing locomotive could be enhanced. With the H7, already a heavy machine, no major structural changes were made. However, Woodard was emphatic about increasing grate area by 6.8 square feet to 66.4 (about the same as a light USRA Mike). In addition, the superheater design was substantially improved, increasing its surface area by a whopping 53 percent. This assured an ample supply of high-temperature dry steam.

The firebox also saw major improvements, including a larger diameter mud ring that surrounded the bottom of the chamber and, internally, use of a brick arch supported by large-diameter tubes. The arch, which projected into the firebox from the front wall, served as a baffle to direct the burning gas initially toward the rear before it flowed into the flues. This provided a longer path needed to allow the combustion processes to continue for as long as possible. This additional length (and time) resulted in a more intense fire that produced more pounds of steam per pound of coal burned. To help the Mikado start its train, a trailing-truck booster engine was used below 15 mph. Other innovations included a smokebox-mounted throttle (replacing the usual location inside the steam dome) as well as lightweight side rods (using high-strength steel) and hollow driver axles and crankpins, both of which decreased the dynamic augment (pounding of rails at high speed).

A cutaway diagram of the modern steam locomotive prepared by Lima for its New York Central H10 Mikado. A careful examination reveals details of virtually all locomotive components mentioned in this book. Of note are the brick arch in the firebox, a trailing truck with booster engines, the outside pipe connecting the steam dome to the superheater header, and tunnel for stoker at rear. Eric Hirsimaki Collection.

As it rolled out of the shop, No. 8000 weighed 334,000 pounds, only 1.8 percent more than the H7. It was a husky-looking locomotive with an Elesco feedwater heater on the crown of its smokebox. At this time such appliances were still relatively rare, with only 234 engines (on 28 roads) so equipped. The most preferred heater designs were the Elesco (cylindrical tank) and Coffin (saddle tank). As with No. 8000, when mounted external to the smokebox, either of these two feedwater heaters substantially changed the locomotive's front-end appearance.

In engineering parlance, feedwater heaters are classified as heat exchangers. Those from Elesco and Coffin were of the *shell and tube* design, while the later models by Worthington were *direct contact* type. The initial advantage claimed by the shell and tube configuration was that the exhaust steam (containing small amounts of oil and grime from valve pistons and power cylinders) did not come into contact with the boiler feedwater and thus there was no possibility for contamination. Later, however, the Worthington designs, which sprayed droplets of feedwater into exhaust steam, would include a process for cleaning the resulting mixture before it entered the boiler. The earliest Worthington design (BL type) was similar in shape to a large pump and was usually mounted near the rear driver (on fireman's side), while the later S and SA models were of rectangular shape and normally recessed into the smokebox. After 1930 the Worthington SA was the most preferred design.

Needless to say, Woodard's and Lima's first step into what has become known as the super power era was a resounding success. Even though the H10's tractive effort was only slightly larger than that of the H7, No. 8000 hauled more and used less fuel. In one especially impressive test, the H10 hauled an unusually long train consisting of 138 cars (9254 tons) between Detroit and Toledo. Its drawbar horsepower was as much as 35 percent greater than that of the H7, and its boiler efficiency was far superior to any ever attained on a locomotive. The NYC people were ecstatic, calling the 8000 a "wonder engine," and after only six weeks of testing ordered 75 duplicates plus the prototype itself. Eventually Lima would construct 115 of the 300 H10s built.

The Future Becomes Reality

Through the success of its H10 design, the small company in Ohio, using engineering talent hired away from a larger competitor, was able to convince a skeptical industry (builders and railroads) that dramatic performance improvements were possible. And Will Woodard had finally showed the world that firebox performance and steaming rate were just as important as tractive effort. But once the H10 was under construction, Woodard and his team turned their attention to the next step, that of building a new high-horsepower locomotive from the ground up. The first public hint of the design concept came in March 1923 when Lima designer George Basford, in a speech to the Pacific Railroad Club, mentioned a 2-8-4 wheel arrangement as "Lima's present thinking."

This speculation was confirmed in late September 1924 when a construction order was issued for a "stock" 2-8-4. The company continued to search for a sponsor, but none was forthcoming, although NYC again agreed to work closely with Lima. By January 1925 Woodard decided to give the new engine its official identity. He directed that it be numbered 1 and be classed as A1. The new locomotive would be lettered for NYC's Boston & Albany Railroad that operated a line across the Berkshire Mountains of western New England.

The main feature of the A1 was its large firebox with a 100-square-foot grate, a size never before used on a rigid-frame locomotive. The huge firebox was supported by an articulated four-wheel truck that served as the mechanical connection between locomotive and tender. The trailing truck carried not only a Franklin-built booster, which added 13,200 pounds of tractive effort, but also a new type of ash pan that improved airflow into the firebox. Among the other Woodard ideas was that the firing rate be kept below 100 pounds/hr per square foot of grate. His team had studied tests of various rates and found that, above 100,

Lima's formal photograph of its revolutionary new type of locomotive, the 2-8-4, finished in 1925. Will Woodard designated his creation No. 1, perhaps having had a hunch that this machine would be a landmark in American steam power development. Eric Hirsimaki Collection.

much of the coal remained unburned and went up the stack as soot. The A1's boiler was considerably larger than that on the H10, mainly to allow for the total evaporative surface to be increased by 15 percent. The ratio of superheat to evaporative surface was also the largest ever used.

To understand better what drove Woodard's thinking on firebox-boiler design, we present in Table 6-1 some of the performance ratios developed by Francis J. Cole of Alco in 1914. Readers with technical backgrounds will notice immediately that these were purely empirical factors and were not like the "dimensionless groups" developed later as the basis for physical modeling. Instead, Cole's analysis of locomotives in the 1910s suggested permissible ranges for these factors as guidance to designers.

The parameters in the ratios of Table 6-1 are self-explanatory, with one exception. The term "gas area" in the second factor refers to the cross-sectional area *inside* tubes and superheater flues. If the gas area was too small, the hot gas flow from the firebox would be impeded, whereas if it was too large, the extra weight of the tubes/flues would lead to gross inefficiency. As defined by Cole, better performance is characterized by *lower* values of all ratios. As is evident in the first three factors, an increase in the grate area will be beneficial, while for the last two ratios, an increase in the evaporative surface (outside area of tubes) and superheater surface is also beneficial. With this insight, we can understand clearly why Woodard and his design group emphasized improvement of the heating process as the key to super power engines.

Another Woodard innovation for the A1 was cast-steel power cylinders with steam passages bolted onto the saddle. His mentor, Alco's Cole, had pioneered this feature in an earlier experimental Pacific. This step alone saved two tons of dead weight and allowed an increase in steam pressure to 240 psi. Steel cylinders later became an industry standard, along with the A1's extra-long valve travel that improved steam flow into the cylinders. Using the same lightweight driver axles and crankpins as in the 8000, the A1 also introduced the use of small tandem side rods, rather than one large rod. In this way, stresses would be smaller in each rod and the overall dynamic loads decreased. In early February the A1 was shown to railroad representatives by Lima president Coffin, who said, "Our 1925 model is the finest piece of machinery I've ever seen." Conversations with the shop forces that built the A1 showed that they were also proud, as they knew the 2-8-4 included virtually every new idea known to designers of that day.

Table 6-1
Typical Cole Performance Ratios

$$\text{Grate demand factor} = \frac{\text{tractive effort} \times \text{driver diameter}}{\text{grate area}}$$

$$\text{Air demand factor} = \frac{\text{gas area (tubes and flues)}}{\text{grate area}}$$

$$\text{Total machine efficiency} = \frac{\text{engine weight}}{\text{grate area}}$$

$$\text{Boiler demand factor} = \frac{\text{tractive effort} \times \text{driver diameter}}{\text{evaporative surface (tubes)}}$$

$$\text{Economy of design} = \frac{\text{engine weight}}{\text{evaporative surface} + \text{superheater surface}}$$

Source: *Lima, the History*, Hirsimaki.

Like the H10, with its high-mounted Elesco feedwater heater, the A1 had a brutish appearance, enhanced by a pair of cross-compound air compressors placed on the pilot deck. Because of the NYC's tight clearances the A1's smokebox had been scalloped on each side to provide clearance for the pumps. As it turned out, this unusual placement improved weight balance and also became a common practice with all builders.

The final specifications for the A1 included a weight of 385,000 pounds (15 percent more than the H10), and a starting tractive effort (with booster) of 86,200 pounds (11 percent more than the H10). Its 63-inch drivers were the same as those of the H7 and H10. On February 11, 1925 the A1 was shipped dead to the New York Central's Selkirk shop near Albany. It had been decided that tests would be conducted on the 60-mile stretch of mountainous track between Selkirk and Washington, Massachusetts. At the West Springfield (Mass.) shops, extensive measuring equipment was attached to the engine and a wooden windscreen was mounted on the pilot deck to protect technicians.

One of the most impressive runs by the A1 was on April 14, when it left Selkirk eastbound with a 54-car train (2296 tons). Approximately 45 minutes earlier an H10 with 46 cars (1691 tons) had also left eastbound. To almost everyone's surprise, the 2-8-4 and its train began gaining on the earlier train, and at Chatham, New York the two trains were abreast on parallel tracks before the A1 pulled ahead. Twenty miles further east, the 2-8-4 was 10 minutes ahead of the H10.

The A1 had handled 26 percent more tonnage and taken 57 minutes less for the trip to North Adams Junction. Measurements showed that the 2-8-4 had an average boiler efficiency of 80.5 percent and a maximum drawbar horsepower of 3890. The water use rate was 20 pounds per horsepower-hour (or 20 pounds/hr of water used for each horsepower produced), while the corresponding coal use rate was 2.44 pounds, both new records of efficiency for steam locomotives. This outstanding performance was soon headlined by

One of the final tasks in finishing a steam locomotive was to determine an official weight. This was an extremely important matter, with many legal effects far beyond the erecting bay. In 1925, when the A1 was completed, the weight was determined by using highly accurate balance scales placed under each axle. Here is the scene in Lima's scale house as a shiny No. 1 sits quietly. Soon she will be charging down the main line of the Boston & Albany, setting records for efficiency and performance. Eric Hirsimaki Collection.

Table 6-2
Locomotive Performance Ratios

	Desired Range	H10	A1
Grate demand factor*	52.7–57.5	60.25	43.7**
Air demand factor	11–13	14	10.6**
Total machine efficiency	120–130	118	114**
Boiler demand factor	850–1000	874	856
Economy of design	75–85	52.5**	53.3

Notes: Smaller values of each factor designate better performance.
        *Multiply given number by 1000.
        **A new record.
Source: *Lima, the History*, Hirsimaki.

every publication in the industry, and was the main topic of conversation at meetings of railroad industry and trade associations. Woodard's super power design concepts would become the new standards for all builders. The A1, which was first proposed as the *Lima* type, finally became *Berkshire* in honor of the line on which she proved herself, and would later operate as a B&A engine. Recalling the earlier definitions of the Cole Performance Ratios, Table 6-2 illustrates the impressive results that Woodard obtained with both the H10 and A1 designs, including three new records for the A1.

Although Will Woodard was clearly a genius at locomotive design, he wasn't perfect. The major shortcoming of the A1 was its 63-inch drivers. This design choice gave the engine a maximum horsepower in the 35–40 mph range. Although New York Central bought 55 Berkshire types for the B&A, the road was still closely tied to Alco, which in parallel to Lima's A1 program was beefing up the performance of the L1 Mohawks. In the process many of Woodard's ideas found their way into this new engine.

Only a month after the A1's successful road tests, the new L2 Mohawk, No. 2700, went through a similar series of tests. With 69-inch drivers, its maximum power occurred in the 45–50 mph range, giving it a clear edge in that all-important category, mainline speed. The result was an order to Alco for 300 L2's. We can only speculate on the outcome of this competition if Woodard had used 65- or 66-inch drivers for the Lima 2-8-4. In fact, the higher boiler efficiencies Woodard pioneered later became the basis for using 69-inch drivers on all new freight locomotives.

In the succeeding months after the NYC tests, the A1 roamed the Midwest, demonstrating its performance on the Illinois Central, Milwaukee Road, and Missouri Pacific, with a side trip to the Chesapeake & Ohio. In each case the host road had specific comparisons in mind. The C&O tests, for example, were on the mountainous Allegheny Division east of Hinton, West Virginia. Representatives of not only C&O, but also Erie and Nickel Plate, were there to see how the A1 stacked up against C&O's heavy Mikados of the K3 class. Although the 2-8-4's performance was solid, there were no immediate orders. However, all three of these roads would eventually purchase Lima engines, spanning four wheel arrangements.

The Illinois Central tests, on the flat profiles of the Chicago-Champaign line, pitted the 2-8-4 against a relatively new Lima 2-10-2. The results gave a significant edge to the A1 in every category. Consequently the road ordered 50 engines plus the A1. Calling them *Lima* types, IC's order was the largest by any railroad. The A1 demonstrated on the Milwaukee Road in the fall of 1925, hauling both freight and passenger trains on the LaCrosse and Illinois Divisions. Unfortunately the road's poor financial condition prevented any future Lima orders. But the A1 was a better salesman on the Missouri Pacific, which ran it in freight service on its Illinois Division in early 1927. The 2-8-4 was working against a standard Mikado and a three-cylinder heavy 2-8-2. Another successful test brought Lima orders for 25 engines.

New York Central No. 3113 class L4a Mohawk represented the height of development for this wheel arrangement on the NYC. With many super power features, its road performance approached that of the later Niagara 4-8-4 (see chapter 9). Eric Hirsimaki Collection.

More Lima Innovation

The national hoopla surrounding the A1's initial performance on the New York Central soon came to the attention of the Texas & Pacific Railroad, which in 1924 was searching for new power. With a fleet of 44 Santa Fe types (2-10-2), it was considering three possible designs for new power: Mallet compound articulateds, three-cylinder, single-expansion engines, or more 2-10-2's. But early in 1925 it approached Lima and began discussing an elongated A1, with five sets of drivers, an idea that Woodard and associates had already been considering. With the impressive performance of the A1 in mind, the railroad quickly settled on an order of ten 2-10-4's, to be known as class I1A. These engines would include almost all of the features of the 2-8-4, and thus the design and assembly were relatively straightforward.

The primary differences were in the firebox, where Woodard replaced the traditional arches with thermic syphons and a combustion chamber. These features had been available for a few years, but Woodard had chosen not to use either of them on the H10 or A1 designs. The result of these changes was that the I1A's firebox contained 9.3 percent of the total evaporating area as opposed to the A1's 6.6 percent. To gain some insight into the physical principles on which the combustion chamber is based, we must consider what occurs during the process of burning. Coal is a hydrocarbon material (i.e., composed of hydrogen and carbon), while burning is a process of rapid oxidation. Therefore during a combustion process, the fuel is oxidized rapidly by incoming air, and the resulting fire produces large amounts of radiant energy (just like a small flame in a home fireplace).

The oxidation process breaks the hydrocarbon fuel into its constituents and oxidizes each one. The products are steam (H_2O), carbon monoxide (CO), and carbon dioxide (CO_2). Carbon monoxide is a product of incomplete combustion, since, if it mixes with air, it will continue to oxidize (burn) into carbon dioxide. Thus, while we know that oxidation at the molecular level is virtually instantaneous, complete oxidation within a large volume (such as a firebox) is much slower and depends critically on the time available for the components to mix before burning can begin.

The combustion chamber in a firebox was nothing more than an extra volume at the front or top of the firebox where the components had additional time to complete the combustion process. Since the inclusion of this extra volume generally meant less length was available for evaporation on the tube surfaces, it might seem that there was little advantage in having a combustion chamber. However, the opposite was actually true. Because the gas produced by the combustion chamber was much hotter than would otherwise occur, the shorter tubes could actually transfer more heat because the rate of heat transfer at the end of the tube (near the smokebox) is only a small fraction of the total.

The Nicholson thermic syphons used by Woodard on the T&P 2-10-4's were another appliance that improved heat transfer to the water. These devices were water channels that passed through the center of the firebox (from bottom to top) and enhanced the convective heat transfer between the hot gas and the water inside (similar to the heating process in tubes that leads to evaporation). The siphon action occurred because, as the heated water rose to the top of the channel, it induced an inflow from the bottom. Thus a continuous circulation of cooler water from the lower part of the boiler toward the top was created. As with other such appliances, these syphons caused some maintenance problems due to surface degradation by cinders and thermal stress cracks. They found favor on some roads and not on others. For example, C&O, Nickel Plate, Rio Grande, Western Maryland, and Baldwin used these extensively, while New York Central, Union Pacific, and N&W did not.

The T&P 2-10-4's used a cast-steel articulated trailing truck rather than the forged design of the A1. And of course the larger engine weighed more and could pull more. Both its weight of 448,000 pounds and its total tractive effort of 96,000 pounds were 16 percent higher than corresponding values for the A1, while its maximum horsepower of 4200 was

Appearing only a year after the revolutionary Berkshire, Lima's first 2-10-4's for the Texas & Pacific solidified the universal design principles of the super power concept. The 70-engine fleet of 2-10-4's amassed by T&P completely changed their mainline freight operations, especially on the 600-mile stretch of demanding desert operations between Ft. Worth and El Paso, Texas. Here is No. 630 (class I1b, 1928) resting at Ft. Worth in the 1940s. Eric Hirsimaki Collection.

Texas & Pacific 2-10-4 No. 605 (class I1; Lima, 1925) charges along the main line near Shreveport, Louisiana with an eastbound train. A. E. Brown, Louis R. Saillard Collection.

24 percent higher. Likewise, when the new engines were delivered in late 1925 (only five months after the order), their performance on the undulating profiles of T&P's 600-mile line between Fort Worth and El Paso was as surprising as those of the A1 some nine months earlier.

Christened the *Texas* type, the 2-10-4's outperformed T&P's 2-10-2's in every category. Average tonnage was up by 44 percent, average speed increased by 33 percent, fuel oil used was down by 43 percent, and maintenance cost per mile was down 29 percent per month. Figures like these convinced the T&P to purchase 60 more of these monster machines over the following five years. As happened with other engine names, some roads were not interested in using the name *Texas* for their 2-10-4's. Burlington, for instance, decided to call them *Colorado* types instead.

Between June 1922 and February 1925, Lima had produced the first super power locomotives using two new wheel arrangements. These would be the prototypes for the final two decades of American steam locomotive development. Within months of the publication of test data for the A1 and I1A, the two larger builders were turning their considerable economic and technical muscle toward the design of this new breed of motive power. Indeed the locomotive industry had seen almost 50 years of design experience become virtually obsolete in less than 3 years, because of the genius of William Woodard, along with the lean and hungry attitude of a small company in Lima, Ohio.

CHAPTER 7

SUPER POWER REIGNS

The period between Lima's production of the 2-10-4 in 1925 and the stock market crash of 1929 saw a flood of new locomotive designs using four-wheel trailing trucks to support jumbo-sized fireboxes. Two more models hit the rails during the first two years after the name "super power" was coined. Alco's progressive engineering team was quickest out of the chute, with its 4-8-4 delivered to the Northern Pacific in 1926, followed closely by its 4-6-4 for New York Central in 1927.

Northern Pacific, like most western lines, was immediately attracted to the 4-8-4 wheel arrangement. Building on Lima's initial success with its Berkshires, Alco produced 12 engines (class A) of this wheel arrangement for NP during 1926, only two years after the Lima A1 had debuted on the Boston & Albany. The success of this powerful and efficient engine opened the door for this configuration to become the workhorse of the super power era. Number 2607 was one of the original group. Eric Hirsimaki Collection.

Workhorses of the New Era

The pioneer A2 class 4-8-4 for the NP was built with an unusually large grate area (115 square feet) to better burn lignite, a low grade of coal plentiful in the West. Baldwin's first 4-8-4 was the S1 class delivered to Chicago & North Western in 1929. Also in that year Alco began delivering the first of Rock Island's R67 class, a group that would eventually num-

Facing page: Rock Island began building its fleet of Alco-built 4-8-4's (class R67b) with 65 engines in 1929–30. By 1946 this class had been expanded to 85 machines, the most for any one American design. Two of the postwar R67b models are shown. Number 5109 (*top*) is at Kansas City in 1944, while No. 5117 (*middle*) speeds westward at Lennox, Illinois with a 100-car train in 1952. As with numerous other 4-8-4 designs, the R67 plans were pulled from storage in 1943 and used in construction of the 10 engines of Milwaukee's S3 class (*bottom*), whose builder's photo clearly shows a similarity in boiler and running gear between the two designs. Top: Robert J. Foster, Joe Collias Collection; *middle*: Joe Collias; *bottom*: Eric Hirsimaki Collection.

ber 65 (largest 4-8-4 fleet of the same design). Later this Granger road would receive 20 larger 4-8-4's, giving it the second-largest fleet of this wheel arrangement (behind only Southern Pacific).

The *Northern* type (for Northern Pacific) would eventually become the standard engine of the super power era, just as the 4-4-0 was in the beginning decades, followed by the 2-8-0, and the 2-8-2. Thirty-one railroads purchased over 900 engines of this type, produced from 70 different designs. They turned out to be equally effective pulling tonnage or tourists, and excelled in moving trains across the vast spaces west of the Mississippi River. Not surprisingly, the *Northern* designation did not resonate with everyone. Other labels for 4-8-4's included *Dixie* (NC&StL), *Golden State* (SP), *Greenbriar* (C&O), *Niagara* (NYC), *Pocono* (DL&W), *Potomac* (Western Maryland), and *Wyoming* (Lehigh Valley).

The year 1930 would see the 4-8-4 break new ground in another area besides its horse-power. The Timken Roller Bearing Company of Canton, Ohio had experienced considerable difficulty in getting roads to substitute its products for older, friction bearings. Finally in 1925, the company arranged with a local railroad (Wheeling & Lake Erie) to permit testing of the new bearings on various types of freight cars. In one head-to-head test between old and new bearings on May 22, 1925, the brakes on two steel boxcars were released on a slight grade. The car with roller bearings began rolling on its own and kept rolling for a mile and a half. Meanwhile, the friction-bearing car required three kicks from a switcher to get it rolling and stopped after 1200 feet. A year later Timken bearings were installed on W&LE locomotive tenders, an advantage since they ran up good mileage but never left home rails.

Finally in 1929, unable to obtain permission from any railroad or builder to allow a demonstration of its bearings on a large mainline locomotive, Timken purchased a stock 4-8-4 from Alco, similar to the engines built earlier for the Delaware, Lackawanna & Western. Officially designated TRBX 1111, but known informally as the *Four Aces*, it carried the

There was nothing unusual about homebuilt Wheeling & Lake Erie 0-6-0 switcher No. 3968 (class B5, 1937), but its tender was another story. The inboard roller bearings on the tender trucks were part of a 1935 operational test for the Timken Company, an on-line industry in Akron, Ohio. Railway & Locomotive Historical Society, J. W. Swanberg Collection.

A scene in Norfolk & Western's Roanoke shops in 1956 provides details of roller bearings fitted to driving axles. Drivers are mounted onto each end of the axle using a large hydraulic press. Phillip A. Weibler.

number under its cab window and the Timken name in large letters on the tender. Since Timken was not constrained by any railroad color scheme, the engine was painted dark green and displayed playing card symbols (club, diamond, heart, and spade) on its sand dome and headlight number boards. After being fitted with the new bearings, it began a nationwide tour during which it consistently impressed railroads with its operating capabilities and the general public with its unusual characteristics. For example, to show how easily No. 1111 could be moved, a photo-op in Chicago's Union Station had three female office workers from the Pennsy team up on a rope-pull to haul the mammoth machine forward a few feet. This was possible because the rolling resistance of a roller-bearing-equipped locomotive was a mere 10 ounces per ton!

In 21 months of roaming the main lines of 13 lines, the *Four Aces* ran off 119,600 miles between Portland, Maine and Seattle with no bearing problems. Timken was quick to tout the significant operational advantages of this new technology, such as more tractive effort

Norfolk & Western 4-6-2 No. 578 (Baldwin, 1912) has carried a local passenger train from Bluefield, West Virginia to Norton, Virginia in 1958. During a check before starting on the return trip, an engine mechanic decided to add some lubricant to the trailing truck journal bearing. J. Parker Lamb.

since friction losses were less, no fear of hot boxes (hot bearings), and better coasting performance (prevented slack from pushing the train into the tender).

To understand what a fundamental change this step represented, we must explain what is known as *hydrodynamic lubrication*. Even the most primitive and rudimentary machines include surfaces that slide over one another. In the beginning, the relative speeds between the two surfaces were small, and thus early lubricants were obtained from animal fats and even water. For railroad bearings, tallow was commonly used. Hence the name *tallow pot* for the fireman who checked bearings on locomotives, or for other workers who attended to journal bearings on cars.

Widely used for many years, the *journal bearing* consisted of a polished shaft of hardened metal surrounded by the journal made

from softer metal (usually brass or bronze). Indeed the large journals used on early locomotive drivers were usually called *brasses*. They were fabricated from two blocks of metal that were smoothed on adjacent edges and soldered together. After the external dimensions were trued, the block was mounted in a large lathe, and a hole was created for the driver axle. The initial clearance between axle and journal was usually around 1/8 of an inch. After all machining was complete, the two halves of the journal were separated by melting the solder. This allowed the journal, which rode within a spring-mounted housing (driving box), to be reassembled around the driver axle.

In practice, there was a hole near the top of the journal through which the lubricant flowed. This thin film of fluid separated the metal surfaces of the rotating shaft from those of the stationary journal. Since the journal surfaces were made from softer metal than the axle, there would eventually be some wear in the axle passage, and it would expand to a slightly larger diameter. If the wear was not excessive, the two journal halves could be resurfaced at their interface, and a new axle passage created. Consequently, when the journal was remounted on the axle, there was again a proper fit.

Looking closely at the thin film of lubricant, we see that the surface of the rotating axle moves in relation to that of the journal, and consequently there is a shearing force transmitted from the axle through the film of liquid to the journal surface. This shearing force, when multiplied by the speed of the axle surface, provides a value for the power dissipated by the shearing force. This power dissipation in each bearing is transformed into heat that affects the properties of the lubricant.

Although friction losses in each bearing may be negligible, the total amount of lost power due to bearing friction was significant since a typical steam locomotive included a hundred (or more) such bearings. The largest, of course, were on the drivers and truck axles, but many others were used in the driving rods, valve gear, mechanical stoker, water pumps, and electric generators. Thus the cumulative effect of bearing losses was significant to the mechanical efficiency of a locomotive. To replace friction bearings, mechanical engineers and metallurgists developed first a ball bearing in which two circular rings (called cages or races) enclosed a group of hardened-steel balls. These would generally be surrounded by a thick lubricant grease that would adhere to all bearing surfaces. We recognize instantly that the energy dissipated by a ball bearing would be only a small fraction of that in a journal bearing of equivalent size.

For heavy machines, a later improvement transformed the moving balls into rollers, which were usually cylinders with a slight taper. It was this type of bearing that Timken installed on its No. 1111. With 14 wheels on each side of the engine and tender, a total 28 roller bearings were needed to allow the three women to move a 700,000-pound engine and tender in the Chicago publicity stunt of 1930. As mentioned, one of Timken's selling points was that roller bearings increased a locomotive's tractive effort, and it pointed to the AAR formula (presented at the beginning chapter 3) for proof. The company noted that the factor representing the machinery efficiency when starting, 0.92, could be increased to 1.0, since there was no bearing friction to be overcome. In essence, omitting the factor 0.92 allowed the tractive effort to be around 9 percent larger. However, in a strict sense the tractive effort is fixed by the power produced by the cylinders and is not affected by fractional resistance. What Timken should have noted was that roller bearings increased drawbar pull due to less friction. However stated, the effect was significant.

Unfortunately, even after the *Four Aces* concluded its national tour, the actual incorporation of roller bearings was a slow process, with only three lines ordering any installations by 1934 because of the lingering effects of the depression. These included a Pacific on the D&H, two Hudsons on the NYC, and two Northerns on the Delaware, Lackawanna & Western. After 1936, however, the majority of new locomotives, slated for long-distance, high-speed service, would include roller bearings, at least for drivers and truck axles. But, as with many other design features, some railroads never adopted this technology to any great extent (examples include B&O, Great Northern, Illinois Central, Frisco, and SP).

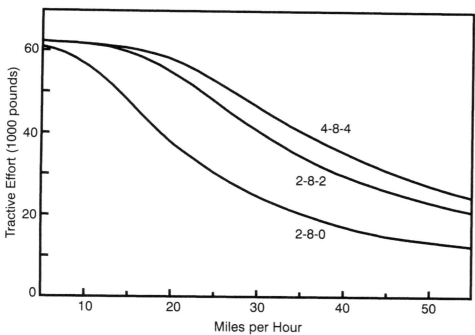

Comparison of mainline tonnage capability of three locomotives, showing the importance of larger fireboxes (and thus larger steaming rates). Note that all engines have virtually the same starting tractive effort. Adapted from *The Steam Locomotive*, Johnson.

However, the *Four Aces* quickly found a home, being bought by Northern Pacific. This groundbreaker was renumbered 2626 and lasted until the diesel era was well under way.

Later, Timken and other manufacturers would show by actual tests that a locomotive could move a train of freight cars equipped with these bearings that was 76 percent longer than one with journal bearings. Evidence such as this led eventually to the end of the old, energy-hungry journal bearings on all rolling stock, although the first use of modern bearings had occurred on some Milwaukee Road passenger cars in 1926.

A 1932 study published by Baldwin compared the mainline performance of three locomotives: a heavy Reading 2-8-0 (with 64,400 pounds tractive effort), a Frisco-modified USRA heavy Mikado, and a moderately sized 4-8-4 (Lehigh Valley class T1). These machines represent the three generations of steam motive power that we have described. A major part of this study was to demonstrate the improvements in pulling power for newer designs. The accompanying graph was a part of this report. It shows the variation in rated tractive effort (proportional to drawbar pull or train tonnage) as a function of speed. In

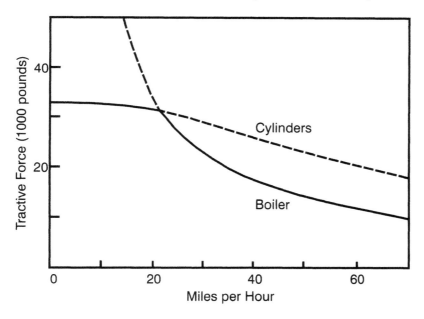

Illustration of the independent effects of boiler and cylinders on overall locomotive performance, which is limited at higher speeds by steam generation rates. Adapted from *The Steam Locomotive*, Johnson.

constructing this graph the computations for tractive effort (chapter 3) were modified to account for the decrease in mean effective pressure (MEP) due to speed. The clear indication of this comparison is that, even though the starting tonnages are nearly the same, the three engines performed quite differently at speed.

We should recognize that there are two primary reasons for the decreases in pulling ability shown by all three types of locomotives. First, we know that train resistance increases with speed (due to axle bearing losses as well as aerodynamic drag) and contributes to a lesser pulling capability. But the major cause for the decreases in drawbar pull at speed is a fundamental characteristic of all steam locomotives. We can demonstrate this statement with the accompanying sketch showing the maximum tractive effort producible by the cylinders and, independently, by the boiler. At low speed we see that there is ample steam available but the power is limited by cylinder volume, while at higher speeds maximum tonnage producible by the boiler eventually falls below the limiting capability of the cylinders. Thus the final performance curve for a locomotive is based on a combination of the limits from a locomotive's two major components mentioned at the beginning of the book, namely the boiler (energy generation) and the cylinders-drivers (energy conversion).

The underlying reasons for both components to decrease with speed are a result of basic principles of physics. For the cylinders, increased speed causes the valve gear to become less able to open and close the valves with a precise timing that would maintain a nearly constant power output. We will delve further into this process in chapter 9. As for energy conversion, the decrease in steaming rate of the boiler is due to the time required to boil water. All common liquids (indeed virtually all substances) possess a molecular property known as *thermal diffusivity*, which determines how quickly heat is transmitted from one part of a fluid to another. This is manifested in the fact that water molecules must remain in contact with hot surfaces inside the boiler for a specific time before reaching their boiling temperature. At low speed the rate of demand for steam is much lower than the rate of production, but as speed increases the demand increases faster than the production. Since there must always be such a limit, no matter how large the boiler, a realistic goal for an engine designer is to move the steaming rate curve upward, closer to the cylinder limits, for the speed range of most importance. Such a change required either a hotter fire or more evaporating surface. This was the goal for all engine designers in the super power era.

Returning to the variation of tonnage for the three types of locomotives, we can gain additional insight by examining a tabulation of the *relative* values of tractive effort based on that of the Consolidation locomotive. Such a tabulation is shown in Table 7-1. It is clear that the 2-8-0, with a low steaming rate (small firebox) can handle only 14 percent of its starting tonnage at 50 mph, but the Mike increases that proportion by 1.7 times to 24 percent. Finally the super power Northern, which has only 2 percent more starting tractive effort, can pull over twice as much as a 2-8-0 at 50 mph. These figures of course provide a reason for Woodard's obsession with larger steaming rates, and his basic concept of super power locomotives.

Table 7-1
Relative Tonnages for
Three Types of Locomotives

Type	Starting	25 mph	50 mph
2-8-0	1.00	0.42	0.14
2-8-2	1.01	0.68	0.24
4-8-4	1.02	0.74	0.29

Source: *The Steam Locomotive in America*, Bruce.

4-6-4 Type

A problem facing the New York Central in the late 1920s was that its Pacific designs had reached their zenith with the delivery by Alco in 1926 of ten K6 engines. These locomotives, whose design was similar to Alco's famous Pacific No. 5000 of 1924, produced a tractive effort (with booster) of 52,600 pounds. However, the weight of all-steel coaches and sleepers, including two diners and a lounge car on premier trains, was beyond even the K6's capacity on high-speed, long-distance schedules.

Paul W. Kiefer was a college-trained engineer with shop experience on the Lake Shore and Michigan Southern. He began his career with that road in 1907 and later worked as

Central's engineering representative at both Baldwin and Alco plants. Moving to the NYC's headquarters in New York City as a designer, he was eventually named chief engineer on January 1, 1926. Barely settled into his new office, he received a phone call from F. H. Hardin, assistant to the president. The terse message was, "Go ahead with the new passenger locomotive design."

While there had been no discussions about wheel arrangements, Kiefer was fully aware of Woodard's success with the B&A Berkshire design, and so he began to consider how to employ the principles of this new super power concept. In general there was some reluctance by the NYC to abandon the six-coupled driving gear in view of the road's many years of developmental experience with Pacifics. Plus the avoidance of a fourth driving axle would help keep down weight and cost (both initial and maintenance).

But even after the NYC engineering group had determined that Woodard's use of a four-wheel trailing truck was the preferred way to support a large firebox, they did not immediately start drawing plans. Instead, following the principles of careful engineering design, they mounted a four-wheel trailing truck under K3 Pacific No. 3284 in November 1926 for a series of tests on weight distribution and tracking characteristics.

The final design specs that went to Alco included a grate area of 81.5 square feet, firebox volume of 428 cubic feet, boiler diameter ranging from 82 to 87 inches, and a total heating surface of 4484 square feet. Most impressive were its 79-inch drivers and a tractive

Late-afternoon summer sunlight emphasizes the running gear of J1d Hudson No. 5363 (Alco, 1929) as it lopes southward through Fairborn, Ohio, en route to Cincinnati with a mail and express train in 1955. J. Parker Lamb.

effort of 53,260 pounds, including 10,900 from a booster. Construction of No. 5200, known as the J1a class, proceeded at a rapid pace, illustrating the longtime cooperation between the builder and its primary customer. The 4-6-4's boiler arrived at the erecting shop floor on January 28, 1927. Four days later came the main frame, followed one day later by the cylinders. In an incredibly short seven days the engine was assembled, steamed up, weighed, and road tested. The next day (February 9) it was completely finished (including painting).

On rollout day, February 14, Alco formally passed the huge new machine over to Patrick E. Crowley, Central's president, who, in a unique ceremony for the nation, christened it the *Hudson* type. One of the features noticed by the crowd that day was the way Alco had hidden the Elesco feedwater heater. Instead of being on the outside of the smokebox as Lima had done with the H10, A1, and I1A, the heater was mounted on a shelf inside the smokebox so that only the upper corners of the barrel were on the outside. Another aesthetic feature was its Commonwealth Delta trailing truck (with a larger rear wheel for the booster engine). On the pilot beam both the air pump and the feedwater pump were hidden behind streamlined shields, and much of the boiler plumbing was covered by its jacket.

The first Hudson turned out to be a lot more than classic symmetry and handsome appearance. Its initial mainline performance also caused many heads to swivel. During its first trials, the 5200 was able to sustain a speed of 75 mph with a train of 26 steel coaches that weighed 1700 tons, producing 4300 hp at 69 mph. In comparison with the road's Pacifics, the J1a produced a 16 percent increase in starting tractive effort (without booster) over a K5. Its thermal efficiency (based on coal usage) was 22 percent better than a K5.

Following the successful introduction of the J1a, a slightly modified version, the J2a, was produced by Alco in 1928 for the hilly Boston & Albany line, where Lima's A1 had made its reputation. This engine had 76-inch drivers (3 inches smaller than J1a) and thus a slightly higher tractive effort, since speed was not as important on the B&A's profiles. The final production series was the J3 version, with a 16 percent smaller cylinder volume than the J1 but a slightly higher boiler pressure, which kept the starting tractive effort essentially the

One of NYC's last operating Hudsons speeds southward through a limestone cut north of Dayton, Ohio with a mail and express train for Cincinnati. Centipede tender is nearly as long as No. 5436 (class J3a; Alco, 1937). J. Parker Lamb.

same. Total production of the Hudson design was an impressive 275 engines, with the three subclasses divided the following way: A total of 205 J1's were built between 1927 and 1931; twenty J2's, half of which came from Lima, were assembled between 1928 and 1931; while the final version (50 J3's) appeared in 1937–38. To satisfy the public's interest in streamlining, as exemplified by the shovel-nosed Burlington Zephyr, NYC installed in 1934 a bathtub-like, shovel-nosed shroud on J1e No. 5344 for service on the Commodore Vanderbilt. Public displays of this engine at major cities along NYC's main line were the highlight of the road's public relations program in these post-depression times.

It should be noted that the Hudson name was not universally accepted. In 1925 C. H. Bilty of the Milwaukee Road designed a 4-6-4 (class F6) he called the *Baltic* type, conforming to European practice. But the official construction orders to Baldwin were delayed until 1929–30, long after New York Central's J1's had captured the name that was synonymous with the NYC. Undaunted, Milwaukee Road always used the European name for its 4-6-4's. Other early Hudsons were delivered by Baldwin to Santa Fe (10 in 1927) and to CB&Q (12 in 1930).

Streamlined Milwaukee Road Baltic-type No. 100 (Alco, 1938) was the first of six engines built by Alco in 1938. They rode on 7-foot drivers and replaced the road's streamlined 4-4-2's on fast passenger trains. Eric Hirsimaki Collection.

2-8-4 and 2-10-4 Types

The next buyer of the Berkshire type, after the A1 design went to the Boston & Albany, was the Erie Railroad, which in 1927–28 received 85 Berkshires of three classes (but similar designs) from all three builders: Alco (25 S1's), Baldwin (35 S3's), and Lima (25 S2's). Counting later deliveries, Erie would eventually roster one-seventh of all 2-8-4's built. These locomotives rolled on 70-inch drivers, a great improvement over the A1's 63 inchers. Also in 1928 Lima sent five 2-8-4's to the Boston & Maine.

The first 2-10-4's to appear after Lima's introduction of this type were delivered by Alco in 1928 to the Central Vermont. These were not true super power engines but rather a way to spread weight over more axles. However, they were the largest steam engines to operate in New England and even outlasted the more famous NYC steam power used on the B&A. In 1929 Baldwin produced its first 2-10-4's, class H1A's for the Bessemer & Lake Erie. The following year Baldwin and Lima split an order of 36 Texas types for the Chicago Great Western.

The Erie Railroad was the first line to embrace the Berkshire type as the backbone of its freight operations. Built by Lima in 1927, No. 3325 was the first of Erie's S2 class (25 engines). The fleet would eventually reach some 105 engines in four subclasses. Eric Hirsimaki Collection.

Also in 1929 the C&O Railroad began investigating the configuration of a large rigid-frame engine that combined the low-speed pulling ability of its simple 2-8-8-2's with the speed of Erie's S-class 2-8-4's. First, it borrowed one of Erie's S-3's, boosted the boiler pressure, and added weight for higher adhesion. After studying records of its road tests with a dynamometer car, C&O decided on a large 2-10-4, partly because its shorter length (compared to an articulated) would allow a longer tender and yet permit the new engine to fit on existing turntables. Soon it approached Lima about designing such a locomotive.

This was the type of challenge that Woodard loved to tackle, and what soon emerged from the drafting boards was a locomotive that was as much ahead of the original T&P Texas type as that locomotive had been ahead of the first Berkshire. The engine's boiler expanded from 100 inches at the smokebox to 108 inches at the rear flue sheet (beginning of the firebox). A 66-inch combustion chamber length gave the firebox a total volume of 825 cubic feet. The result was a steaming rate of 100,000 pounds per hour that translated into 5000 drawbar horsepower. In late 1930 Lima began delivering the first of 40 Texas-type engines. Classified as T1, they rode on 69-inch drivers, had a grate area of 122 square feet, and a tractive effort of 108,680 pounds (including 15,000 from a booster). Not surprisingly, they were the heaviest two-cylinder engines to date (566,00 pounds).

Here's how the T1 solved C&O's need for power *and* speed. Prior to the arrival of the big 2-10-4's, the road would couple 140 cars of coal to a simple 2-8-8-2 at the Russell, Kentucky yard, and then had to shove the train up the 0.7 percent grade to the Ohio River Bridge at Limeville. Fourteen hours later the hoppers would complete the 236-mile trip to Toledo. Once the T1's took over, the same size train required no pushers and the trip was made in 13 hours, even as the engine was consuming 13 percent less coal and 10 percent less water than the 2-8-8-2. Often the road added 20 more loads (total tonnage of 14,000 tons) that required a couple of short stints of pushing. Despite this, T1's still pulled more than 17 million tons out of Russell each year. They would eventually be displaced by an even more spectacular locomotive (as we will see in the next chapter). Needless to say, the T1 became the prototype for all future Texas-type engines (in particular those for AT&SF and the Pennsylvania Railroad).

Articulated Types

The large and efficient boiler-fireboxes advocated by Woodard also led to the further evolution of the simple articulated locomotive. As noted earlier, the first generation of articulateds, whether compound or simple, were not high-speed machines, largely due to

---

(*Facing page, top*): Bi-coastal Berkshire: The only 2-8-4's on the Southern Pacific were ten locomotives purchased from the Boston & Maine in 1948. Constructed as coal burners by Lima in 1928, they were converted to oil, which was carried in the whale-back tenders built for early cab-forward Mallets (4000 series). Here is No. 3500 in Los Angeles in 1949. Gerald M. Best, Louis R. Saillard Collection.

(*Facing page, middle*): Lima's 1930 design for Chesapeake & Ohio's T1 class 2-10-4's brought this wheel arrangement to a new level of capability that revolutionized C&O coal train schedules and also became the prototype of two other Texas types (Santa Fe and Pennsy) in the final generation of American steam power. Here is No. 3033 leaving Fostoria, Ohio with a coal train in 1934. Clyde E. Helms, Jay Williams Collection.

(*Facing page, bottom*): Missouri Pacific Berkshire No. 1912 was among a group of 25 built by Lima in 1930. The 63-inch-drivered engines ran only a decade before the railroad rebuilt them into 75-inch-drivered 4-8-4's, confirming the Northern's almost universal appeal during the super power era. Eric Hirsimaki Collection.

the dynamic forces arising from the side-to-side oscillation of the leading driving gear at speed and from the rotating components (drivers and rodding). These forces and their control were only vaguely comprehended in the early years simply because a fundamental scientific understanding of dynamic loads had yet to be developed.

The first simple articulateds of the super power age were produced in 1928 when Alco began delivering a batch of 2-8-8-4's to the Northern Pacific, a company that, as we have seen, was always anxious to push the envelope of locomotive design. This wheel arrangement gave the road essentially a "double Berkshire" to handle its mountainous routes in the Pacific Northwest. The dozen engines of its Z5 class were named *Yellowstone* types and, like the road's pioneering Northern types, carried unusually large fireboxes. The Z5's grate area of 182 square feet was never exceeded, and its starting tractive effort of 153,400 pounds (including 13,400 from a trailing truck booster) was the largest ever for a simple articulated. For a number of years these were the world's largest locomotives.

The depression years between 1931 and 1934 dealt a major blow to locomotive builders, who suffered serious losses, along with all other sectors of American industry. With the financial picture brightening a bit in 1934, railroads once again started ordering super power machines. Consequently, engineering design innovations came forth at a rapid pace between 1935 and the beginning of World War II. Although diesel-powered passenger trains would appear in the mid-1930s, steam power, especially the super power locomotives, still ruled American main lines.

The 18 Yellowstone types, produced by Baldwin for the Missabe Road in 1941 and 1943, were among the most powerful engines ever built (in terms of drawbar force). They allowed the DM&IR to increase train tonnages by 30 percent, and tirelessly hauled iron ore for nearly two decades. In 1959 No. 228 (class M4) is ready to leave Fraser, Minnesota in late afternoon with 190 empty ore jennies. William D. Middleton.

Side view of Missabe Road Yellowstone-type No. 223 (class M3; Baldwin, 1941) at Two Harbors, Minnesota in 1959 highlights details of running gear and all-weather cab on these behemoth engines. Phillip A. Weibler.

Duluth, Missabe & Iron Range 2-8-8-4 No. 227 (class M3; Baldwin, 1941) climbs Saginaw Hill near Grand Lake, Minnesota in 1959 with 171 loaded ore jennies. William D. Middleton.

A moderate number of 2-8-8-4's were built just before or during World War II. Lima constructed 12 Yellowstone engines for Southern Pacific in 1939. These were similar to the famous cab forwards, but since they burned New Mexico coal, they were of conventional design, and also the heaviest steam locomotives ever owned by the SP. Two years later, Baldwin turned out eight mammoth 2-8-8-4's (M3 class) for the Duluth, Missabe & Iron Range, while ten similar M4's came from Eddystone in 1943. It is interesting to note that these engines utilized super power concepts to optimize drawbar pull rather than horsepower, since the DM&IR hauled only one commodity at low speed. During the latter part of the war, B&O wanted new diesels, but was told by the War Production Board (WPB) to buy large steamers, and thus it acquired 20 EM1 class engines from Baldwin in 1944–45. Such were the vagaries of a wartime bureaucracy.

Baldwin's first production of simple articulateds occurred in 1935 when it rolled out two batches of 2-6-6-4 engines for the Pittsburgh & West Virginia and the Seaboard Air Line. The three P&WV class J1 locomotives, with Belpaire fireboxes and 63-inch drivers, pioneered this wheel arrangement, and their strong performance resulted in four class J2 engines two years later. In contrast, the five SAL locomotives ran on 69-inch drivers and were designed as dual-purpose engines, although they were used almost exclusively on freight trains. Their success over the road prompted Seaboard to order five more only two years later. They, along with Clinchfield's 4-6-6-4's (see below), were the only super power articulateds to operate in the Deep South.

One of the most widely used simple articulated designs was conceived in the early 1930s when Union Pacific vice president Otto Jabelmann began studying his road's needs for larger locomotives. He thought that UP's profiles between Cheyenne and Ogden demanded the optimum combination of speed and power, which was available only with a new type of articulated engine. To get the high-speed tracking capability, he felt that a four-wheel lead truck was needed, whereas a six-coupled driving gear was light enough to balance easily and yet provided 12 drivers on the rail for power. He also realized that all of the eight-wheel articulateds produced previously were too slow for UP's needs.

Thus he and his engineering staff sketched a layout for a new wheel arrangement, the 4-6-6-4, and sent it to Alco in early 1936. Both the builder and the railroad knew that the secret to success would be good weight balance (to keep the front gear from slipping), as well as controlling the lateral oscillations of the front drivers. Alco was able to design an

The first high-speed simple articulated engines to operate in the Deep South were Seaboard's Baldwin-built 2-6-6-4's of the R1 and R2 classes. Number 2502, shown at the road's Howells yard in Atlanta in 1947, was part of the first order for five engines in 1935. David W. Salter.

Despite its steep grades and heavily curved main line, Clinchfield Railroad opted for the high-speed 4-6-6-4 design in 1943 when it ordered eight machines from Alco (class E1). Three years later it acquired six more (class E3) from the Denver & Rio Grande Western, which had received them through a wartime allocation. They were also built by Alco but to the Union Pacific 3900-series design. Here we see examples of both designs. Number 656 carries a six-axle tender, while No. 870 (former Rio Grande) uses the more modern pedestal (centipede) design. Note the large coaling trestle used at Clinchfield's primary shop in Erwin, Tennessee. Hoppers were pushed to the top and thus could be unloaded directly into locomotive tenders. Ron Flanary Collection.

improved suspension system just as had been required to make the early 4-4-0's usable. Following usual super power practice the builder also used lightweight main and side rods, and crankpins. Upon arrival from Alco in late 1936, the new high-speed articulateds, named the *Challenger* type, were put to work on the Sherman Hill–Wasatch region, augmenting (and often replacing) lanky Alco-built 4-12-2's, the nation's longest rigid-frame engines (albeit with a number of flangeless drivers). This first group of 4-6-6-4's had 69-inch drivers, 235 psi boiler pressure, and weighed 566,000 pounds. They produced a starting tractive effort of 97,400 pounds.

Copies of these early Challengers were constructed by Alco for the Clinchfield Railroad, Delaware & Hudson, and Western Pacific. However, during World War II Union Pacific ordered 65 improved Challengers from Alco, bringing its total to 105 (of around 250 built). These new locomotives had 70-inch drivers, a slightly higher boiler pressure, and

The Challenger wheel arrangement was conceived by Union Pacific's Otto Jabelmann and produced by Alco in 1936. Although some design details changed with later models, the overall capabilities of these dual-purpose machines were a perfect fit to the long-distance demands of UP's routes west of Omaha, Nebraska. These two photos compare the evolution of the 4-6-6-4 from No. 3902 in 1936 to No. 3949 in 1944. Eric Hirsimaki Collection.

weighed slightly more (due to substitution of strategic metals). Wartime allocations also sent part of the UP Challenger order to the Rio Grande, but since the Alco models were incompatible with the Rio Grande's Baldwin-built 4-6-6-4's, they sold them to the Clinchfield Railroad. Other roads getting some of the total Challenger production included Western Maryland (from Baldwin), while Alco delivered this type to Northern Pacific and Spokane, Portland & Seattle.

More Northerns

During the six years before World War II there were similar advances in the development of two-cylinder power, which were becoming faster and more powerful as the designs were refined. Once again the Northern type led in production. Among the notable 4-8-4's that appeared during this time was the second-generation of Southern Pacific's famous GS (*Golden State*) series. Six GS2's, built by Lima in 1936, introduced the popular and widely admired Daylight color scheme to steam power. Incidentally, the shroud and color design was Lima's idea, confirming that the builder understood aesthetics as well as outstanding performance. While the GS2's had 73-inch drivers, the 44 engines of the succeeding classes (GS3, 4, and 5) had 80 inchers. Their main accomplishment was a reduction of running time for the Coast Daylight between Los Angeles and San Francisco from 12 hours in 1923 to 10 hours. In total there were 60 engines in the GS2 through GS6 classes, with the last 10 (GS6) being non-streamlined machines, built during wartime.

Although some railroads, such as Pennsylvania, built many locomotives at company shops, it was still a rather unusual occurrence when, in the mid-1930s, CB&Q ordered 28 boilers from Baldwin to match those on the eight Northerns the company had delivered in 1930. Between 1936 and 1940 the road's West Burlington shops completed its impressive O5A class. A similar situation developed in 1937 and again in 1942 when Cotton Belt's Pine Bluff shops assembled two blocks of five 4-8-4's, identical to the ten it had bought from Baldwin in 1930.

Southern Pacific's Lima-built Daylight 4-8-4's were considered by many to be the most beautiful of the Northerns. Starting in 1937, SP eventually acquired 50 such engines in its classes GS2 through GS5. Presented here in appropriately scenic settings are GS4 No. 4449 (*top*) and GS5 No. 4458 (*bottom*). The former engine became well known in modern times after its rebuilding to pull the Bicentennial Train that toured the nation. It was photographed near Alpine, Texas en route from New Orleans to Los Angeles in 1984. Number 4458 was captured in 1952 near Chatsworth, California with the Daylight (No. 99) from San Francisco to Los Angeles. *Top*: J. Parker Lamb; *bottom*: Stan Kistler.

Using boilers fabricated at Baldwin, Cotton Belt's Pine Bluff shops constructed two groups of five 4-8-4's that were identical to ten engines delivered by Baldwin in 1930. Number 812, shown at East St. Louis in 1937, was part of the first group of homebuilt engines completed in 1935. They were easily the largest power on the St. Louis Southwestern in the steam era. C. W. Witbeck, David S. Price Collection.

Most lines in the South never invested in super power machines, especially 4-8-4's. One of the few that did was Atlantic Coast Line, with its busy passenger routes to Florida. ACL bought 12 R1-class machines in 1938 from Baldwin, while its northern connection (Richmond, Fredericksburg & Potomac) received a half-dozen 4-8-4's from Eddystone some four years later. One of the region's shorter roads, the Nashville, Chattanooga & St. Louis, actually introduced 4-8-4's to the South in 1930 when it purchased 5 *Dixie* types from Alco, and later 20 more during wartime (1943–44). All of these were smaller-sized Northerns.

The war years (1941–45) brought astronomical traffic levels to American railroads, which scrambled to buy the motive power necessary to move the constant flow of trains. Deliveries of 4-8-4's soared because of the Northern's power and versatility. Due to the urgency of getting machines out of the erecting shop and into the departure yard, in a number of cases recent designs were revisited and duplicated. For example, in 1943 Missouri Pacific bought 15 Northerns that were virtual duplicates of Rio Grande's five M68 class, built by Baldwin in 1937–38. Also during 1943, Alco turned out 25 copies of Rock Island's R67B class (65 engines built in 1929–30) for use by two other roads. Delaware & Hudson received 15 for its class K62, while Milwaukee Road got 10 for its S3 class, one of which has been preserved, rebuilt, and is currently in excursion service.

The South's first 4-8-4's were NC&StL's five J2-class machines, built by Alco in 1930. Capped stack and Vanderbilt tenders were common on the NC. Eric Hirsimaki Collection.

Missouri Pacific's N73-class 4-8-4's included 15 engines built by Baldwin in 1943 to alleviate wartime traffic demands. They were virtual duplicates of Denver & Rio Grande Western's M68 class constructed a few years earlier (1937–38). We see No. 2201 (*top*) when new at St. Louis and later at speed (*bottom*) on a southbound train at Bixby, Illinois in 1954. *Top*: Robert J. Foster, Joe Collias Collection; *bottom*: Joe Collias.

Brothers at heart: Despite the fact that the 4-8-4's shown here are vastly different in appearance, they are mechanically equivalent. Both were constructed by Lima in 1943 using plans for the Southern Pacific GS2 class, a result of emergency wartime allocations by the War Production Board. In all there were 10 Western Pacific engines (*top*), eight Central of Georgia locomotives (*bottom*), and 16 Southern Pacific machines built in one large order to help relieve wartime traffic demands. These photos illustrate clearly the influence of accessories (such as feedwater heaters), cabs, and tenders on a locomotive's appearance, irrespective of its basic mechanical specifications. *Top*: Eric Hirsimaki Collection; *bottom*: Frank E. Ardrey.

Nothing illustrates the construction chaos during World War II better than the convoluted case of some Southern Pacific 4-8-4's. It began with SP ordering 16 engines (GS3 class) from Lima in 1943. At about the same time Western Pacific ordered a half-dozen 4-8-4's from Lima patterned after the C&O class J3 machines, while Central of Georgia placed an order for 8 Northern types from Baldwin. When the War Production Board saw orders for 30 Northerns of three designs from two builders, it considered this an intolerable inefficiency. Thus, it decreed that all engines would be from an existing design (SP GS2), and that Lima would be the sole builder. In the end SP received 14 engines, while WP and CG received their requisite allocation. While locomotives for the two western carriers were almost identical in appearance, the Central of Georgia engines were completely unrecognizable as a GS2 design since they received no shrouds. In addition, they carried different appliances (especially feedwater heaters) and pulled short eight-wheel tenders.

Among the most notable of wartime Northerns were those of Santa Fe and Union Pacific, both built with 80-inch drivers and large tenders for long-distance runs. The AT&SF's magnificent 2900s were built by Baldwin in 1943–44. Because of the shortage of high-strength steels, a lower-grade metal was used for side rods and other parts. To achieve the

The pinnacle of Santa Fe's passenger power was represented by the 30 machines of its 2900 class. Weighing a whopping 510,150 pounds, they were the heaviest 4-8-4's ever built. Number 2903, with mechanical stack extension raised, prepares to leave Victorville, California in 1950. Stan Kistler.

Running gear on Union Pacific 4-8-4 No. 809 (*top*) glistens in the morning light of a winter day in Sidney, Nebraska. Engine is headed west with a manifest in 1956. Builder's photo from 1944 shows sister engine No. 841 (*bottom*) in original condition without smoke deflectors. *Top*: Stan Kistler; *bottom*: Eric Hirsimaki Collection.

New Haven's 10 Hudsons
(class I5) introduced
streamlined passenger
power to New England.
Shown here at Baldwin's
Eddystone plant before
delivery in 1937. C. W.
Witbeck Collection.

necessary strength, the substitute parts were larger and weighed considerably more than
they should have, making these 30 locomotives, at 510,150 pounds, the heaviest 4-8-4's ever
built (almost 8 tons heavier than the road's 3765 series).

To minimize fuel and water stops over the 1765-mile run between Kansas City and Los
Angeles, they pulled a gigantic 55-foot tender (total capacity of 31,500 gallons of fuel and
water) carried on two eight-wheel trucks. A major external feature of the wartime engines
was their side rods, which were tapered in each direction from the second (main) driver.
They also featured mechanically operated stack extensions that lifted smoke in high-speed
operation. Union Pacific's last ten 4-8-4's, built by Alco in 1944, were almost identical to
four others outshopped five years earlier. They carried 23 tons of coal and 23,000 gallons
of water in a five-axle pedestal tender with a four-wheel lead truck.

Final Period of Production

The decade after 1935 saw some famous Hudson types ordered. New Haven bought ten
streamlined engines from Baldwin in 1937. These class I5 machines were called *Shore Line*
types and powered heavy NH passenger trains between Boston's South Station and New
Haven where electric catenary began. The same year Santa Fe put into service six high-
stepping 4-6-4's with 84-inch drivers. The class engine, No. 3460, was delivered with a

(*Facing page*): A fascinated youngster studies the running gear of streamlined J1e Hudson
No. 5344 (Alco, 1931) (*top*) stopped briefly at Michigan Central's Ann Arbor station in 1940.
When new, this engine wore a bathtub-shaped cowling for NYC's Commodore Vanderbilt
streamliner, but in 1939 this Henry Dreyfuss cowling was applied at Cleveland's
Collinwood shops. The lower photo shows a sister streamlined Hudson No. 5452 (class J3a;
Alco, 1938), shorn of its shroud, heading out of Dayton, Ohio on a 1955 run between
Cincinnati and Cleveland. By then the Scullin disk drivers were the only clue to its
ancestry as one of America's early streamlined locomotives. *Top*: J. Parker Lamb Collection;
bottom: J. Parker Lamb.

streamlined cowl that featured the popular bullet nose. Although these machines normally pulled the Chief between Chicago and La Junta (Colo.), engine No. 3461 illustrated its durability in 1937 by running from Chicago to Los Angeles with mail train No. 8 at an average speed of 45 mph (with sprints to 90 mph).

In 1938 two famous Alco 4-6-4's appeared. During that year Milwaukee Road's F7-class Baltic types, six engines with 8-foot drivers and a shovel-nosed cowling, began service along with the last and finest of the NYC's Hudsons. Alco produced 40 engines of the J3a class that featured a 43-inch combustion chamber, roller bearings throughout (a first), and the more efficient Baker valve gear (replacing the Walschaerts design). These machines produced almost one-quarter more drawbar pull at 70 mph than the original J1's of a decade earlier. To promote its plush passenger service, NYC ordered the last ten J3's with streamlined cowls designed by Henry Dreyfuss. By 1945, however, accessibility had become more important than appearance, and the streamlining was removed. Nevertheless, from 1941 to 1950 two other Hudsons received a different shroud, featuring stainless steel fluted side panels on the engine and tender. These engines were used on the Empire State Express, one of NYC's premier trains.

The C&O was able to obtain eight Hudsons (class L2) from Baldwin in 1942, and in 1946 converted some Pacifics to light Hudsons. Finally in 1948 it ordered what would be America's last 4-6-4's, the five L2 machines arriving from Eddystone with poppet valves, which were more efficient than piston valves controlled by conventional valve gear. The Baldwin-built machines of 1942 were the nation's heaviest Hudsons at 439,500 pounds. These engines were used mainly for high-speed service on C&O's low-grade lines. In the meantime (1943), Wabash decided to work around WPB restrictions on new locomotives, and converted some 1925-era, three-cylinder Mikados into 80-inch-drivered 4-6-4's with shrouds covering the running boards, streamlined stack covers, and elephant-ear smoke deflectors (see following section).

Unable to purchase new passenger locomotives during 1943 wartime controls, Wabash's Decatur, Illinois shops rebuilt a group of Alco three-cylinder Mikados (class K5) into seven high-drivered, semi-streamlined Hudsons (class P1) that were later equipped with the large smoke deflectors and stack cowling shown in this 1944 photo at Decatur. Highlighted by a blue-and-white color scheme, they became the road's premier passenger power until the end of the steam era. David Price Collection.

The Nickel Plate Road was known for its fast freights powered by a 70-engine fleet of Berkshire types. Here we see one of these famous engines in its final months of service during 1958, as No. 747 (class S2; Lima, 1944) accelerates an eastbound train after a stop at State Line Tower in Hammond, Indiana. The 2-8-4's compact and efficient design belies its tremendous power, a legacy of the genius of Lima designer Will Woodard. J. Parker Lamb.

The Berkshire type was also very popular during the post-depression period. In particular, those roads controlled by the Van Sweringen brothers (C&O, Erie, Nickel Plate, and Pere Marquette) became heavy users of these workhorse engines. Mention has already been made of Erie's stable of 105 Berks that began in 1929. But the Nickel Plate (including the Wheeling & Lake Erie) topped that figure with a total of 112 engines, including 65 from Lima and 47 from Alco. All of these engines had 69-inch drivers. The Lima deliveries began with 15 S1's in 1942, and continued with 30 S2's in 1943–44, and a final order of 30 S3's in 1948.

The Chesapeake & Ohio started purchasing Lima-built 2-8-4's (*Kanawha* types with 69-inch drivers) in 1943, and by 1947 received its last order, bringing the total number of K-class engines to 90. Even the smallest Van Sweringen road, Pere Marquette, got into the act with 39 Lima-built Berks between 1937 and 1944. Furthermore, C&O's experience with these locomotives impressed its neighbor Virginian Railway, which ordered five duplicates of the larger road's K4 class from Alco in 1946.

Louisville & Nashville, one of the few southern region roads to purchase engines with four-wheel trailing trucks, wanted to buy 4-8-4's, but its South Louisville shops would not

Fresh out of the paint shop, Louisville & Nashville 2-8-4 No. 1960 (class M1; Lima, 1942) poses for a company portrait. The Berkshires enabled the coal-hauling L&N to increase its train tonnages by nearly one-third. L&N Railroad, Ron Flanary Collection.

Illustrating the Berkshire's versatility, L&N No. 1963 (class M1; Lima, 1944) heads out of Cincinnati Union Terminal in 1945 with Florida train No. 18, the Flamingo. This machine represented one of the final designs developed at the Lima Works. W. Terrell Dickey, Ron Flanary Collection.

accommodate such a long engine. So instead it began building a fleet of 2-8-4's with 15 Baldwin locomotives in 1942 and 1944. The last order for 22 Berks went to Lima, and they were completed in 1949. In retrospect it seems entirely appropriate that the machine that started the super power era would bring down the curtain on all steam locomotive production at the two companies responsible for 88 percent of the 2-8-4's built. With the delivery of seven Pittsburgh & Lake Erie class A2a Berkshires in the summer of 1948, the famous Schenectady erecting shops would soon be modified to build other forms of motive power. In fact, with its tender shop already dismantled, Alco contracted with Lima to construct tenders for this final order. A year later, in May 1949, the Ohio company's 71-year steam engine production would end with the shipment of No. 779, last of the Nickel Plate's S3-class machines.

Interestingly, four eastern lines purchased 4-8-4's during this last chapter of production. These included Western Maryland (12 J-class engines from Baldwin in 1947) and C&O (14 J3a's from Lima in 1948). In addition 30 Northerns were assembled by the Reading Railroad shops between 1945 and 1947. However, most notable was New York Central's S-class Niagara, constructed in 1945–46.

Designed by the same Paul Kiefer–led team that produced the road's J-class Hudsons, the S class was the pinnacle of excellence in NYC's long devotion to high-performance steam engines. Its design was solidly based on the accumulated knowledge of two decades of super power locomotives, namely increasing steam generation capability and overall thermal efficiency while decreasing the weight per horsepower. Similarly, mechanical efficiency was increased by the use of roller bearings, along with lightweight rodding and improving counterbalancing to decrease track dynamics.

A feature emphasized by NYC in the S class was an "overbuilding" of the engine to provide capability over that expected in normal service. This meant that the locomotive was not operated near its limits in everyday operations. This practice not only reduced maintenance requirements but also provided a reserve of extra power to make up delays when necessary. As a consequence, these machines were known for their durability, with one engine (No. 6024) running 700 miles a day to chalk up 228,849 miles in 11 months before its initial shopping. Moreover, the Niagara's running gear used coil springs on the equalizer system and lateral motion boxes on the first and third driver axles. These features, plus a high factor of adhesion (4.5) allowed the S class to run about 190,000 miles between tire turnings as compared with 100,000 in older designs.

In 1945 No. 6000, the only S1a, was built by Alco as a prototype, using 75-inch drivers. Soon the diameter was increased to 79 inches and, after more tests, the 25 production models (S1b) carried the taller wheels that allowed them to produce up to 5050 drawbar horsepower at 63 mph. In order to use the largest boiler diameter and still stay within the NYC's restricted clearances, the design team eliminated the steam dome, while providing a grate area of 101 square feet. The resulting tractive effort was 61,750 pounds, while the weight per horsepower was reduced to 93 pounds, as compared with 123 pounds in the road's K5 Pacific and 97 pounds in the J3 Hudson. The Niagara's performance is further discussed in chapter 9.

The pinnacle of development for New York Central locomotives was the postwar S1-class Niagara. Number 6000 was the forerunner, a single S1a model that carried 75-inch drivers and a 275 psi boiler pressure. Eric Hirsimaki Collection.

During the last decade of steam locomotive production, the 2-10-4 was not a big seller. For many railroads it had become a mid-range engine, since most could use Northerns and Berkshires when speed was important, while simple articulateds satisfied the need for extra power. Despite this, two of the nation's largest lines acquired virtually all of the production during this period. In the late 1930s Santa Fe asked Baldwin to build a large Texas-type engine patterned after the C&O T1 class built by Lima. The result was the delivery in 1937 of ten powerful engines in the 5000 class. With 74-inch drivers and a 310 psi boiler pressure, these monsters weighed 538,000 pounds and had a starting tractive effort of 93,000 pounds.

Unlike the T1 and many other 2-10-4's, these engines did not carry boosters (less maintenance). While the initial engines burned coal carried in a twelve-wheel tender, when AT&SF went back in 1943 for 25 more 2-10-4's to alleviate wartime power needs, it bought oil burners that used the same 16-wheel tender mentioned earlier in connection with the 2900-class 4-8-4's. These 5011-class locomotives were legendary for their pulling capability, developing 5600 drawbar horsepower at 40 mph. Fittingly, they represented Santa Fe's final order for steam power, retiring in 1957 after being used as helpers out of Belen, New Mexico.

Among the largest 2-10-4's were the 25 engines of Santa Fe's 5011 class, built by Baldwin in 1944 and patterned after C&O's pioneering T1 design (Lima, 1930). Here No. 5028 pulls out of San Bernardino, California in 1951 with a brakeman on the footboards to throw switches in the yard. Stan Kistler.

During the summer of 1956 the Pennsy leased a group of Santa Fe 5000's to operate coal drags between Columbus and Sandusky, Ohio. Number 5035, the last of this 25-engine series, rests at the Columbus yard, sitting beside one its contemporary rivals, the Pennsy J1-class 2-10-4, along with an older Decapod. J. Parker Lamb.

One of ten oil-burning 2-10-4's, Kansas City Southern No. 901 (Lima, 1937) lifts a thick plume of smoke as the train charges southward near Page, Oklahoma in the late 1940s. Preston George, Joe Collias Collection.

(*Facing page, top*): Pennsy J1-class 2-10-4 No. 6412 charges along the main line with an eastbound manifest at Westville, Ohio in 1956. J. Parker Lamb.

(*Facing page, middle*): Side view of Pennsy J1-class 2-10-4 No. 6487 shows large firebox along with running gear details. Engine is heading a northbound coal train near Worthington, Ohio in 1956. J. Parker Lamb.

(*Facing page, bottom*): Pennsy J1-class 2-10-4 No. 6496 leads a northbound coal train near Lewis Center, Ohio in 1956. Coal is heading from Columbus to Lake Erie docks at Sandusky, Ohio, and engines were in their last months of service. J. Parker Lamb.

Not quite as powerful at speed (due to 70-inch drivers) were Kansas City Southern's ten Texas types of the S class produced by Lima in 1937. Half were delivered as coal burners and half used fuel oil. Their job was to move freight across the Ozark and Ouachita Mountains between DeQueen, Arkansas and Pittsburg, Kansas. They routinely sped along the flats at 60 mph but could lug 1800 tons up a 1.8 percent grade. Sadly, they were the last 2-10-4's produced by the company that introduced this wheel arrangement.

The largest order for 2-10-4's also came as a result of the wartime traffic crunch. The Pennsylvania Railroad, whose Juniata shops were the birthplace of virtually all PRR designs and much of its production, was not allowed by the WPB to develop a completely new locomotive. Instead, it had to settle for a virtual duplicate of C&O's T1a class. However, wartime expediency resulted in Lima assisting Altoona with special tools and dies to speed production in 1943. In fact, Lima was supposed to construct an additional 25 engines, but the order was cancelled by the WPB. Despite the lack of Pennsy's usual Belpaire firebox, its J1-class 2-10-4's were powerful machines, with 70-inch drivers and 110,100 pounds of tractive effort (including 15,000 from a trailing truck booster). Many lasted until the end of PRR steam in 1958, with 25 put in reserve for future use (that never came).

As we close this discussion of the super power era, some readers will recognize that no mention has been made of many well-known locomotives. This oversight will be corrected in the next chapter.

Evolution of Smoke Management

One of the most prominent appearance features of a steam locomotive is its smokebox, called the *front end* by designers. The smokebox contains the throttle valve and piping to admit high-pressure steam to the valve chests as well as the piping to permit the exhaust steam and combustion gas to exit through the stack. Somewhat surprisingly, to get smoke out of the stack without secondary problems was something of a challenge.

From the early days of wood-burning fireboxes through the 1880s, when bituminous coal was introduced, there was a continuing problem of tiny, hot embers being lifted from the grate by the draft of air and transported into the smokebox, and then through the stack itself. The result was a prolific production of lineside fires. To combat this problem, various kinds of spark arresters were devised, beginning with the large *balloon* stacks of the 1840s. These early designs used a conical stack configuration above the smokebox, not for the sake of appearance but because of its effect on the internal flow of gas.

Experiments on the flow patterns of gas carrying small particles showed that as the flow passed upward into the conical section, the flow velocity decreased to a level where the particles could not be carried by the flow and would fall by gravity to the bottom of the stack. Later, various types of deflector plates and wire mesh were placed inside the large stacks to capture a greater percentage of the embers. Eventually the high-maintenance balloon stacks were discarded, and separation of embers was attained through the use of baffles and mesh placed inside the smokebox. This was easily possible since, as stacks became shorter, smokebox diameters became much larger. Grate designs were also improved so as to minimize the generation of buoyant embers leaving the firebox area.

Modern short stacks, which appeared in the 1930s, usually included a rounded lip at the top. Although this was largely an ornamental feature, it inadvertently helped solve another problem that had developed as train speeds increased. In many cases the smoke plumes from some engines did not rise above the train but blew back across the cab, hampering both the visibility and breathing of the crew. Although the designers had no understanding of the *aerodynamics of blunt bodies*, the rounded lip at the top of the stack was instrumental in lifting the smoke above the train. The physical reason for this success was that the exhaust flow from the stack interacted with the incoming airflow about the front of the locomotive (including the lip of the stack) to produce a swirling, *vortex flow* pattern

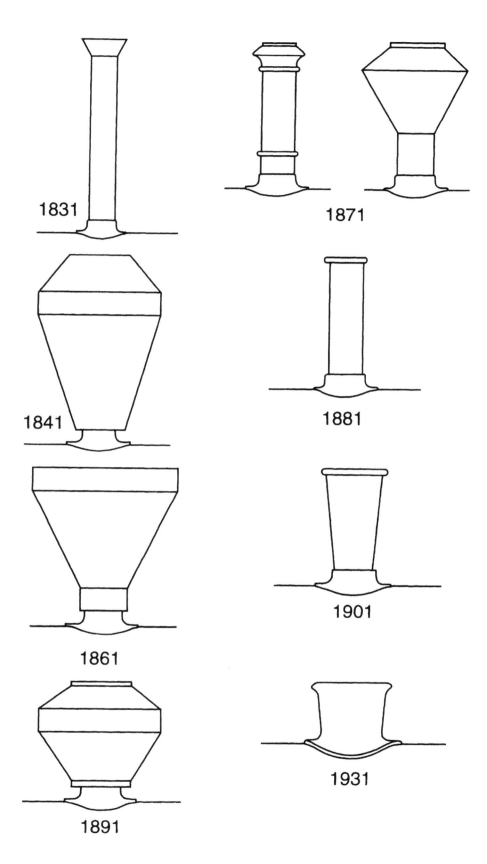

1831

1871

1841

1881

1861

1901

1891

1931

Variation of smokestack configurations during the era of wood-burning locomotives (1831–1891), and for coal- and oil-burning locomotives (1871–1931). Adapted from *The Steam Locomotive in America*, Bruce.

New York Central L4a Mohawk No. 3127 (Lima, 1943) gets coal and water at Galion, Ohio in 1855. "Elephant ear" smoke deflectors were applied after World War II. Drop coupler was used as a safety measure since it prevented the coupler from snagging debris in a wreck. J. Parker Lamb.

on each side of the stack. The vortex flow patterns behind the stack were corkscrew-like flows that both contained the smoke (kept it from spreading) and directed it on a path above the train.

The smoke-lifting capability of the rounded lip on straight stacks was improved by English designs that incorporated a larger lip that, rather than being circular in cross section, was triangular. These so-called *capped stacks*, which were often highly decorated, became widespread in Great Britain and European locomotives. In the United States only a few railroads specified this feature after 1910. Notable users were Delaware & Hudson, Nashville, Chattanooga & St. Louis, and Texas & Pacific.

During World War II the German railway system began using separate smoke lifters on many of its engines. These were large plates, placed parallel to the sides of the smokebox but displaced away from the surfaces by one to two feet. The plates formed the incoming airflow into high-speed sheets that flowed upward around each side of the stack, carrying the smoke above the engine. This design was brought to American railroads after the war and used widely in high-speed engines such as NYC's Mohawks, B&M Pacific and Mountain types, and Northerns of D&H, NYC, UP, and WP. Even UP's later Challengers received this treatment. The American designs usually incorporated much larger deflection plates than those from Europe. Attached to the outer edge of the running boards, they were often called *elephant ears*.

Other roads found that mounting a *skyline casing* on top of the boiler was very effective as a smoke lifter. The shroud enclosed both the stack and domes, creating a smooth top contour that produced an upward flow pattern across the engine. Notable examples were Southern Pacific's Daylight 4-8-4's, as well as their wartime cousins on the Western Pacific, along with some of SP's non-streamlined 4-6-2's and 4-8-2's.

Southern Pacific class P10 Pacific No. 2482, shown at Sacramento, California in 1950, was one of three such engines fitted with skyline casings and side skirts in 1941. With a paint scheme similar to that on the famous GS2 Daylight engines, the 4-6-2's were assigned to the San Joaquin Daylight. By the early 1950s the skirts and paint had vanished, but the skyline casing remained attached as an effective smoke lifter. Similar smoke control devices were used on SP's 4-8-2's. J. Parker Lamb.

A third design, less popular than the others, was an open-top cowl that surrounded the stack and was slightly taller than the stack. When viewed from above, the cowl was stream-lined in shape (usually an oval). As in the straight stacks, the top edge of the cowl had a rounded lip that served to produce a larger vortex flow pattern than the stack alone. One of the major proponents of this lifter design was the Union Pacific, which installed them on its second series of Challengers as well as all of its Big Boys.

One major railroad completely eschewed the aerodynamic approach to smoke lifting. Santa Fe used mechanically controlled stack extenders on its 4-8-4's and 4-6-4's. Another famous engine, the Pennsy K4, received experimental applications of three types of smoke lifters. At various times, locomotives of this design were fitted with full streamlining (two designs), skyline casings over stack and domes, and small elephant ear deflectors.

(*Facing page, top*): Southern Railway 4-8-4 No. 6495 (class Ts1; Alco Richmond, 1919), with Wimble smoke duct, was assigned to the mountainous Rat Hole Division between Cincinnati and Chattanooga, so named because of its many tunnels. Louis R. Saillard Collection.

(*Facing page, middle*): The streamlined shroud covering Frisco's light Pacific No. 1026 (Baldwin, 1919) includes a special fin at top of the stack to keep smoke lifted above the locomotive. Photo at St. Louis in 1939. Robert J. Foster, Joe Collias Collection.

(*Facing page, bottom*): In 1946 C&O's Huntington, West Virginia shops rebuilt two Hudsons (class L1) into streamlined power. Brightly painted boilers led to their nickname, "Yellowbellies." Forward slanted nose was later copied for shroud on steam turbine No. 500. Eric Hirsimaki Collection.

CHAPTER 8

THE PINNACLE OF DESIGN

In this chapter we highlight six locomotive designs that displayed a high level of engineering innovation and, with few exceptions, were associated with a single railroad. All reached their ultimate development during the last decade of steam power production. As we have noted, there were many instances where the same (or similar) designs were used on numerous roads, but occasionally the specific needs of a railroad led to unusual designs. For most of these cases, the specific need was to traverse mountainous terrain with heavy trains in the shortest time.

Union Pacific 4-8-8-4

Selecting the first locomotive on our list is, in today's parlance, a no-brainer. It is one of the most famous and yet the rarest example of a super power engine (only 25 built). Looking westward, we find once again the legacy of Otto Jabelmann, a genuine western hero, at least as far as the Union Pacific was concerned. Born in Cheyenne and destined to be a UP man, he began as a crew caller, later became a roundhouse foreman, and eventually a UP vice president. As we have seen, the articulated locomotive was a much more complex piece of machinery than a rigid-frame engine, due largely to the dynamic loads produced above 40 mph by the transverse oscillations of the forward driving gear. Superimposed on this were the sympathetic movements of a lead truck that was supposed to guide the front engine into curved sections of track. Consequently, virtually all of the articulated locomotives prior to 1930 were drag engines.

(*Facing page, top*): From the day it left Alco's plant in 1941, the Big Boy design was hailed as the pinnacle of American steam locomotives. And the mainline performance of these 25 engines did nothing to diminish their reputation. Here is No. 4017 waiting at Rawlins, Wyoming in 1956 for its next assignment. Stan Kistler.

(*Facing page, bottom*): A common image of UP's Big Boy shows it charging along the main line with a manifest, such as No. 4021 running eastward in late afternoon near Rock River, Wyoming in 1956. Stan Kistler.

A close-up view of the Big Boy's running gear at sunset is the best way for one to appreciate the magnificence of this machine. Number 4023 shown at Laramie, Wyoming in 1954. Stan Kistler.

But that all changed in 1936 when Jabelmann sketched out the design of the first high-speed articulated, the 4-6-6-4 configuration that later displaced older engines such as the 9000-series *Union Pacific* types (4-12-2). In addition he put together the specs for UP's 800-series 4-8-4's in 1938. These were typical "western" Northerns, tall drivered (80 inches) and big boilered for long-distance, high-speed running.

About the time that the quartet of early 800's began to appear in 1939, Jabelmann was already at work on his next challenge from the UP operating department, which, duly impressed with the success of the 4-6-6-4's at work, wanted to push the envelope even further. Following are the size and performance guidelines Jabelmann was given for the new engine.

a. Design the largest and most powerful locomotive possible within existing clearances and axle loads of 67,500 pounds.
b. Design it to move 3600-ton trains from Ogden to Green River (ruling grade 1.4 percent) without a helper.
c. Design it for safe operation at speeds up to 80 mph.

With this mandate Jabelmann and his engineering design staff started with the Challenger and added two more axles for power. They worked closely with Alco to develop an even better system of suspension, known as "lever control." The builder found that the transverse oscillations of the front engine caused the entire locomotive to rotate about a vertical axis located at the last driver. Thus the designers fixed the transverse location of this axle and allowed all other axles to move laterally, but controlled their movement with a resistance that increased toward the front of the locomotive. Moreover, the front running gear was allowed extreme vertical flexibility, with all axles (including the lead truck) equalized on each side and the two sides cross equalized at the front and at the main pivot point connection with the rear driving gear. The effect was essentially an enlargement of the early concept of the three-point equalization of a 4-4-0, in which the lead truck was given much greater flexibility than the drivers. This improved suspension design made the big engine quite rigid on tangent track yet able to glide around curves with a restrained movement, free of the dangerous oscillations experienced by most eight-coupled articulateds. More than its sheer size, this was the most significant technical advance included in the 4-8-8-4.

As with other major locomotive projects discussed here, the speed with which plans were drawn, steel components fabricated, and engines assembled by builders of this period is astounding. The shop crews at Schenectady pushed No. 4000, the first 4-8-8-4, out the door less than two years after Jabelmann began his design study in Omaha. This period included a short nine months after Alco signed a contract to produce 20 of the 144-foot-long behemoths whose boilers were constructed of steel plate 1⅜ inches thick. Although the road could have called these locomotives the *Wasatch* type or the *Sherman* type, instead it resurrected the whimsical label *Big Boy*, first scribbled in chalk on the smokebox door by a workman in the Schenectady erecting bay.

Clearly this machine was no "boy" when it came to specifications and performance. With 68-inch drivers, a 300 psi boiler, a 19-foot-long firebox with a 150-square-foot grate, the 4-8-8-4 could lug 100 car trains over Sherman hill at 35 mph, while tonnage was still at a respectable 4200 on a 1.4 percent grade at a speed of 20 mph. Its weight of 772,200 pounds was the largest ever published for a locomotive anywhere. (However, as we shall see later, there are "published" weights and "unpublished" weights.) When running wide

Norfolk & Western was so proud of it final locomotive designs that it ordered a formal portrait of the "big three" at Roanoke at the end of World War II. Here the queen of the fleet is flanked by a high-speed A-class 2-6-6-4 and a Y6-class Mallet compound. N&W Railroad, William D. Middleton Collection.

A rebuilding program in the 1980s brought two of Norfolk & Western's famous big three designs out of storage and onto the main line for excursion service. In 1987 both Class A No. 1218 and class J No. 611 were operated on adjacent tracks during a national convention of rail enthusiasts. Here the articulated leads an empty hopper train through an **S** curve near Salem, Virginia, while the 611 moves a long excursion train in parallel. Jay Williams.

open the Big Boy consumed 22 tons of coal per hour along with 100,000 pounds of water, and at 41 mph showed a peak drawbar horsepower of 6290 (essentially the same as an N&W class A). The last five Big Boys were built during 1944.

Because of its length, the 4-8-8-4 was restricted to the line between Cheyenne (Wyoming) and Ogden (Utah). When the Challengers came on line, some older turntables had to be fitted with temporary extensions that allowed the last two tender axles to be pushed upward to clear the tracks around the table. But with the Big Boy it was necessary to build four new ones with 135-foot spans (at Cheyenne, Laramie, Green River, and Ogden).

Beginning with its inaugural deadheaded trip in September 1941 from Schenectady to Omaha (via NYC and C&NW), the mammoth 4000 was a magnet for local press coverage, inspiring some 520 newspaper articles in 45 states. The title "biggest locomotive" was the recurrent theme of these written pieces, which also used this occasion to congratulate the nation for its technological success, clearly symbolized in this powerful machine. With the encouragement of Union Pacific, along with its outstanding performance on a highly visible line, the Big Boy became a national symbol as "America's greatest locomotive."

Norfolk & Western's "Big Three"

Three designs solidified Roanoke, Virginia as the place where American steam locomotion made its last stand, with the support of its staunchest adherents. As noted previously, the Roanoke shops began in 1891 as the Roanoke Machine Works and by 1895 had built 152 small first-generation engines for its corporate parent N&W. As the size of locomotives began to outgrow the capacity of the shops, the railroad ordered its motive power from major builders, especially Richmond and Schenectady. However, in 1912–15 the shops were expanded so that they were able to construct 14 Pacifics (E class) and three twelve wheelers (M class). The next big job was 16 Mountain types (K class) in 1916–17. Further shop expansion occurred at the beginning of World War I.

With the smaller locomotives complete, the shops were ready to tackle a large engine. Their new task was to develop a more powerful version of the Z-class compound 2-6-6-2's, the road's primary heavy freight engine. By 1919 chief mechanical engineer J. A. Pilcher and his staff had designed and produced five prototypes of the Y2 class, a compound 2-8-8-2. After testing these engines, some further improvements were made, and an order for 20 Y2a's was given to Baldwin. During the USRA period (1917–20), most railroads were allowed to choose which wheel arrangements best suited their needs. The N&W chose only two models, taking 10 Mountain types and 50 compound 2-8-8-2's (called Y3's, as they were an improvement over earlier Y2a's).

In a rare move for the railroad industry, the N&W began a program after World War I to develop and train more motive power craftsmen and technicians. Special classes were held at shops throughout the entire system, and the result was a new generation of technical leaders who were enthusiastic about the challenges of building and maintaining ever more powerful locomotives. This is one of the few documented cases in which railroad management realized that even when highly competent engineering talent was available to conceive and design new motive power, their capabilities had to be supported by dedicated people in the foundries, boiler shops, and erecting bays. No doubt this tradition was partially responsible for the significant accomplishments on the N&W during the next three decades.

Another important step in labor relations occurred during the 1928–35 period when the shops built 20 Y5 compounds that were not needed at the time but which kept the labor force active during the depths of the depression. This move paid off handsomely when, in 1934, N&W's upper management decided that it would embark on a new initiative to design and construct a state-of-the-art high-speed freight locomotive.

Soon the engineering team of J. A. Pilcher, G. P. McGavock, and C. H. Farris, after reviewing the newest locomotives in use and recent technical advances in locomotive technology, begin sketching out the specifications for a 2-6-6-4 engine, carrying the designation *Class* A. They intended to employ a one-piece, cast-steel main frame with integral cylinders (developed only recently by General Steel Castings), roller bearings on all axles, as well as the advanced lubrication methods developed by the Nathan Company. The Class A's would have mechanical lubrication at 238 points and pressurized lube at 98 locations. By keeping the hundreds of moving parts lubricated at all times, frictional losses were decreased, and the time lost by hand lubrication was virtually eliminated.

The first of ten new 70-inch-drivered Class A's rolled out of the shops in late May 1936, and just as Lima's pioneering A1 had done 11 years earlier, it immediately set new records for efficiency and low maintenance. Dynamometer tests showed that its massive boiler-firebox could produce 6300 drawbar horsepower at 45 mph, and that it could sustain a 6000 hp rating between 32 and 57 mph. It could even move a passenger train comfortably at speeds up to 70 mph. Soon the entire industry realized that "those N&W fellas down in the Blue Ridge Mountains" had developed one of the nation's most versatile locomotives. A total of 43 Class A's would be built, the last 5 between 1949 and 1950. These are distinguished by the large rodding that housed roller bearings.

Buoyed by the success of their Class A design, the N&W engineering group next turned its attention to the road's workhorse, the Y5-class 2-8-8-2 compounds that had evolved during 1930–33 from the Y3's of USRA design. Rather than switch to a simple engine, the road decided that, since this locomotive was intended as a complement to the fast 2-6-6-4—namely to pull long coal trains in mountainous territory—a compound design was still appropriate. Thus the main emphasis of the engineering team was on upgrading the Y5 to include the advanced features from the Class A design such as cast-steel main frames, roller bearings, and lubrication.

The first of 25 Y6's were produced in 1936 with 57-inch drivers and a boiler pressure of 300 psi (compared with 270 in the Y3 and Y4 classes). This combination yielded a starting tractive effort of 152,000 pounds (simple) or 127,000 (compound). Tests proved that, at 25 mph, the Y6 would produce 5500 drawbar horsepower, while its top speed was 50 mph.

Norfolk & Western Class A No. 1242, equipped with roller bearings on its side and main rods, sits on the ready track at Roanoke between runs in 1956. Phillip A. Weibler.

Norfolk & Western coal train headed for tidewater fights up a short grade near Bluefield, West Virginia in 1958 behind Y6b-class Mallet No. 2183, which carries an auxiliary water tank behind tender. Use of these canteens enabled N&W to drastically decrease the number of en route water stops. J. Parker Lamb.

Close-up view of Norfolk & Western class Y-6a Mallet No. 2136 shows small trailing truck nearly invisible beneath the engine's mammoth firebox. Phillip A. Weibler.

138

PERFECTING THE AMERICAN STEAM LOCOMOTIVE

Empty Norfolk & Western
coal hoppers head south
from Columbus, Ohio in
1955 behind Class A 2-6-6-4
No. 1208. J. Parker Lamb.

With this increase in performance, the shops then began to modernize the road's fleet of older 2-8-8-2's and ended up with 191 engines that were either pure USRA (Y3 class) or improved copies that had 58-inch drivers. A final production of 30 Y6b's appeared between 1949 and 1952. These N&W designs, the only Mallets produced in America after 1935, had taken this nineteenth-century concept about as far up the ladder of technology as was possible in the mid-twentieth century.

The third and final major project of the N&W design team began in the late 1930s when the road decided it needed something more powerful than a 4-8-2 for its passenger trains. Designers McGavock and Farris began analyzing the performance of 4-8-4's on other roads as a prelude to settling on the specifications for the new J class. For this high-speed engine they added new features such as lightweight rodding (including roller bearings), lightweight power pistons, hollow piston rods, and aluminum crossheads. By decreasing the weight of moving parts, the resulting dynamic loads on both the locomotive and the roadbed were drastically reduced. When it came to streamlining, these proud Virginians decided there was no need to hire a famous industrial designer from the Northeast. They turned instead to one of their own, the multi-talented tool supervisor F. C. Noll, who also had an artistic flair.

When the first five class J's left the shops between October 1941 and January 1942, the engineering and production staff were confident that these were the best locomotives they had yet produced. Although the J's initial boiler pressure was 275 psi, after initial tests it was decided to increase the tractive effort by raising the pressure to 300 psi and adding a trailing truck booster for an additional 12,500 pounds. This gave these high-drivered (70 inches) Northerns a starting tractive effort of 82,000 pounds, the most of any 4-8-4.

The lubrication system on the J's was especially impressive, with 230 points of mechanical lubrication and 72 more with pressure fittings. With a full supply of lubricant, these speedsters could run an astounding 1300 miles without attention. Although its usual maximum speed was 80 mph, on one test the J led a 15-car train along a straight and level track at 110 mph, a tribute to the great balancing of drivers and the low weights of other moving parts. During World War II the road built five more J's, but due to a metal shortage did not install any streamlining until war's end. The final three J's were completed in 1950, and by 1954 the first two (Nos. 600 and 601) had already run off 2 million miles.

After World War II the N&W continued to stress availability, always a major drawback with steam engines, which usually required a high level of inspection and maintenance

Norfolk & Western's Powhatan Arrow heads out of Bluefield, West Virginia behind J-class No. 607 in 1954. Phillip A. Weibler.

To facilitate rapid inspection and servicing of engines between runs, N&W constructed large "lubritorium" buildings at its major engine terminals after World War II. These were long enough to accommodate two or three locomotives on each track. A 1946 view of the two-track structure at Williamson, West Virginia shows streamlined 4-8-2 No. 134 moving out while another locomotive remains inside. Norfolk & Western, William D. Middleton Collection.

Builder's photo of C&O Allegheny No. 1625 shows unusually sleek appearance for such a large locomotive. Eric Hirsimaki Collection.

Doing what it was designed for, C&O 2-6-6-6 No. 1624 (class H8; Lima, 1941) is in charge of a long string of loaded hoppers on the mountainous line near Hawks Nest, West Virginia in 1956. Phillip A. Weibler.

between runs. It built special *lubritorium* structures as well as long shop buildings where a large group of engines could be serviced simultaneously. On the main line it eliminated 17 water stations by adding auxiliary water tanks to freight locomotives. Using this device, engines could generally cover an entire crew district (about 110 miles) without a water stop. This change alone produced an astounding increase of 31 percent in the road's *gross ton-miles per train hour*. For each train this standard measure of performance is obtained by multiplying the train tonnage by the average speed. Based on our earlier definition of horsepower, we see that this figure is proportional to the average horsepower produced in moving trains. Thus, the sum of all of these data for individual trains is the gross amount for the entire railroad over some specified time interval (month or year).

The last locomotive built at Roanoke was not one of the three discussed so far, but a humble 0-8-0 switcher. Always an opportunist, N&W bought five Pennsy Pacifics during World War II, and, after neighboring C&O dieselized in 1950, it purchased 30 relatively new 0-8-0's built by Alco and Lima. These shifters performed so well that the Roanoke shops constructed 45 copies. This production ended in December 1953, closing out a 26-year period in which 3000 skilled workmen turned out 295 new or rebuilt locomotives and in the process brought American steam locomotives to their highest level of technology.

Chesapeake & Ohio 2-6-6-6

The next engine in our pantheon was a Lima product, and its story is one of technical triumph and organizational failure. It began in the summer of 1940 when members of the Advisory Mechanical Committee (AMC), working out of the Cleveland headquarters of the lines controlled by the Van Sweringen brothers (C&O, Erie, Nickel Plate, and Pere Marquette), came to western Ohio. Their mission was to discuss with Lima the design for a new, more powerful freight locomotive to better move C&O's coal traffic through the Allegheny Mountains.

The AMC functioned as an interested third party between the builder and the user lines. While its performance had generally been satisfactory in the past, it would not prove so in this instance. Prior to the 1940 meetings there had been some thought that C&O should merely increase its fleet of 2-10-4's (class T1) built by Lima in 1930. However, the C&O motive power department had been very impressed with the performance of 2-6-6-4 and 4-6-6-4 locomotives in fast-freight service. The AMC finally settled on a beefed-up version of N&W's Class A. To assure the highest possible steaming rate, this new locomotive would carry a mammoth firebox on a six-wheel trailing truck, and thus the 2-6-6-6 configuration was born. The Lima engineering staff, going back to the early Woodard era, had pushed for use of a six-wheel trailing truck to a number of roads without success. Indeed, Woodard's original plan after finishing the Texas & Pacific 2-10-4's in 1925 was to build the next super power locomotive as a 4-8-6, but the idea never resonated within the industry and was later shelved (see chapter 9).

An official order from the C&O for ten class H8 engines, to be known as the *Allegheny* type, was signed in September 1940. After some disagreement about the engine's weight, a figure of 724,500 pounds was put into the contract. However, during the preparation of the final erection drawings, this issue escalated even more as the AMC engineers kept adding what their Lima counterparts deemed were unnecessary changes that increased the weight. For example, AMC wanted much heavier rodding because they "felt" it was needed, even though Lima's stress calculations did not agree. This move caused the driver counterweights to be heavier. The committee also wanted thick-wall, cast-steel steam delivery pipes rather than the usual seamless pipe. But the most serious matter was the size of the cylinder castings, which carried a thin bushing (metal lining) that could be replaced after some wear. Again, AMC insisted that a much thicker bushing be used. This increased the size and weight of the cylinder castings by a considerable amount.

When the first Allegheny was weighed in late 1941, Lima engineers were not surprised when the scales tipped at 778,000 pounds, some 27 tons over that specified in the contract! However, key AMC officials later entered the scale house alone and presumably re-weighed the engine. They then announced the "official" weight as 724,500 pounds. And that's the way the matter stood for over two years. In the meantime another ten Alleghenys were delivered in 1942.

In 1944, however, C&O's management became concerned about the weighing irregularities after learning that two of the AMC officials involved in the matter had transferred to Lima. This and other factors led C&O to file a lawsuit against Lima in late 1944. The final settlement was very costly to the builder, causing the locomotive to receive undeserved scorn inside the corporate offices as a "good idea that went bad." Despite the litigation, C&O was quite happy with the performance of these big engines and ordered 25 more in 1944, with a final order of 15 being delivered in late 1948, giving the road a fleet of 60 of these unique locomotives.

C&O's neighbor and sometimes rival, Virginian Railway, had also been impressed with the Allegheny's performance and decided to order eight engines for delivery in mid-1945. When its class AG 2-6-6-6's were ready for shipping, VGN set up the delivery route via the C&O connection at Deepwater, West Virginia. But the C&O people objected, saying that AG's weight of 753,000 pounds was too heavy for their roadbed. To which the Virginian men laughed and replied, "Don't you boys know you've been running engines just like these for four years?"

In many respects, the 2-6-6-6 design was Lima's finest machine, with a grate area of 135 square feet, 67-inch drivers, a tractive effort of 110,200 pounds, and a factor of adhesion of 4.5. Their magnificent boilers had a diameter of 109 inches (9 feet), a size exceeded only by two contemporary engines and two early compounds. Total evaporating surface was 7200 square feet for the first models and 6800 for later ones. In addition there was a 118-inch-long combustion chamber to improve heat transfer in the firebox and thus increase the steaming rate. The last 15 machines were fitted with eight over-fire jets along each side of the firebox. These devices injected streams of air about 4 feet above the grate that greatly improved the circulation of gases within the firebox and thus produced a hotter fire with less smoke. The tender, carrying 25 tons of coal and 25,000 gallons of water, rode on seven axles (four-axle truck on rear).

But the star-crossed Alleghenys ran into another unusual circumstance once they began service on the C&O. At the time of their delivery there was a serious lack of coordination between the motive power department, the freight traffic department, and the semi-autonomous division superintendents. Consequently the new, super power engines were not subjected to the usual performance tests under a wide range of conditions so that new train lengths and helper districts could be established for the 2-6-6-6's. Instead, tonnage ratings for the H8's were set even before the engines were delivered. They were based on extrapolations (educated guesses) of the performance of current locomotives, the T1 Texas types on the Russell, Kentucky–Toledo run and the simple 2-8-8-2's (H7a) between Handley, West Virginia and Clifton Forge. Indeed, Lima conducted the only dynamometer tests two years after the Alleghenys began service, and despite a record-setting performance no change was ever made in their tonnage ratings.

One of the earliest dynamometer runs was an acceleration test with No. 1608 in August 1943 near Edgington, Kentucky. Pulling a train of 160 loads (14,083 tons), representing the heaviest ever seen on the Northern Subdivision, the engine started off with 117,500 pounds of drawbar force. After six minutes the train had gone a mile and the speed was 19 mph. Five minutes later the speed was at 29 mph. As it approached the Limeville bridge its speed was at 31 mph, but on a 0.7 percent approach grade it fell to 13.5 mph. Once off the bridge it accelerated again to 24 mph on the 0.2 percent grade to a coaling stop at Robbins. Two additional acceleration tests were carried out in late 1943 with No. 1651 (then brand new) and No. 1608 again. The results were virtually the same as for the August runs. Yet the operating department, at the time concerned primarily about the T1's stalling on the Limeville grade, forbade any crew from "running the hill" without a helper. Yet the H8's had proved they had enough muscle to climb the grade from a dead stop, while pulling 10 percent more tonnage than a T1, without any assistance!

The dynamometer crew was especially elated the day near Circleville, Ohio when No. 1608 produced 7498 drawbar horsepower at a speed of 46 mph with a train of 14,075 tons! It is reported that some of the Lima engineers shed tears of joy when they realized that their

A spic-and-span Virginian 2-6-6-6 (class BA) rests between runs at Princeton, West Virginia in 1958. Virtual duplicates of the earlier C&O Alleghenys, the eight VGN engines provided ample power for coal trains headed eastward from Roanoke to tidewater. Phillip A. Weibler.

In 1911 Baldwin constructed 12 cab-forward compounds (class MM2) for passenger service on mountainous lines using a 2-6-6-2 configuration. To improve tracking at higher speeds, they were soon converted to 4-6-6-2's and became the prototypes for all later cab-forward engines. Three of these were also converted in 1929 to simple operation (class AM2), including No. 3906 shown here at Portland, Oregon in 1947. Don H. Roberts, Louis R. Saillard Collection.

locomotive had bested the N&W's Class A record of 6300 hp (virtually the same as the Big Boy). Sadly, however, no changes in operating patterns were ever made to recognize and utilize the H8's unusual capabilities. C&O's indifferent attitude about the H8's performance is also illustrated in its lack of attention to the trailing truck, whose rear wheel was made 7 inches larger in diameter than the front pair in order to accommodate the installation of booster engines. Curiously, these devices, which would have allowed the H8's to start even longer trains or same length trains on steeper grades, were never installed.

On the Virginian Railway the 2-6-6-6's, known as *Blue Ridge* types, were well received, but again no detailed performance test data were gathered, largely because these powerful machines were assigned to the powder-puff profiles between Roanoke and Sewell's Point (Norfolk). Electric locomotives already ruled the road's most torturous grades between Mullens (W.Va.) and Roanoke (134 miles). What the railroad wanted when it acquired the 2-6-6-6's was more speed on tidewater-bound coal trains than its drag-era articulateds could produce. Using tonnage calculated by the VGN mechanical department, the AG class engines were assigned a conservative rating of 13,500 tons between Roanoke and Victoria (110 miles with a ruling grade of 0.2 percent) and 14,500 tons between

Early Southern Pacific cab-forward Mallets of the MC6 class (Baldwin, 1923) are illustrated by 2-8-8-2 No. 4032 shown at Portland, Oregon in 1956. These 20 engines were converted to simple distribution as the AC3 class. Don H. Roberts, L. R. Saillard Collection.

Victoria and Norfolk (essentially the same tonnage as on the C&O north of Russell). Coming out of Norfolk the limit was not tonnage, but length. A train of 165 empties was a mere 4500 tons. Clearly the Alleghenys were never challenged by any of these ratings, and crews routinely made or bettered their scheduled times.

Viewing the entire operating career of the 2-6-6-6's, we see that, unlike the five other engines mentioned, these Lima machines were never pushed to their limits or had their true growth potential exploited. Citing C&O's lack of interest in the H8's performance capabilities, some observers have suggested that the road might as well have gone with its original plan and just ordered more T1's. Thus, for railroad historians and locomotive aficionados, there will always be many *What happened?* and *What if?* questions surrounding these magnificent machines that never had a chance to show their true mettle.

During its final months of operation, Baldwin-built cab forward No. 4253 (class AC11, 1942) was in pusher service on the Santa Margarita hill of Southern Pacific's Coast Line. Here the disk-drivered engine waits in late afternoon at San Luis Obispo, California for its next assignment. J. Parker Lamb.

Southern Pacific's Cab-Forward Configuration

The last entry on our pinnacle list is like none of the five preceding engines, either in its appearance or its evolution of development. Unlike the others, it did not spring forth from a special design project after the super power era was in full bloom. Instead the cab-forward layout goes back to the first decade of the twentieth century, and is due to the original Central Pacific alignment across the Sierra Nevada from Roseville, California to Sparks, Nevada. The line, built during the Civil War with extremely primitive construction techniques, passed through many tunnels as well as snowsheds, needed to shelter rails from the heavy snowfalls that were typical on this mountain range.

Starting with light American types, Central Pacific used virtually every type of first-generation rigid-frame locomotive during the first forty years of its struggle to move tonnage across the Sierra summit. In the beginning it required up to five 4-4-0's to nurse twenty 20-ton cars over the hill. Later power included small Moguls and Consolidations, but in 1881 CP's chief designer, George A. Stoddard, was asked by master mechanic Andrew J. Stephens to think big and look at a 4-8-0 arrangement. The result was Sacramento-built Central Pacific No. 229, completed in 1882, and immediately tested on the Sierra. Its performance was herculean in comparison with the smaller engines, pulling 20 loads (420 tons) at 10 mph over the summit. The road soon ordered 25 more from the Cooke Works. Unfortunately, as often happened during this period, Stephens, at the urging of President Leland Stanford, pushed the ratio of driver axles to firebox size too far when the road's Sacramento shops built a 4-10-0 in 1884. Named *El Gobernador* (the governor), this design, like many others mentioned, did not have the steaming capacity for successful operation on either the Donner line or the less strenuous Tehachapi crossing.

In still later attempts to get more power, SP employed compound 2-8-0's and 4-8-0's (both cross compound and Vauclain designs). A standard power configuration around 1900 consisted of three pairs of 2-8-0's, which could lug 60 to 70 cars up the hill at 12 mph. Finally, the road ordered 17 oil-burning 2-8-8-2 Mallets from Baldwin. Designed to pull 1110 tons at 10 mph, these behemoths were expected to conquer the challenges of Donner Pass. Classified as MC-1 (for *Mallet Consolidation*), the first two test engines were delivered in May 1909 and crews quickly learned two things. These were indeed the strong mountain pullers that were needed. But the large boilers created two major problems. Forward visibility on tangent track was poor, and became worse inside tunnels and snow sheds due to the massive amount of exhaust.

Conditions inside the cabs were so severe that the road even tried out a makeshift respirator system (remarkably similar to scuba diving gear) that tapped high-pressure air from the engine, reduced its pressure, and purified it. Crews would then wear masks that allowed them to breathe this fresh air while traversing tunnels and show sheds. The first attempt to modify the engines was the installation of deflectors that directed smoke at a 30-degree angle (from horizontal). However, these did not prevent the exhaust from reflecting off the tops of tunnels and into the cabs.

As often happened during this period, design innovation came from a variety of sources. First, Hugo Schaefer, a master mechanic for the Santa Fe, read about the SP engines in the April 30, 1909 issue of the *Railroad Age Gazette*. His letter to the editor on May 14 suggested the possibility of mounting the cab in front for improved visibility. This idea came to the attention of W. R. Scott, SP's assistant general manager, as well as Julius Kruttschnitt, director of maintenance and operations. Both of these officials recommended that the mechanical department investigate such suggestions.

Soon Taylor Heintzelman, superintendent of motive power, and Frank Russell, chief designer from San Francisco, held a brainstorming conference with a group of technical people from the Sacramento shops. Heintzelman reportedly began the meeting with a blunt ultimatum, "These engines were bought to run over the mountains and we've got to see that they do." Clearly it was time for serious innovation, and the ensuing duscussion also brought forth another idea. Charles Browning, a chemist, noted that he had seen in Sausalito a narrow-gauge 4-4-0 on the North Pacific Coast Railroad with its boiler pointed in reverse and its cab mounted over the front cylinders. As the discussion developed, Heintzelman grasped the practicality of this new design, and asked Russell to start working on it.

Soon the motive power office in San Francisco was abuzz with the preparation of new drawings for modifying the previous 17-engine order to Baldwin. Chief mechanical engineer Howard Stillman, remembering the El Gobernador fiasco, was somewhat skeptical, but saw no other possible solutions. It is said that, in later years, some of the Baldwin engineering staff had attempted to take credit for the cab-forward idea. But old-time SP men never let that claim go unchallenged.

The 15 new MC2-class cab-forward 2-8-8-2's (Nos. 4002–4016) were completed in late 1909 and set up in Sacramento during February and March of 1910. They immediately proved themselves on the Sierra Nevada, doing the work of two consolidations at speeds as low as 4 mph. They could take 28 loads across the summit at speeds approaching 10 mph and, when double headed, could make 15 mph with twice the load.

But these early cab forwards were not without problems, as one would expect. Initially there was resistance to their use by engine crews who, being accustomed to having their cabs protected by a long boiler, thought the new engines were death traps. One engineer told his road foreman, "I don't want a caboose in my lap some day." The stern reply was,

Running eastward with an extra train, flat-faced AC6 class No. 4133 breezes through
Ferrum, California in 1950, leaving a GS4-led passenger special in the siding. Stan Kistler.

Cab-forward No. 4227 (class AC10) is westbound with train No. 801 near Mojave, California
in 1952. Stan Kistler.

"Mister, if you do your job right, that won't happen." At first a few crewmen even refused to take them out, but after seeing both their greater power (which meant shorter runs) and much improved cab conditions, they soon accepted, and later admired them.

However, a more serious operating problem occurred when the fuel oil flow between the tender and the firebox was reduced. This often happened on steep grades when the oil level was less than a foot from the tank bottom. With a higher liquid level (or with the train on a flat profile), the fuel tank bottom pressure was sufficient to push oil to the firebox. To cure this problem, the Sacramento shops sealed the oil tanks and then applied 5 psi air pressure above the liquid level to push the oil toward the burners in the firebox. Incidentally, the tenders also used steam lines to keep the oil warm enough to flow easily.

From its original fleet of 15 MC2's, the cab-forward fleet grew to 47 by 1913, with a dozen engines in the MC4 class and another 20 in the MC6 class. (There were no MC3 or MC5 groups.) But in 1927 George McCormick, general superintendent of motive power, decided to see if these compounds could be converted to simple operation and thus extend their service lives. MC6 No. 4041 was selected and received, in addition to four new cylinders, a rebuilt boiler using 210 psi superheated steam that increased its tractive effort from 85,040 to 90,490 pounds. The performance of this new AC3 (for *articulated Consolidation*) and its rebuilt companion No. 4028 convinced SP that all future engines would be simple articulateds. Eventually all of the cab-forward Mallets would be converted to the AC2 and AC3 classes. These would later be dubbed "sport models" by operating crews.

Then in 1928 Superintendent McCormick directed the mechanical department to begin planning an even more powerful cab-forward engine using a four-wheel lead truck. With super power concepts now firmly established for new locomotives, Baldwin designers were able to bring the cab-forward design to its pinnacle. Clearly the unique configuration of the AC's confounded the Whyte classification system. While they are usually referred to as 4-8-8-2's, from a mechanical standpoint they are equivalent to a Yellowstone wheel arrangement and are so designated in the summary of super power production given below.

The first ten of these second-generation cab forwards arrived from Baldwin in 1928, and in the ensuing 16 years the Southern Pacific would build a roster of 195 of these "backward-running" Yellowstones, the largest fleet of engines from the same base design in the super power era. The first 51 of the larger engines were distinguished by flat-faced cabs with top-mounted bells. However, starting with the AC7 series (25 engines in 1937) the cabs were made more streamlined and the bells hidden behind the cowling. These latter AC's carried 250 psi boilers and a tractive effort of 124,300 pounds, 6 percent higher than the AC4 and AC5 classes that used 235 psi pressure. Southern Pacific added another 28 engines in 1939, and then, to cope with wartime traffic, purchased 90 more, culminating in 20 AC12's in 1944. The final engine of this order (No. 4294) was SP's last new steam locomotive. Counting the earlier compounds that were rebuilt as simple engines, the total number of cab forwards was 256, spread over three wheel arrangements, including 12 AM2's (*articulated Moguls*). These were 4-6-6-2's that had originally been bought for passenger service as 2-6-6-2's.

It is surprising that the cab-ahead concept did not spread to other lines that used fuel oil in mountainous territory. The best possibility came in 1930 when the Western Pacific was thinking about buying simple 2-8-8-2's. Some of the road's management wanted the cab-forward design, but the enginemen, like their earlier SP counterparts, reacted negatively when asked for their opinion. Eventually the road decided on conventional engines. Some years later, old hands from the WP were heard to remark that this decision was probably a mistake, especially after they had run the AC's on detour operations through the Feather River Canyon.

But no one can deny the legacy of these uncommon locomotives, whose basic design followed the adage "Necessity is the mother of invention." They battled the fury of the Sierra Nevada for 46 years, overcoming the constant challenges of mountain grades and Mother Nature's harshest blows.

Summary of Production

The entire scope of the super power era comes into focus if we examine the total production of locomotives by type and by builder, as is done in Table 8-1. We see that Alco produced the most Hudsons, Challengers, and Big Boys, while Lima constructed the most Berkshire, Texas, and Allegheny types, and Baldwin led in Northerns and Yellowstones. As noted earlier, Northerns were by far the most popular wheel arrangement, followed by Berkshire, Hudson, and Texas types, while Yellowstones barely edged out Challengers for the top spot in simple articulateds, due mainly to the inclusion of SP's largest cab forwards in the former category. Northerns and Berkshires were also one–two in the number of roads ordering, with Hudsons coming in third. It is not surprising that, as originator of the super power concept, Lima's share of total production was 23 percent, considerably larger (by 6 percent) than its general market share.

Another interesting statistic is that only four roads purchased over one-third of the total production, with New York Central at 365 leading Southern Pacific (281), C&O (220), and Pennsylvania (205). In contrast the "Other" category in Table 8-1 includes some of the last-ditch efforts to save steam power from extinction. (See next chapter.)

Table 8-1
Summary of Super Power Locomotives

Type	Alco	Baldwin	Lima	RR Shops	Total	RR's Using
4-6-4	289*	75	14	27	405	15
4-8-4	330	383*	96	108	917	31
2-8-4	166	75	368*	—	609	17
2-10-4	20	106	141*	125	392	9
2-6-6-4	—	17	—	43*	60	3
2-6-6-6	—	—	68*	—	68	2
2-8-8-4	1	254*	12	—	267	4
4-6-6-4	225*	27	—	—	252	9
4-8-8-4	25*	—	—	—	25	1
Other	—	28	—	55	83	3
Total	1056	965	699	358	3078	

*Indicates largest producer of type.
Source: *Lima, the History*, Hirsimaki.

A 1949 book by New York Central's Paul Kiefer summarizes that road's motive power evolution from second-generation Pacifics and Mountains (Mohawks) through Hudsons and Northerns (Niagaras) of the super power era. These data provide a most graphic summary of the performance increases that came from the ideas of Woodard and others after World War I, and brought American locomotives to their pinnacle. The variations of drawbar force for five NYC engines are presented in the upper part of the accompanying graph. The lowest drawbar force was of course generated by the early 4-6-2, constructed before Lima's A1. In contrast the L4 Mohawk was in fact a contemporary of Lima's H10 design and thus, even though technically a second-generation engine, contains many of the performance-enhancing features espoused by Will Woodard. As is evident, its pulling effort is only slightly smaller than that of the Niagara.

The corresponding drawbar horsepower variations in the lower graph indicate not only the significant boost in power attributable to super power designs but also the corresponding increases in the speed at which the peak horsepower was produced. We see that it ranged from 40 mph for the Pacific, to 50 for the J1 Hudson, to around 60 for the J3 Hudson, Mohawk, and Niagara. It was data such as this that convinced progressive railroads to quickly embrace super power designs.

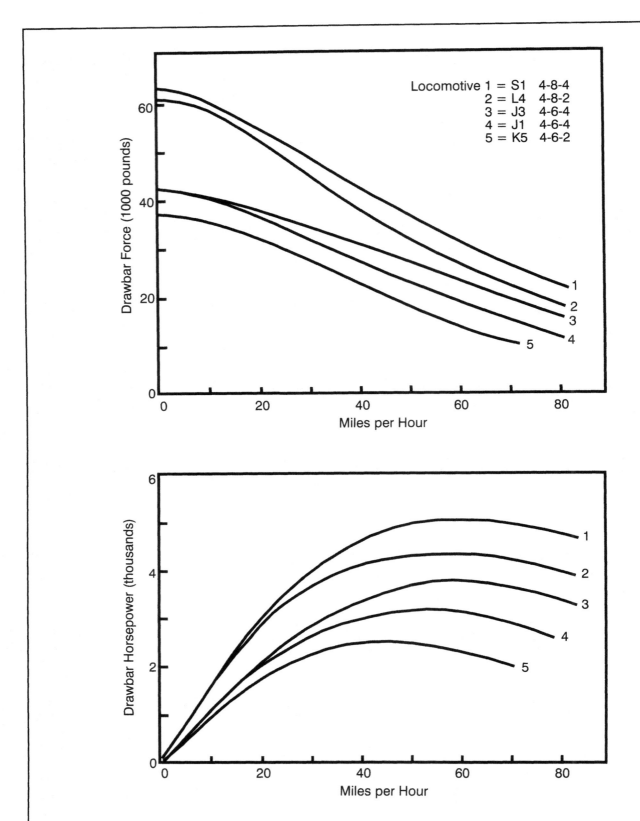

Performance data for five New York Central locomotives provide evidence of the technical advances made during the super power era. The upper graph shows the variation of drawbar force with speed, while the curves in the lower graph indicate the comparable horsepower variations. It is seen that designers were able to increase the rate of steam production at high speed, and this produced higher performance in mainline operation. Comparing the curves for two Hudson classes shows the significant effects of various improvements over the life of a single design. Adapted from A *Practical Evaluation of Railroad Motive Power*, Kiefer.

To bring about a long-needed national recognition of technical progress in the twentieth century, the American Society of Mechanical Engineers began a campaign in 1971 to designate "national engineering landmarks" that represent the extremely broad range of technology covered by the mechanical engineering profession. Between 1973 and 1989 a total of 135 sites were selected, of which 19 were related to rail transportation. A few of the sites, representing eighteenth-century technology, were located outside the Unites States.

Not surprisingly, the list includes three steam locomotives whose construction dates span virtually the entire super power era. The oldest is Texas & Pacific 2-10-4 No. 610 (1927), the first engine of the second order of 15 Texas types, which is on display at the Texas State Railroad Historical Park in Rusk (near Tyler). Next is cab-forward No. 4294 (1944), the last new steam engine delivered to the Southern Pacific, whose home is the California State Railroad Museum at Sacramento. The youngest of the trio is Norfolk & Western J-class No. 611 (1950), which was retired to the Virginia Museum of Transportation in Roanoke. Both it and the T&P locomotive continued operating careers in excursion service after being rebuilt following their initial retirement. Their encore performance allowed another generation of train watchers to be impressed with these examples of mechanical art at its pinnacle.

During 1939 Pennsy K4s No. 5399 (Juniata, 1924) served as a test bed for the Franklin poppet valve control system, which was a prototype of that used later on the T1 duplex. In 1940, Lima also made substantial modifications to the engine's vintage steam delivery system, producing in the process the most powerful Pacific locomotive in history. Note poppet valve control boxes on a lengthened pilot beam. Eric Hirsimaki Collection.

CHAPTER 9

STEAM TECHNOLOGY'S
FINAL THRUSTS

In chapter 5 we reviewed some of the experimental machines that preceded the pinnacle of development during the super power era. But there was also another period of major experimentation during the latter part of the American steam epoch, as builders and a few railroads struggled to produce new designs that could compete with the encroaching diesel-electric locomotive. These experiments fell into three major categories: poppet valves, duplex locomotives, and steam turbine power sources.

Poppet Valves

The most fundamentally important control system on a steam locomotive is that which modulates the valve motion. Earlier we described the evolution of valves from low-speed, low-pressure slide valves to the more modern piston valves, which served quite satisfactorily until reciprocation rates (driver rpm) began to climb in the 1940s. During the last decade of steam locomotive production, designers tried out many ideas for getting steam into and out of the power cylinders in a precise way during high-speed operation, but none was completely successful. From an engineering perspective, these failures confirmed that a reciprocating machine has an upper limit on speed.

The major physical reason for such a speed limit on reciprocating steam engines is that the large moving parts (power pistons and piston valves) have tremendous inertia and resist rapid changes in direction. For example, after the power piston stops at the end of one stroke, it must almost instantaneously accelerate to high speed (over 1000 feet per minute) in the opposite direction, then decelerate and stop again, before repeating this motion. During a very brief part of each stoke, a carefully measured amount of steam must be admitted in a way to act on the entire piston face. On the reverse side of the piston, the exhaust steam must be allowed to exit the cylinder in an equally brief period after it has expanded to a predetermined low pressure. At high speed the usual piston valves and associated valve gear cannot respond to these rapid movements in a precise way. The result is that the steam does not enter or exit the power cylinder with the proper timing, and thus the power produced in each stroke is diminished.

The most obvious solutions envisioned by designers were to reduce the mass (and inertia) of the piston valve, and also replace the inertia-laden valve gear linkage with a smaller, but functionally equivalent, control system. Naturally they turned for guidance to the most common high-speed reciprocating machine of that period, the automobile engine. In such engines, each power cylinder receives air through an intake valve and exhausts through an outlet valve. Indeed, contemporary designs often have four valves per cylinder in an attempt to operate better at high reciprocation rates. The valves themselves are thin (and precisely machined) disks that are activated by an integrated push rod (tappet). This configuration is known as a *poppet valve* and, when enlarged to 6 inches in diameter with foot-long tappets, it became the heart of a new type of locomotive valve gear system. Many competent mechanical engineers spent years in futile attempts to perfect a robust and reliable poppet valve control before the end of steam locomotive production.

As we noted in previous discussion of outside valve gears, a locomotive engineer could control the cutoff position and thus the admission phase of steam delivery, but he had much less control over the exhaust phase. With the poppet valve system on a locomotive there were separate intake and exhaust valves (often four per cylinder), driven by separate cams. The system thus provided a more precise timing of all events associated with steam passage through the cylinder.

Just as an automotive engine drives its valve motion using a cam shaft connected to the crankshaft by a timing chain, a locomotive must contain the same functional elements, with the timing chain being replaced by another type of mechanical signal from the driving gear. One of the earliest poppet valve gears was created by the distinguished Italian engineer Arturo Caprotti in the 1920s. In this design there was a long connecting rod between the eccentric crank (main driver) and the cam chamber at the cylinder.

His first American installation was in 1928 when B&O rebuilt one of its P7 Pacifics for a trial period that lasted only a year. The following year Caprotti gear was installed by Baldwin on one of Pennsy's two experimental K5 super Pacifics, which the road hoped would be able to compete directly with the NYC's new J-class Hudson. With the other K5 using Walschaerts gear, it was possible to make a clear comparison of two valve gears. Unfortunately, the result for Caprotti's design was the same as in the B&O trials, and it was replaced after a year. One of the main complaints was its lack of robustness, due to the larger sizes and loadings of American engines as compared with their European counterparts. Incidental to its performance was the nickname given to the Caprotti-equipped K5 engine. It was generally called *Mussolini*, a name that in these years before World War II did not carry as much negative connotation as it would later.

The next American effort to develop a reliable and accurate poppet valve control was undertaken at Franklin Railway Supply, beginning in 1937. This effort was led by none other than Will Woodard, who, as was mentioned, worked simultaneously for Lima, Franklin, and other parts of the Coffin-Allen group of companies. Like most designers, Woodard had long been intrigued by the potential performance improvements offered by poppet vales, and had even proposed a 4-4-4 locomotive using the system in 1934. Like many of his other forward-thinking concepts, it was ahead of its time, and completely ignored outside the company.

But Pennsy's continued interest in making a quantum jump in the capabilities of its primary passenger locomotive, the sturdy K4 Pacific, caused the road to contract with Franklin to equip one of these engines (No. 5399) with its new poppet valve control system. First, the engine was fitted with a new cast-steel cylinder saddle that contained separate steam chests for each valve chamber. Then a large control box was mounted on a lengthened pilot beam. It was located on the centerline of the engine so as to produce symmetrical connections to the cam boxes adjacent to the steam chests.

During its first series of road tests in the fall of 1939, No. 5399 performed brilliantly. Dynamometer car data displayed an increase of 24 percent in drawbar horsepower at 60 mph (as compared with a conventional valve gear) and a whopping 60 percent increase at 80 mph. (Recall the graphs of NYC engine performance in the previous chapter that showed decreases in horsepower with speed.) Later tests at the Altoona test lab confirmed these results.

However, PRR then sent the locomotive to Lima for other improvements in its steam-generation capability, including a front-end throttle (like the A1), a new superheater, and an improved boiler tube design. Although 5399's performance was improved still further, by mixing two sets of experiments on one locomotive, Pennsy had made it difficult to interpret the cause of improvements. Thus many skeptics argued that most of the improvement in performance came as a result of modernizing a 1913 design, rather than installing poppet valves. For evidence they pointed to a series of NYC tests of a poppet valve–equipped S1 (4-8-4) whose performance was improved only marginally.

As would be expected, however, the K4 test data convinced Franklin that its new valve control system offered a fundamental improvement in high-speed operation of steam locomotives. It promoted specific proposals to the Pennsy (rebuilding an M1 Mountain type into a Northern with poppet valves), as well as to Southern Pacific (equipping some Daylight 4-8-4's then under construction), but no new programs could be initiated because of the outbreak of World War II. However, as we shall see in the next section, poppets would see their only mass installation within the next five years. Sadly, Will Woodard would not participate in further developments of this system due to his death in 1942 at age 69.

In 1940 the New York Central decided to try poppet valves in its Niagara design, ordering No. 5500 from Alco. Although its performance was solid, it was not spectacular; mostly it was too late to stem the tide of dieselization. Eric Hirsimaki Collection.

Duplex Designs

A *duplex engine* seeks to overcome one of the major weaknesses of large, fast locomotives such as the 4-8-4, namely the large dynamic forces produced by pistons and side rods. Even the latest methods of balancing drivers were insufficient to prevent continuing road-bed damage, a major problem. Baldwin's chief engineer, Ralph P. Johnson, recognized a potential solution as far back as 1932 when he proposed to the B&O a locomotive that split the eight-coupled drive gear of a 4-8-4 into a pair of four-coupled engines, each with its own smaller power cylinders and valve gear. The result was a rigid-frame 4-4-4-4 locomotive, in which the second set of cylinders was placed between the second and third drivers, thus lengthening the rigid wheelbase. Incidentally, the year 1932 also marked the introduction of the first experimental duplex engine in France.

Although initially rejecting Johnson's design, the road later decided to pursue this approach at its own Mt. Clare shops in Baltimore. The *George H. Emerson*, a 4-4-4-4 named for the B&O's chief of motive power, was completed in May 1937. In an effort to minimize the long wheelbase, designers had used opposed pistons, with one set of power cylinders near the cab. The *Emerson* also contained a water tube firebox of a design patented by the chief of motive power. But, like Baldwin's 4-10-2 No. 60000, this locomotive was overtaken by events, for the B&O also began receiving its first passenger diesels from ElectroMotive Division (GM) in 1937. B&O president Daniel Willard quickly realized the potential of this new form of power and called a halt to further steam development.

But the duplex concept did not die with the B&O experience. It was immediately picked up by an independent-minded railroad, thoroughly dedicated to the steam locomotive. Despite this, it had stubbornly resisted locomotives using Woodard's concepts, and at this time had *never* used a mainline engine with a four-wheel trailing truck. That of course is a description of the Pennsylvania Railroad, which prided itself on designing and building its own locomotives at Altoona. (As we have seen in an earlier section, the World War II emergency finally forced PRR to build 2-10-4's based on a C&O design.)

After extensive conversations between its own designers and representatives of the three builders, Pennsy settled on a passenger engine of epic proportions: a 6-4-4-6 wheel arrangement weighing over 300 tons and running on 84-inch drivers. With a cast-steel main frame longer than that of a UP 4-12-2, this monster machine would be capable of generating 6000 hp and moving a 1200-ton train at 100 mph. Engine No. 6100 (class S1) left Altoona in 1939 wearing Raymond Loewy-styled streamlining similar in appearance to the shrouding he had applied to one of the road's K4 Pacifics in early 1936. The S1, after receiving much national publicity at the New York World's Fair, proved to be both fast and powerful but, in many ways, was "too big" for everyday work and extremely slippery. Indeed, it was known by Pennsy power people merely as the "big engine." During the war years its fancy skirt was stripped away to facilitate maintenance, and eventually the engine was scrapped in 1949, after a short ten-year operating career.

Not surprisingly, Baldwin's Ralph Johnson had not been a strong supporter of either the B&O or PRR duplex designs, and in 1939 convinced his company to build its own design as a rolling salesman just as Vauclain's No. 60000 had been in 1926. Before starting construction, however, the company's sales staff scurried around to court potential buyers with specs, drawings, and artist renderings of the radical styling by Otto Kuhler. Finally in July 1940 Pennsy signed up for two 4-4-4-4's to be called class T1.

These engines were designed to pull eleven 80-ton cars at 100 mph, and contained lateral motion pedestals on the first and third drivers to allow passage through 17-degree curves. The 80-inch-drivered T1's weighed slightly more than Santa Fe's 3780-class Northerns and slightly less than Northern Pacific's A3's. Their 16-wheel streamlined tenders (when loaded) weighed 80 percent as much as the engine itself. The first T1 (No. 6110) was delivered in late April 1942 and the second one a month later. Soon they were making a strong showing on trains in the Harrisburg-Chicago passenger pool.

After 120,000 miles of service, No. 6110 was sent to the Altoona dynamometer lab in April 1944, and exhibited a maximum of 6100 drawbar horsepower using a 15 percent cutoff. Sensing that it had the steam equivalent of the highly successful GG1 electric locomotive, the road ordered 50 more T1's in 1944, splitting the order between Baldwin and Altoona. Unfortunately this turned out to be a colossal miscalculation by the railroad. For only two years after the last T1 was delivered in August 1946, PRR president Martin Clement announced that "By May of this year [1948] we expect all of our through passenger trains west of the electrified territory to be dieselized." This statement was part of a press release announcing a $16 million order for diesel locomotives (both passenger and freight).

In parallel with the T1's development, Baldwin and PRR were also crafting a duplex engine for freight. Wanting five sets of drivers on the rail within the shortest wheelbase, the experimental Q1 design, like B&O's *Emerson*, employed opposed power cylinders, which also helped diminish dynamic loads from the piston strokes but produced other problems by locating the rear cylinder saddle near the firebox. A single prototype, with a 4-6-4-4 configuration, was built in 1942 for testing. It was a hefty engine, weighing as much as a typical Challenger, and had a tractive effort of 115,800 pounds (including 15,000 from a booster). With less streamlining than the T1, it kept the same long-distance 16-wheel tender.

Not completely satisfied with the Q1, the road ordered a Q2 model in 1944. On this engine the power cylinders were conventionally located. Carrying the six-wheel engine in the rear, this 4-4-6-4 configuration had even less shrouding than the Q1. At the Altoona test lab, the Q2 performed brilliantly, producing almost 8000 indicated horsepower at 57 mph with a water evaporation rate of 137,500 pounds per hour, causing the road to proclaim that the Q2 was "the most powerful steam locomotive in the higher speed range." Soon Altoona was at work on an order of 25 more Q2's that were completed in 1945.

Pennsy's immense and impressive S1-class duplex, unveiled in 1939, was known simply as the "big engine." With its 6-4-4-6 wheel arrangement, it proved capable of moving heavy passenger trains at sustained high speeds, but because of its size and advanced features it was highly incompatible with current engine technology. Eventually it faded from service and was scrapped after a decade. Charles T. Felstead, Eric Hirsimaki Collection.

Pennsy's original T1 duplex locomotives (Nos. 6110–11) of 1942 (*top*) were encased in a Raymond Loewy–designed shroud that featured an attention-getting prow of revolutionary shape. However, as often happened with streamlined engines, the demand for accessibility to mechanical components necessitated that the production series (Nos. 5500–49) (*bottom*) have a more modest shroud. These two photos illustrate the changes in appearance of these revolutionary engines. *Top*: Railway & Locomotive Historical Society, Harold C. Volrath Collection; *bottom*: Eric Hirsimaki Collection.

Pennsy's first attempt at building a duplex freight locomotive was Q1 class 4-6-4-4 No. 6130 (Altoona, 1942), which featured opposed power cylinders to minimize the rigid wheelbase. Here is the experimental engine (*top*) waiting an assignment in Chicago in 1946. As an improvement on the Q1 design, the Q2 class (Altoona, 1946) discarded the opposed cylinders and employed a 4-4-6-4 wheel arrangement. Number 6176 (*bottom*) provides details of this successful entry in American steam power's last period of development. *Top*: R. B. Graham, Eric Hirsimaki Collection; *bottom*: Eric Hirsimaki Collection.

The Q2 and J1 (2-10-4) engines were the Pennsy's most modern freight locomotives. They also represented two designs with the same operating goal, fast freight. The Q2 was somewhat larger and produced about 2000 more horsepower than the J1 at the Altoona test plant. The duplex could also operate at higher speeds simply because it was designed for lighter dynamic loads. This is illustrated clearly by the relative piston thrust values. Each of the J1's pistons produced a thrust of 178,300 pounds, whereas the two Q2 pistons shoved with 92,000 (front) and 133,000 pounds. Thus in many respects, the Q2 represented a significant improvement over the J1, whose roots went back to a 1930s Lima design. The Q2 gave a good account of itself during its short operating career, which helped bring down the curtain on the American steam epoch.

So what went wrong with the T1 and other passenger duplexes? Were the designs flawed? Were the testing lab results not indicative of road performance? As to the first two questions, these locomotives (of both B&O and PRR) were well designed and constructed. But the sober reality is that the T1 was a revolutionary new design that was rushed into production while still in the prototype stage. In contrast with most other major roads, Pennsy had *not* been building or operating super power locomotives for a decade when the diesel locomotive began to make inroads just before World War II. Thus it hurried through the T1's shakedown period, in which final flaws are normally removed from a new design. With the diesel at the doorstep, PRR did not have the luxury of doing what most roads had done, testing one of two prototypes extensively in road service before signing a production contract. Observers of the period noted that the railroad had indeed put too much credibility in the test lab data, forgetting that these carefully controlled running conditions are a far less rigorous experience than everyday mainline operation.

And there were some problems with the mechanical aspect of these duplexes. For example, there was a serious disagreement between Baldwin and PRR about the T1's valve gear. The builder preferred the reliable Walschaerts motion, while the road wanted to plunge headfirst into mass production of the Franklin poppet valve control system it had tested on K4 No. 5399. Baldwin's argument was that it was unwise to couple two major experiments (duplex drive and valve gear) into one engine since it would be virtually impossible to sort out the source of many operating problems. This reasoning, ignored by Pennsy due to time constraints, is fundamental to any scientific study of "cause and effect." Actually one T1 was later converted to Walschaerts gear but was never tested thoroughly. No such problem existed with the slower Q1 and Q2 engines, which carried this traditional valve gear.

Like the road's pioneering duplex, S1 No. 6100, Pennsy's geared steam turbine engine was also a 6-8-6. Number 6200 (S-2) was constructed in 1944 by Baldwin-Westinghouse. It was an impressive performer but, like the S1, too far advanced for its times. Eric Hirsimaki Collection.

As to the problem of high-drivered duplexes being slippery, after some study a mechanical committee of the Association of American Railroads recommended that these designs have larger factors of adhesion, since driver slip usually means that there is too much power for the weight (on drivers). Clearly, both of these problems on the T1 could have been solved had enough time been available to tackle the weight control difficulties separately from the valve control problems.

From our contemporary perspective, we can see clear evidence that Pennsy's corporate culture as "The Standard Railroad of the World" had promoted an attitude of arrogant independence in locomotive development. Although a very wealthy railroad, it chose to follow an extremely conservative and fiscally cautious policy with new engines. Instead of participating in the evolution of Northern and Hudson types, it attempted to modernize its Pacific and Mountain types that represented 30-year-old technology. This process was partially successful, but was not a long-term solution. Indeed, it left PRR with virtually no "knowledge base" of design or operating experience on super power locomotives when it tried to bypass the 4-8-4/4-6-4 period and jump directly into large duplex designs. These engines were much more complex pieces of machinery than conventional locomotives. As with any new engine configuration that is designed to cure one set of problems, the duplex also created another set of new challenges.

The downside risk of pushing "too far and too fast" is illustrated by comparing the T1 design to a contemporary machine, New York Central's S1-class Niagara (4-8-4). The more revolutionary duplex did not come close to the NYC engine's performance or its reliability. We noted earlier that NYC bought a prototype engine for extensive road testing and modification before ordering a 25-unit production run from Alco.

Although these were the technical aspects of the duplex's shortcomings, what really led to the short careers of the T1 and Q2 were external factors, mainly the overwhelming superiority of the diesel and Pennsy's mounting deficits due to soaring costs and aging steam power. Sadly, the corporate gamble on duplex steamers had cost PRR $25 million that it could ill afford to lose.

Steam Turbine Prime Movers

As we have seen, none of the final designs of reciprocating steam locomotives were able to effectively slow down the steady encroachment of highly efficient diesel-electric power. Most lines capitulated quickly and completely to this new motive power concept, but there were three roads on which such a switch represented nothing less than an assault on their corporate identity. Each had over a century of tradition as a hauler of large amounts of coal behind coal-burning locomotives. Before releasing their grip on steam power technology, these three wanted to investigate one more option, a non-reciprocating engine that was already being used in many other applications, including ships and stationary power plants. The power source was the steam turbine, and the three lines were, not surprisingly, Chesapeake & Ohio, Norfolk & Western, and Pennsylvania.

Pennsy was the first to try this propulsion system in 1944 when it ordered a large turbine-powered engine from Baldwin that contained two rotary machines built by Westinghouse Electric Corporation. At first glance, No. 6200 (class S2) resembled a conventional PRR locomotive with Belpaire firebox, four 68-inch drivers connected by side rods, and a large 14-wheel tender. But instead of power cylinders above the lead truck of its long 6-8-6 platform, it contained two circular housings sitting on the main frame between the second and third drivers. The larger housing was on the right side and contained an impulse-type turbine (6500 hp) that was connected to the main driver by a set of gears similar to those in an electric locomotive. This provided power for forward motion, while a similar 1500 hp turbine (for backup movements) sat on the left side of the engine. The S2 weighed 580,000 pounds and had a tractive effort of 70,500 pounds.

We have seen that the duplex engines brought with them a new set of operating problems, and the same was true for gear-drive turbines. Although they operated well on the main line, they were not compatible with the variable speed requirements on a railroad. For example, just as inertial effects limit reciprocating machines at high speeds, turbines operate best at very high rotational speeds, and their rotary inertia resists attempts to change speeds rapidly. Thus these turbine locomotives performed well at high speed, but were poor at low speed. Consequently the S2 was in the shop frequently and was finally stored for a while before being scrapped in 1949.

While this Pennsy experiment was in progress, the C&O decided to investigate a significantly different design in 1947. It ordered three turbine locomotives from Baldwin and Westinghouse Electric that used a DC generator to drive traction motors just as in a diesel-electric locomotive. These mammoth machines were built on 100-foot-long main frames with a wheel arrangement similar to a large electric locomotive. The leading power truck was a 2-D (4-8-0) type, whereas the rear one was 2-D-2 (4-8-4). In the usual notation for electric motive power, this would be a 2-D+2-D-2 wheel arrangement.

The lack of symmetry in the running gear was a result of the loadings. The front part of the locomotive carried a 29-ton coal bunker, while the rear was taken up with a rearward-facing, conventional boiler supplying steam at 300 psi. The cab was placed behind the coal and ahead of the firebox, while the trailing tender carried only water. All of the machinery was shrouded with a streamlined cowling that featured an unusual forward-slanting nose fairing.

Unlike the Pennsy engine that used an *impulse turbine*, a distant relative of the ancient waterwheel, the C&O locomotive was powered by a rotary machine of the *reaction type*. In this design, pressure differences produced by the steam flow drove the rotor at a speed of 6000 rpm and produced 6000 hp to drive four 1000 kW direct-current generators that fed eight traction motors. These hefty locomotives weighed 857,000 pounds (without tender) and had a starting tractive effort of 98,000 pounds.

Since the design of such hybrid locomotives was at the edge of postwar technology, it is not surprising that there were many problems with the C&O engine, especially with its weight distribution and the accessibility to machinery. Just as with the PRR turbine, we can only conclude that these machines were nothing more than a short-lived and unsuccessful experiment.

The final part of this "three-act turbine drama" was played out by the Norfolk & Western, which, only a year after all locomotive production ended at its Roanoke shops in 1953, received a prototype machine from the now Baldwin-Lima-Hamilton Corporation. Like the C&O machines, it was 106 feet long (plus a 55-foot water tender), carried 20 tons of coal in a large bunker at the front, used a reaction turbine to drive DC generators, and weighed a million pounds with tender. But it was an entirely different machine mechanically. First, it contained a Babcock & Wilcox water tube firebox that produced 600 psi steam. It also utilized a more conventional truck arrangement that included 12 traction motors on four C-type trucks (thus a C-C+C-C). It was also quite different in overall appearance, its boxy hulk covered with a typical black N&W shroud. It was indeed a strong contrast to the highly contoured and brightly painted C&O turbines.

On the locomotive roster, it carried the number 2300 and the classification of TE1 (for turbine electric), but in everyday life it was known as *Jawn Henry*, a variation of "John Henry," that mythical icon of hard labor on the railroad. And like the other turbine-powered locomotives, it could pull heavy trains economically, even outperforming Y6b's on coal trains while using less fuel. Not surprisingly, on level gradients it was no match for the speed of a Class A engine. In the May 1953 issue of *Trains* magazine, editor David Morgan reported his experiences while riding the TE1 between Bluefield and Roanoke: "*Jawn* rides smoothly and makes the dynamometer car needles move with gusto. Once while starting, the tractive effort [drawbar force] measurement read 224,000 pounds. Impressive!"

The first of three Chesapeake & Ohio steam turbine–electric locomotives sits in Chicago prior to its debut at the 1949 Railroad Fair. Covered with a rakish, brightly colored shroud, the gigantic machine represented a level of technology that was far ahead of the period. Consequently, there was insufficient time for it, or any other steam turbine project, to mature before diesel-electric capabilities had overtaken them. Charles Vesely, C. K. Marsh Jr. Collection.

With its classification lights still wrapped in a factory-applied covering, N&W's first steam turbine–electric, No. 2300 (*Jawn Henry*), poses at Roanoke for its portrait in 1954 while a passenger train glides past behind No. 605 (J-class 4-8-4). Norfolk & Western, William D. Middleton Collection.

Running as N&W Extra 2300 east, recently delivered steam turbine *Jawn Henry* lugs an
endless string of loaded hoppers through Christiansburg, Virginia in the summer of 1954.
Coal bunker at front of locomotive is evident in this overhead view, as is the head
brakeman's shanty on the water tender, an anachronism for such a modern locomotive.
Norfolk & Western, William D. Middleton Collection.

However, *Jawn Henry*'s problems were much the same as the other two designs, namely high initial cost, high maintenance expense, and even its length (would not fit N&W's standard 115-foot-long turntables without uncoupling the tender). Despite these potential pitfalls, the road's operating department wanted to keep testing these engines and even prepared a proposal to the board of directors in 1956 to purchase five more TE1's.

What happened next speaks forcefully of the corporate culture of railroads and especially about how difficult it was for the Big Three coal roads to abandon steam power. Shortly before the N&W board was to gather and decide if additional turbines would be ordered, there was a meeting of the operating committee to review the proposal. President Robert Smith had invited both vice president and general counsel Stuart Saunders and assistant general counsel John Fishwick to the meeting. In the ensuing discussions, Fishwick pointed out that the proposal had neglected depreciation and similar financial considerations that influenced the bottom line of overall cost. Consequently, if only the cost of operations was considered, the TE1 would be economical, while by normal accounting practices it would not.

Saunders recalls that "I made it clear that I would *not* support the operating department's proposal, agreeing with John that it did not present a true picture of overall financial impact. I also mentioned that I thought the turbine locomotive was too long, and that crews had difficulty seeing hand signals." According to Saunders, President Smith reacted to these objections with extreme agitation, and in his anger kicked a spittoon across the room. Clearly this was a case of "old habits die slowly and with great anguish." Smith, who first worked for the N&W before graduation from college and who had come up through the operating department, represented the hallowed traditions and culture of the *old* N&W. In contrast, the two lawyers, Saunders (17 years with N&W) and Fishwick (an 8-year veteran), did not carry this cultural baggage, and could view the matter of motive power in a more unbiased and objective light. However, even after N&W began ordering diesels in 1955 the TE1 labored on for two more years before being retired, thus ending American railroading's 11-year fling with steam turbines.

We can recognize that the experimental machines described here, both duplex rod engines and turbines (geared and electric drive), were based on the fundamental premise of the steam age, namely that each train is pulled by only one piece of propulsion machinery. We have also seen that steam-powered locomotives had reached a physical limit on size, and that all attempts to make them even larger were not economically feasible at that time. In the next chapter we will discuss an alternative concept, motive power modularity.

Steam and Diesel — Face to Face

The unusual circumstances of World War II brought the development of both steam power and the newer diesel-electric locomotives into direct competition. Once the wartime traffic onslaught had ended, the nation's railroads were left with worn-out rolling stock and battered roadbeds. It was now time for the management of each railroad to look seriously and carefully into its own crystal ball and decide, among other things, what form its next generation of motive power would take. Among the specific questions were these: Could steam power, with which all railroads were very familiar, continue to be developed? Given its limited wartime service, was the diesel-electric machine really tough enough to handle the rough usage inherent in railroad transportation? And above all, what were the economic consequences of each choice?

Although every major railroad made detailed economic studies that compared the operation of steam and diesel power fleets, only one railroad dared to publish it results. In 1947 New York Central's Paul W. Kiefer, chief engineer of motive power and rolling stock (mentioned earlier as the father of the Hudson and Niagara designs), gave an invited presentation to the Institution of Mechanical Engineers in London on the occasion of that group's centennial celebration. Believing that the extensive data generated during the preparation for that presentation would be valuable to the railroad industry, the Central allowed it to be published in book form in 1949. It represents the most thorough postwar comparison of steam and diesel power ever made public.

Kiefer and his staff compared overall performance of motive power on the basis of two measures: *availability* and *utilization*. The first measure was the percentage of time a locomotive is available for duty, while the other is the corresponding percentage of time it is in operation. Data on motive power performance itself was gleaned from train operations in the fall of 1944 and spring of 1945. The results showed clearly that three-unit 4500 hp freight diesels and two-unit 4000 hp passenger diesels were equal in performance to steam locomotives of comparable size.

A more controlled test series was carried out in October and November of 1946 in which four two-unit passenger diesels were compared to an equal number of 4-8-4's (Niagara types) on three round-trip runs between Harmon (N.Y.) and Chicago. Incidentally, one of the Niagaras was the last of this model constructed and was equipped with poppet valves. Monthly mileages for the two types of power during this period were 29,021 (diesel) and 26,168 (steam).

Extrapolating this data (taken in favorable weather conditions) to an annual cycle with periods of severe cold, the NYC study found that the average monthly mileages would be reduced to 27,000 (d) and 24,000 (s). Moreover, the annual availability percentages would be 74 (d) and 69 (s), while the corresponding utilization numbers were 70 (d) and 63 (s). A particularly telling statistic was that which indicated the effect of winter weather on steam power. The data showed that, on an annual basis, steam would be unavailable for nearly a month (28 days) while diesel power would be lost less than half this time (12 days). The annualized costs of operating each type of power were nearly the same, with the diesel slightly ahead at $1.11 per mile compared to steam at $1.22.

A parallel study of freight train operations showed that two four-unit 5400 hp diesels performed slightly better than a pair of steam locomotives of equal power. From annualized data, the average monthly mileages were 10,000 (d) and 8500 (s). Availability numbers were 73.5 (d) and 65.7 (s), whereas utilization percentages were 70.1 (d) and 63.5 (s).

While a significant study, this NYC report could not address a more fundamental question, namely the effect of future increases in the power available in individual diesel units. Thus, one should remember that this was a comparison of the best technology of the steam era with what we now consider to be a relatively primitive machine in the early stages of the diesel power era. The evolutionary advances in diesel locomotive development would eventually allow a fleet of these engines to provide the same operating capability as a much larger fleet of steam locomotives. Nor did this annual operating summary attempt to describe the overall economic effect of reducing labor costs associated with steam engine maintenance and operation of an extensive water supply system. However, these studies were done by virtually every railroad (along with builders) and provided further incentives to change. Consequently most railroads moved rapidly in the late 1940s to begin shrinking the lines over which steam power was used, allowing complete dieselization to gradually encroach over the entire system.

What Might Have Been

Every locomotive design group included a few forward thinkers whose role was to plan five to ten years away and envision new engines that included emerging concepts. One such man, of course, was Lima's Woodard, who, soon after completing the first Texas & Pacific 2-10-4 in 1925, told his group to begin thinking about even more powerful machines. Among those configurations that were rendered as schematic designs were a 2-6-8-4 (a high-speed 2-6-6-4 with slightly more power), and three designs that included six-wheel trailing

One of Lima's last attempts to advance steam locomotive development was its 4-8-6 proposal of 1947. To illustrate the concept, an artist airbrushed a photo of a C&O class J3a 4-8-4 to show double Belpaire firebox, six-wheel trailing truck side frame (with but four wheels on the rail), and a poppet valve control system. Like many other last-ditch efforts, it was overlooked by the nation's railroads, which were already buying large numbers of new diesel-electrics. Eric Hirsimaki Collection.

trucks. The smallest was a 4-8-6, followed by a 4-10-6 and a 2-12-6. The 4-8-6 schematic also included a trailing truck booster with two axles connected by side rods, similar to D&H's tender truck boosters on its experimental 2-8-0's. These sketches were soon filed away due to a lack of interest brought about by the depression-era economy.

But in 1947, with the Ohio builder finishing its last two major domestic orders (Berkshires for Louisville & Nashville and the Nickel Plate), the clock was ticking down on Lima steam production. The locomotive design group, now led by Woodard's successor Bert Townsend, revived the 4-8-6 platform and added some contemporary twists. These included a double Belpaire firebox, poppet valves with a new control system (using rotary cams rather than oscillating ones), and a high-speed trailing truck booster (useful up to 35 mph). Most intriguing was the firebox with Belpaire "bulges" on both top and bottom. Not surprisingly, this concept quickly came to be called the "double bubble." The traditional Belpaire configuration, with its nearly vertical sides, provided a much stronger structure than the conventional rounded-top firebox. Moreover, the additional bulges also provided more heating surface.

Lima publicized the new 4-8-6 design in June 1947, and within the next year it built a scale model of the new boiler to confirm its analysis of the anticipated improvements. But for various reasons, the company did not mount a serious marketing effort for the new locomotive. However, it did hold some discussions with the New York Central regarding a project to rebuild a Hudson with the double Belpaire. But of course time *did* run out on Lima's steam locomotive business, as well as that of the other two major builders. So we are left to wonder what *might* have happened if some of these advanced features had been available a few years earlier to woo steam's most ardent supporters, roads such as C&O, NYC, and Pennsy.

Another intriguing concept that was never actualized goes back to 1937 while B&O was working on its experimental duplex *George Emerson*. B&O president Daniel Willard came through the Mt. Clare shops to inspect the 4-4-4-4's progress and, in a moment of reflection about the major goal of duplex designs (reducing dynamic loads on running gear and track), mused on the future of steam power.

He remarked that "the ideal steam locomotive would have a constant torque power unit for each driving axle." In his opinion such an arrangement would get rid of track pounding, once and for all. It was just like Willard to peer far ahead of present technology. While serving as B&O's chief executive, his road had boldly experimented with high-speed articulateds, water tube fireboxes, poppet valves, and finally the duplex design he was inspecting that day. And so, as soon as the big duplex rolled out of Mt. Clare in June 1937, the back room design group began looking seriously at what "Uncle Dan" had been musing about.

What they came up with was a sketch for a 60-inch-drivered, 112-foot-long 4-8-4 with a water tube firebox and a streamlined bullet-nosed cowl. Beneath the side skirt of No. 5800 (class W1) one found the secret of this new engine, namely that behind each driver was a small, fully enclosed, two-cylinder steam engine powering a geared axle. These were Besler *steam motors* that were similar in design to Franklin booster engines. Each delivered about 9000 pounds of starting tractive effort and 700 hp at high speed. Their gear ratio of 55:19 assured that, instead of the 4 power impulses (per revolution) for a conventional two-cylinder locomotive, the four Besler motors would deliver 92 impulses per revolution. Hence the term "constant torque" power sources.

Number 5800 would have weighed about the same as a small 4-8-4 (such as on NC&StL), had a tractive effort of 72,500 pounds, and a maximum horsepower of 5000. It also utilized an outside main frame that gave it another attractive feature. If any one of the motors failed, the engine could be taken to a drop pit where the entire wheel-axle-motor assembly could be changed out quickly, exactly the type of advantage that the diesel builders were claiming at the time.

In common with many such proposed designs, this one appeared at the wrong time in B&O's history. As noted earlier, just as the *Emerson* began testing, Dan Willard realized that the road's future power needs would be laid on the diesel side of the ledger. However, any steam aficionado will regret that an ambitious company such as Lima or Alco didn't have a chance to actually build one of these locomotives with modular steam engines.

A 1962 scene depicts what was a typical fate for steam locomotives on short lines. This Atlantic & Western engine was merely shoved onto an empty track and allowed to rust away. The road's turntable (foreground) and a gas-powered motor car have met a similar fate. J. Parker Lamb.

CHAPTER 10

AMERICAN STEAM IN PERSPECTIVE

The steam locomotive has been one of the most admired machines in the history of technological development. Whether viewed from afar or close up, it has never failed to elicit a strong emotional response from observers. Many generations of photographers, whether on professional assignments or as dedicated rail enthusiasts or casual observers, whether recording still or cinematic images, have found the steam locomotive to be an inspirational subject. Similarly, novelists and poets have often woven their literary works around steam-powered trains, as have many popular song writers. Fortunately, in the first decade of the twenty-first century, there still exist many restored and operating steam locomotives throughout the world, while even more have been cosmetically rebuilt, and many are preserved away from gradual deterioration caused by the elements.

It is estimated that 176,000 steam locomotives were built for American railroads between 1831 and 1953, with the peak coming in 1905 when 6265 engines were ordered. The year 1932, with the nation in the depths of the Great Depression, saw the lowest total: only a single order, by the Great Northern Railway, for three homebuilt Mikados. The American experience was a rather haphazard process that included nearly a hundred different companies (plus 70 railroad shops) building 40 types of locomotives for over a hundred railroads. Because each builder and each railroad used its own set of specifications for performance and for the incorporation of appliances (auxiliary machinery), there were virtually no standard designs, only similar configurations that could be adapted to a variety of special needs. While this feature gave steam locomotives a special charm for those who admired railroads from afar, it was also a highly inefficient process, both technically and financially.

In order to provide a framework for our discussion of technical evolution, we have identified five distinct periods in the steam epoch of American railroads. Each of these periods came to an end when the introduction of newer design concepts made older machines obsolete. First, there was the remarkably short *period of transition* between the appearance of imported locomotives from Great Britain in 1829 and the development in the 1840s of the American type (4-4-0) as the standard locomotive in the United States and later on many European rail systems. We have identified the *first generation* of locomotives as those with fireboxes of limited size and no trailing trucks that grew from the 4-4-0 to the 2-10-0 and the 4-8-0 types. Early Mallet compound articulateds (0-6-6-0, 0-8-8-0, and 2-8-8-0) also appeared during this period.

The *second generation* of locomotives appeared during the first 15 years of the twentieth century, and were characterized by larger fireboxes that rode on two-wheel trailing trucks. They evolved from high-speed 4-4-2's into long and powerful (but relatively slow) 2-10-2's and 4-12-2's. Both simple and compound articulateds (2-6-6-2 and 2-8-8-2) were also produced during this period. However, the most widely used second-generation engines were 2-8-2's and 4-6-2's.

A national need to operate heavier and faster trains produced the *third generation*. These circumstances required locomotives with much larger steam generators (boiler-firebox), the first of which was delivered in 1922. This period, called the super power era, was manifested in large locomotives with four trailing wheels, and ended in 1949 when the three remaining commercial builders ceased production of mainline locomotives. Although the Norfolk & Western's Roanoke shops continued production for another four years, no new designs were developed.

We have also identified a *fourth generation* that began in 1937 and lasted for two decades. During this time a number of novel steam locomotive concepts were proposed as evolutionary refinements of super power machines. Many were built and tested, but none was commercially successful, mainly because by 1940 America's railroads were in early stages of a transition into a new *first generation of diesel-electric power*. It takes little insight to realize that these generational transitions have continued, irrespective of the type of propulsion being used.

Why Steam Power Vanished

Laying aside the nostalgic view of technical history, we wish to conclude our discussions of locomotive development with some remarks about why it was inevitable that steam locomotives, which grew out of society's needs in the eighteenth century, would eventually be supplanted by newer technologies that were more efficient and more economically viable. As we noted in the beginning, the working fluid for a steam engine is water. An integral part of any steam locomotive was the tender that carried a supply of this fluid along with the solid fuel that was also needed. If we could discard the carrying of water and instead use a free and abundant working fluid, we would be able to dispense with a large amount of "parasitic power" needed to pull the tender, along with the storage structures and water-processing equipment. Moreover, if we could replace the solid fuel with a more energetic liquid fuel that required less storage volume, we would gain additional improvement. And finally, if we could discard the large mechanical transmission system embodied in the power cylinders, rodding, and valve gear, and replace it with an easily modulated electric motor attached to each axle, we would achieve much greater mechanical efficiency.

Thus we see that the highly efficient and easily throttleable diesel engine, which runs on air and a relatively inexpensive liquid fuel, and drives an electric generator powering a set of precisely controlled traction motors, provides an alternate form of railroad propulsion that is technically superior to the steam locomotive on virtually every count. One of the greatest differences in the two forms of power is due to the use of electric motors instead of large machine elements in the power train. We recognize instantly that the primary duty of a steam locomotive is largely fixed during its manufacture. For example, an 0-8-0 cannot be used to pull a passenger train at 60 mph, while a 4-6-4 does very poorly as a yard engine. In contrast, an early diesel unit of the 1950s could be used individually to switch cars in a yard. Within a short time after completing this duty it could be connected, both physically and electrically, with a group of other units to provide a propulsion system with greater power than a Union Pacific Big Boy. The next day it could be working a local freight or passenger run. Mechanical engineers would call this feature "flexibility due to modularity."

If there was one characteristic that sped up the acceptance of diesels by railroads without robust roadbeds, it was their modularity and their consequent multiple-unit capability that gave those lines a way of achieving enormous pulling power on light roadbeds. Thus

The definition of cold: Dead Illinois Central 2-8-2 No. 1563, once a member of the road's ubiquitous Mikado fleet, is covered with snow and ice during its first winter after being retired in Champaign, Illinois in 1957. It will not see another winter. J. Parker Lamb.

To many devotees of the steam locomotive, Norfolk & Western's Shaffer's Crossing roundhouse in Roanoke served as its final shrine, honoring the pinnacle of achievement of mechanical art. But the inevitable wrecking ball began taking its toll on the structure in 1962, when it was razed to make room for a diesel locomotive servicing facility. Framed in a window, the road's last Y6 compound, recently retired and now unnumbered, will soon be devoured by scrappers with cutting torches. J. Parker Lamb.

rail lines of the South, most of which never owned an engine with a four-wheel trailing truck or had robust roadbeds on which to run them, eagerly switched to the newer diesel-electric locomotives as rapidly as possible. Modularity within each diesel-electric locomotive also gave it an advantage in maintenance and repair. Railroads could replace/repair engines, generators, and traction motors in relatively short times as compared with the major repairs of a steam locomotive. Indeed the entire gamut of structures and personnel, classified under the heading of support infrastructure, always pointed toward the new technology as superior.

Any observer of America's railroad industry for the past half-century can see that the steady evolutionary processes have continued irrespective of the type of motive power. Examples of diesel-electric power of the 1950s are now, just like steam locomotives, venerated icons of a past era, and worthy of preservation in museums or running in excursion service.

Interestingly, during the last decades of the twentieth century, American locomotive builders experienced other mechanical limits. Diesel prime movers, in parallel with automotive engines, were first offered in straight-six and straight-eight designs. These were superseded by V-12, V-16, and V-20 models. While 3000 hp V-16 engines proved to be extremely reliable, the larger 20-cylinder 3600 hp models of the 1960s suffered from problems with dynamic loads that caused excessive flexure of the long crankshaft, and they eventually became a maintenance headache.

Beginning in the late 1980s, new technology allowed V-16 designs to be gradually increased in power to the 4500–6000 hp range, and there were even some attempts to produce a 6000 hp prime mover with a V-20 configuration, but the same problems of crankshaft flexure arose again. Moreover, even though hundreds of 6000 hp units are operating in the year 2002, it is clear that there is still the problem with *bigness*. This characteristic, which beset the large postwar duplex designs, the later experimental steam turbine locomotives, and even the two-engine diesel units pioneered by the Union Pacific in the 1960s, remains as a practical limit in American railroad utilization.

Modern diesel-electric power units represent a new era in railroading, as well as a new era for the mechanical engineering profession, which is increasingly concerned with electro-mechanical systems. Contemporary mechanical engineering designers are accustomed to the incorporation of electrical and electronic components into machines. The latest AC-drive locomotives with alternators, rectifiers, inverters, and microprocessor control systems are but the latest step in the evolution of railroad propulsion. It is a process that will continue as long as parallel sinews of steel stretch toward the horizon. And those innovative mechanical engineers, along with their electrical engineering counterparts, will always be there to "push the envelope" toward the next performance breakthrough.

Smokebox details of NYC H10 Mikado include compound air pumps on either side of the cylinder saddle. Superheater header is at top of boiler, with steam pipes running to each valve chest. Below header are individual superheater tubes that fit inside larger-diameter flues. Lima Locomotive Works, Eric Hirsimaki Collection.

DESCRIPTION OF STEAM LOCOMOTIVE COMPONENTS

Boiler Assembly

The word *boiler* normally refers to three major components: smokebox, firebox, and evaporator. These are contained in a thick-walled boiler shell that was fabricated for early locomotives by riveting together large pieces of high-temperature steel. During the later stages of American locomotive development, welding technology had progressed to the point where it would produce vessels capable of withstanding much higher pressures than early riveted boilers.

The smokebox is at the front of the locomotive and thus is referred to by designers as the *front end*. Inside the smokebox is an *exhaust nozzle* that projects exhaust steam upward through the *smokestack* at a high velocity, while also ejecting hot gas from the firebox, an action that also creates the draft necessary to pull air into the fire. Also inside the smokebox are sections of wire mesh (spark arresters) that serve to trap any hot embers, which otherwise might escape out the stack into the environment and cause lineside fires. Inside the top of the smokebox, immediately ahead of the front *tube sheet* (tube holder) of the evaporator section, is a *header* (chamber) in which steam from the *superheater* tubes is collected. The front-end *throttle valve* directs steam from the header through two supply pipes into the *power cylinders* below the smokebox. Early throttle valves were at the top of the boiler ahead of the steam dome (see below).

The stack is at the top of the smokebox, while the *smokebox door* is a hinged (but bolted) opening at the front of the locomotive. Some engines have headlights mounted on their smokebox doors, while others have a large cast number plate (or railroad logo) on the door with the headlight mounted at the top of the smokebox. Feedwater heaters were often located at the front of the smokebox, either inside or outside. Other models were placed below the boiler and adjacent to the running gear. The function of this device was to preheat water from the tender before it was injected into the evaporator.

The *evaporator-superheater* portion of the boiler assembly contains many small-diameter *boiler tubes* in the bottom half of the shell. In the upper half are larger-diameter tubes (*flues*), within which are located additional small tubes bent into a U shape, with the bend of the U at the rear of the evaporator (ahead of the firebox). These are the *superheater tubes* that lead to the header mentioned above. Most boilers have a *steam dome* constructed at the highest part of the boiler assembly. This is the initial collection point for steam before it enters the superheater. The steam dome is a part of the high-pressure boiler shell, while

Before heading to a scrapping facility, a locomotive was generally stripped of all but the largest and heaviest components. Photos taken at this stage allow one to view the usually unseen details of an engine's essential elements, namely the boiler, cylinders, and running gear. This photo shows the end for a 4-8-2. This is the same Western Railway of Alabama No. 186 shown in chapter 4. J. Parker Lamb.

the sand dome (usually nearer the front of the engine) is merely bolted onto the outer part of the shell. There is also a *safety valve dome* near the rear of the boiler assembly (above the firebox).

The *firebox* (furnace) is a thick metal chamber, which is attached to the boiler shell at the rear of the evaporator section. The firebox protrudes below the evaporator section, although most of the upper surface of the firebox is separated from the boiler shell so that water can circulate around the heated surface of the furnace. There are three major types of firebox shapes in common use, all of which use long bolts (*staybolts*) to connect the firebox shell to the main boiler shell, and thus provide structural integrity for the entire firebox-boiler assembly. The most common firebox shape is cylindrical at the top, matching the curvature of the boiler shell. Another shape is exhibited by the *Belpaire* design, which contains longitudinal blisters at the top in order to provide improved structural strength and larger heating surfaces. These give the firebox a nearly flat upper surface. The

Mammoth firebox and boiler of class Y Mallet compound are illustrated in this photo at Norfolk & Western's Roanoke shops in 1954. Tunnel for stoker screw is visible below firebox. Phillip A. Weibler.

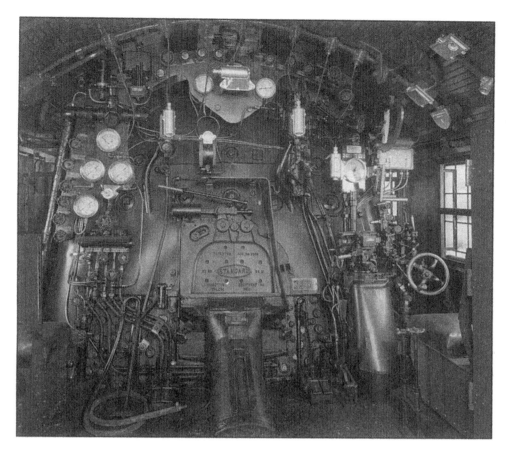

Backhead details of New York Central L4 Mohawk shows firebox door in center, just above stoker tunnel. Engineer's controls on right side show throttle lever swinging down from roof. On the engineer's left are brake valves, while directly to his front is the reversing mechanism controlled by a wheel (in lieu of the commonly used floor-mounted lever). Lima Locomotive Works, Eric Hirsimaki Collection.

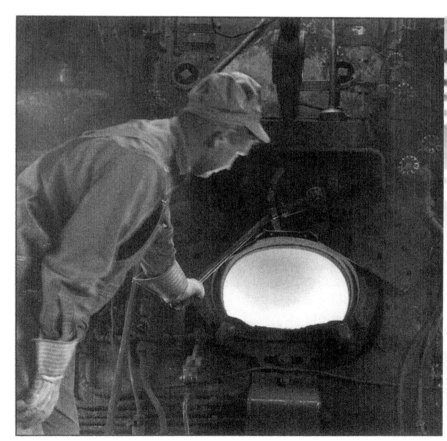

Fireman checks firebox in Missabe 2-8-8-4 before leaving Fraser, Minnesota in 1959 on a run to Proctor with loaded ore jennies. William D. Middleton.

Wooten design is characterized by its extreme width at the bottom, in order to burn slow-burning anthracite and low-grade coal. The top of the firebox is called the *crown sheet*, while the rear area (inside the cab) is the *backhead*, on which are located the throttle, brake, and other locomotive controls used by the engineer and fireman.

The engine cab is usually of an open design characterized by a long roof section that covers an open deck, located partially on the cab and partially on the tender. There is a large opening on the cab's rear wall behind the firebox. This opening allows the fireman to face backward toward the coal pile in the tender. After scooping up a shovelful of coal, he turns and steps toward the fire door (on rear of firebox) and tosses the coal onto the grate, being careful to spread the loads of coal evenly around the grate. While this was difficult work at best, once large engines were developed, it was no longer possible for even a strong and sturdy fireman to supply coal at the rate needed. Thus mechanical stokers were developed that, using a large screw-thread feeder, forced coal into a crusher, which eventually sprayed it onto the fire area. Open cabs were generally not used in extremely cold climates for obvious reasons. Thus a closed cab was developed that had side doors, and a rear wall that was fastened to the tender by a covered vestibule (similar to the openings between passenger cars).

The interior of the firebox is protected by firebrick or similar refractory, while the exterior of the boiler shell, along with much of the associated piping (but usually excluding the smokebox), is covered in asbestos insulation and finally with a sheet-metal jacket. Also inside the firebox are devices that either produce a hotter gas or that increase the heat transfer to the evaporating water. The earliest method of producing a hotter gas was through a *brick arch*, which was supported by water-filled tubes. The arch is attached to the lower front of the firebox and extends upward and toward the rear but is not connected to the rear of the furnace. Its function is to keep the hot gas inside the firebox for as long as possible so that its temperature will be extremely high as it enters the evaporator tubes. In

As part of its preparation for the next trip, each steam locomotive needed to have its ash pans cleaned. At Baltimore & Ohio's Dayton, Ohio roundhouse in 1955, a Mikado gets this treatment as a hostler sprays the grates with a steam jet. Hot coals are seen just below trailing truck. J. Parker Lamb.

essence the arch directs the hot gas toward the rear before allowing it to flow forward into the tubes. The water tubes supporting the arch place evaporating water closer to the fire, and thus speed up the evaporation rate. It was also found that, merely by providing an open space between the front of the firebox and the rear of the evaporator section, additional heating of the gas occurred. This extra space is known as a *combustion chamber* since it facilitates the mixing of the combustion components, which produces a hotter gas. An additional type of heat transfer augmentation device was also used extensively. It is termed a *thermic syphon* and consists of two thick-walled flow channels that span the furnace from top to bottom. These also allow evaporating water to be exposed to the hottest part of the flame.

The *grate* (flame holder) forms the bottom of the firebox and supports the hot coals during the combustion process. An *ash pan* below the grate catches the residual material, which is flushed out by water jets during servicing of the locomotive. Surrounding the bottom of the firebox is a pipe called the *mud ring* that serves both structural and heat transfer roles. For oil-burning locomotives there was no need for a grate or an ash pan. Instead, the bottom of the furnace was lined with firebrick that contained air intake holes. The fuel injector/burner faced backward from the lower front of the firebox and sprayed an atomized jet of warm fuel toward the rear, which was also lined with firebrick to protect against the intense heat generated by the flaming jet. Oil fires were generally hotter than coal fires due to the difference in each fuel's chemical constituency.

Running Gear Assembly

The purposes of the running gear are to support the weight of the locomotive and also to provide a mechanical conversion of the steam into propulsion. There are three types of wheels that support a steam locomotive: *leading wheels* (trucks) below the smokebox, *driving wheels* (drivers) below the evaporator, and *trailing wheels* below the firebox. Not every locomotive contains all three types. For instance, American locomotives of the Civil War era generally have no trailing wheels since the firebox is small. Conversely, locomotives designed for low-speed work in classification yards generally contain no leading or trailing wheels so as to put the entire engine weight on the driving wheels and thus produce greater pulling power. The *Whyte* classification of wheel arrangements counts the number of wheels in each group, and the resulting three-number code (such as 4-6-2) provides a convenient identification for each general type of locomotive.

A locomotive's wheels ride on the *main frame*, which supports the boiler assembly, while the heart of the conversion machinery is a pair of *power cylinders* at the front of the engine. Inside each cylinder is a large disk-like *piston*. Early locomotives had main frames composed of two side frames fabricated from riveted and bolted members, with cross braces between the two sides. Modern engines used large cast-steel main frames that also included the housings for the power cylinders. These were both stronger and lighter than earlier frames.

The front and rear support wheels are much smaller than the driving wheels since the latter must supply virtually all of the propulsive thrust. The power train begins with the *piston*, which is pushed from one end of the cylinder to the other by periodic introduction of high-pressure steam. The piston motion is transmitted outside the power cylinder by a *piston rod*, which is guided by a *crosshead*. The latter can be either an "alligator" type, consisting of two parallel guide bars above and below the crosshead, or the Laird design that includes only an upper guiding bar. The latter design was used in many modern locomotives since the single guide bar generates less friction than the twin-bar type.

In order to translate the reciprocating motion of the piston rod into rotational motion of the drivers, there is a main driving rod (*main rod*) connecting the crosshead with a *crankpin* on the main driver. The crankpin is located away from the centerline of the driver

Two workmen at Chesapeake & Ohio's Huntington, West Virginia shops use sledge hammers to force flanged tire onto a driver. The ring of tubing produces small jets of flaming gas to heat tire around circumference until it expands enough to be forced over the driver. C. K. Marsh Jr. Collection.

(eccentric position), thus assuring that the driver will rotate when the piston rod is moved. The main driver transmits its rotational motion to the other drivers through a *side rod* connecting crankpins on all drivers. Early driving wheels were spoked in order to save weight. The standard spoked design, developed by Baldwin Locomotive Works, was used on the vast majority of locomotives before 1930. Many modern engines employed *disk drivers*, which are more rugged and can be balanced easier. There are three types of disk drivers—*Baldwin, Boxpok,* or *Scullin*—each with a slightly different appearance due to the configuration of holes on the sides of the driver. The Boxpok design was the most common of the three. While appearing from the outside to be solid, a disk driver was actually hollow, being composed of two thinner disks fastened together.

When the drivers are rotating, there is a lack of balance due to the weight of the crankpin, side rods, and valve gear that are located on one side of the driver. To achieve proper balance, each driver requires a *counterweight* placed on the opposite side of the driver from the crankpin. For spoked drivers, these counterweights are usually crescent shaped, but on early locomotives other shapes were used. Driving wheels are fabricated without flanges (blind). This necessitates the use of a steel *driver tire* (with flange) that will eventually become thinner with wear, and can be easily replaced. The process of replacing driver tires is called "sweating." It involves heating the tire with a gas flame until thermal expansion causes its inside diameter to expand to a size slightly larger than the outside diameter of the blind driver. The hot tire is then slipped over the driver and allowed to cool, resulting in what is known as a "shrink fit." When worn, the old tire is severed at one point with a gas-fired torch, taken off the driver, and discarded.

Each driver axle is surrounded by a lubricated bearing, which in turn rides inside a bearing housing. Older locomotives use *journal bearings* (called friction bearings), while *roller bearings* (much lower friction) are used on most modern engines. In order for a locomotive to be able to ride properly on undulating trackage, it is necessary for each driver to have an independent suspension (a way to move up and down independently of the other wheels). This is accomplished by mounting the wheel *bearing housings* inside vertical guides. The housings are connected to springs and are also interconnected with a series of *equalizer bars* that allow the vertical movement of each driver axle to be reflected in coordinated movements of axles on either side. All wheels on one side of the locomotive are often cross-equalized with those on the opposite side. Thus each axle can move both up and down, but this feature also allows each end of the axle (left and right) to move independently.

At the front of the locomotive main frame is a metal assembly known as the *pilot*. It was called a *cowcatcher* in the first years of locomotive development since its primary purpose at that time was to push stray livestock off the railway. Early pilots were constructed of steel straps or pipe (sometimes old boiler tubes), while solid-steel pilots were used on later designs. For snow removal during winter, some roads mounted small plows over the regular pilot, while others constructed the steel pilot in the shape of a plow. For slow-speed switching locomotives, it is customary to provide wooden *footboards* in place of a pilot. These allow the switching crews to step easily onto and off a locomotive during their work. The pilot or footboards are attached to the *pilot beam*, which in turn is fastened to the front of the main frame. At the rear of the main frame, beneath the engine cab, is the *footplate* that helps support the cab and also serves as a bearing surface for the front of the tender. The engine and its tender are permanently coupled using a heavy member known as a *drawbar*, which is connected on each end by large pins. This coupling is disturbed only when the engine is in the shop for heavy repairs.

Controlling the flow of steam into the cylinders requires a complex mechanical system known as *valve gear*. Most early locomotives used the *Stephenson* valve gear configuration, which was originally imported from England. It was fitted to the driving axles between the side frames and is thus called an "inside" valve gear. The most common valve gear used in the United States after 1900 is the *Walschaerts* design. It and the later *Baker* valve gear were attached to the driving wheels on the outside in order to simplify maintenance.

Movement of the valves on each side of the smokebox must correlate with the rotational position of the drivers. Moreover, the valve position must be adjustable so that the loco-
motive can be operated in a reverse direction and, when operating at speed, the engineer can control the length of time that steam is flowing into each cylinder during each stroke of the power piston. These requirements dictate that the valve gear must be connected mechanically to three points: piston rod, driving wheel, and the valve rod (stem). In addition, there must be a control rod from the engineer to effect a reverse movement.

Using the photograph of the Baker gear valve show here, along with the Walschaerts design pictured in chapter 2, one can follow the interconnections between the different links. We see that the *eccentric crank* is mounted at an angle to the diameter of the wheel. It drives the *eccentric rod*, also connected to the *reverse link*, which oscillates as the wheel rotates. Connected to the reverse link is the *radius rod*, which can be slid

Close-up view of valve gear on N&W 4-8-4 No. 607 at Bluefield, West Virginia in 1954. Note the use of Baker valve gear and roller bearings on side and main rods. Mechanical lubricator (box near side skirt) is driven off the crosshead motion by small rods connected to the vertical combination link. Phillip A. Weibler.

up and down on the reverse link. The radius rod connects to the valve stem via the *combination lever*, which is connected to the piston rod. At the end of the steam era, an advanced type of valve gear, incorporating *poppet valves* (similar to automobile engine valves), was developed. Although it worked well, it required much more maintenance.

Locomotive Tenders

A necessary component of a complete steam locomotive is the attached car that carries fuel and water. That part of the tender closest to the engine cab contains fuel (coal or oil) in order to minimize the distance to the firebox. Water tanks are most commonly of a "box" design, giving the tender a completely rectangular shape when viewed from the side. However, there are a number of other configurations, most notably the cylindrical tank used with the *Vanderbilt* tender, which also employs a triangular fuel bunker (when viewed from the side). Other variations included the *"whale back"* tender, in which the water tank was flat at the bottom but cylindrical on the sides and top. This also gave increased rearward visibility. On a few designs this shape is reversed, with a cylindrical bottom and a flat top. The motivations for using cylindrical tanks included ease of fabrication as well as minimization of corrosion at the rectangular corners. Switching engines required only small tenders, since they were never far from a supply of fuel and water. However, the switch crew's need for good rearward visibility generally dictated that the coal bunker be narrower than the tank, and sometimes that the tank be sloped downward at the rear.

Another physical feature of tenders is the presence of a brakeman's shanty or "doghouse" on freight locomotives. Since there is often no room for a third person in the engine cab, the brakeman rode in this tiny enclosure, which is usually located on the tank immediately behind the fuel bunker. Eventually engine cabs were enlarged to accommodate the head brakeman, and doghouses were discarded. These structures are not needed on passenger locomotives, as the head brakeman is generally stationed in the first coach.

Because fuel requirements are related directly to the size and purpose of the locomotive, tender sizes vary widely, and this is reflected in their wheel configurations. The most common truck arrangement was a pair of two-axle trucks similar to those on freight cars. However, when passenger locomotives began running longer distances between refueling, their larger tenders required two three-axle trucks. Eventually these became common for any long-distance engine. An even larger configuration for so-called super power locomotives was the 14-wheel pedestal tender, which included a two-axle leading truck followed

New York Central U3a-class 0-8-0 No. 7820 was a USRA design constructed by Alco Brooks in 1918. Downward view at Cincinnati in 1956 displays typical narrow coal bunker that afforded crews more rearward visibility. J. Parker Lamb.

by five separate axles riding on independent, movable pedestals. The motivation for this design was to spread the weight of the tender more evenly over the roadbed. The largest tenders for American locomotives rode on two four-axle trucks, while slightly smaller ones used one three-axle and one four-axle truck.

Water and fuel were loaded into the tender from storage structures along main lines. Each tender contained a covered opening on top of its tank, into which the fireman inserted a downspout from the storage vessel, constructed of wood in the beginning. In engine terminals these water storage tanks were generally remote to the tracks so that the lineside downspout was fed by pipeline. Generally, locomotives needed water more often than coal; so some lines with high-speed passenger trains sought to eliminate intermediate water stops by loading water into the tender while the train was moving. The collection system involved the use of a movable scoop on the bottom of the tender. This device was lowered into a long pit (track pan) filled with water while the train was speeding along the main line. In contrast, loading of coal could not be done except while the engine was stopped. However, some railroads constructed large *coaling towers* beside the tracks so that high-speed trains need not go into a yard. A pivoted chute (trough) could be swung down to allow coal to flow directly into the tender bunker. In major engine terminals, large-capacity coaling towers were often constructed with the capability of loading three or four locomotives simultaneously. To fill these large towers, some lines constructed *coaling trestles* (long bridges) on which hopper cars were parked and emptied directly into the storage bins.

Wooden water tanks were a ubiquitous part of the railroad landscape during the steam era. This one is on a lightly used Illinois Central branchline in southern Illinois, and is located near a stream, from which a nearby pump fills the tank. J. Parker Lamb.

The fireman's expression suggests that he is in for a long wait while he fills the tank of Missabe Road Yellowstone No. 228 at Fraser, Minnesota in 1959. Note rear bell on tender deck just behind fireman. Yard in background is full of both empty and loaded ore jennies. William D. Middleton.

SERVICE AND REPAIR FACILITIES

For completeness we describe briefly the types of maintenance and repair facilities used during the steam power era. In general, due to their incorporation of innumerable mechanical devices and sliding connections, steam locomotives were extremely labor intensive, requiring constant attention. This required an army of thousands of workers throughout the United States. Indeed, the overall cost of labor for steam locomotive repair and maintenance was one of the major factors in the eventual demise of these machines.

The actual size of a New York Central Hudson's drivers and associated machinery is better appreciated when viewed up close. In a classic scene from the steam era, the engineer uses an oil can with long spout to reach some spots he thinks should have a little more lubricant before he departs the Dayton passenger station for Columbus and Cleveland in 1955. J. Parker Lamb.

Baltimore & Ohio's Dayton roundhouse was still active into the mid-1950s. Here is Q4b Mikado No. 4604 (Baldwin, 1922) preparing to head into a stall for storage and servicing until its next assignment in switching or helper service. J. Parker Lamb.

In the early years of American railroads, a crew change point was established every 110 miles (or thereabouts) because this was considered "one day's work" for the crewmen. Generally, it was also necessary at this location to provide extensive lubrication of the running gear, replenish fuel and water, and often clean the ash pans below the firebox. As better-built engines came on the scene, some of this servicing could be deferred to alternate stops. However, at least once per day the locomotive would go to a major shop and receive a thorough cleaning and inspection (and minor repair) before being prepared for its next 24 hours of operation.

For overall public safety, government regulations required that the locomotive be taken into a roundhouse shop periodically (usually monthly) and receive an even more detailed examination of critical parts of the engine, especially boiler components such as tubes and firebox. An annual pressure test of the boiler, to check for leaking tubes and flues, was mandated by safety laws. Most local shops are arranged in a circular layout known as a

At the end of its operating career, B&O Mikado No. 4604 was fitted with footboards on its pilot beam in order to facilitate its use as a switcher and mainline helper. In 1955 the engine is parked on the Dayton, Ohio turntable. J. Parker Lamb.

Major repairs to Nickel Plate's fleet of Berkshires were made at the road's backshop in Conneaut, Ohio. This scene shows 2-8-4 No. 747 (class S2) in the midst of a major overhaul. With the engine supported on temporary wheels, the leading and trailing trucks are seen directly beside the locomotive. The white paint covering the main frame and wheels allows machinists to inspect for small cracks that require attention. Clearly visible in the frame are the rectangular openings for the driver axles and bearings (driving boxes). These later parts are stacked on the cart above the large white wheel (bottom of photo). Photo taken only a few months before the shop closed in late 1958. Jim Shaughnessy.

roundhouse, in which engine stalls are arrayed around a *turntable*. This configuration provided a compact and efficient venue for light repairs, and provided rapid turning of locomotives, which could operate on the main line in only one direction. When heavy work was required every four or five years, the locomotive was taken to a *backshop*, which usually included a high-bay *erecting floor* having a dozen (or more) parallel tracks for holding engines. A heavy lift crane is mounted near the top of the building in order to remove a boiler from its running gear, or lift an entire locomotive off its wheels. Since a turntable is not appropriate for a long building with parallel tracks, another transport device, the *"transfer table,"* is used. This consists of a low platform, carrying the locomotive, that itself could move on two rails parallel to the shop building and thus position an engine in front of each door to the backshop.

In addition to the erecting floor, a large backshop complex usually incorporated a boiler shop, a driver and truck shop, a general machine shop, a foundry, and other support facilities necessary to completely disassemble and rebuild a steam locomotive. Some railroads even bought locomotive components and assembled new engines on site.

REFERENCES

Alexander, Edwin P. *The Pennsylvania Railroad; A Pictorial History.* Bonanza, 1967.

Baldwin Locomotive Works. *Catalog of Locomotives.* 1915. Reprint, Specialty Press, n.d.

Beebe, Lucius. *High Iron.* Bonanza, 1938.

Bilty, C. H. "The Hiawatha Story." *Trains*, December 1950, pp. 26–30.

Brown, John K. *The Baldwin Locomotive Works, 1831–1915.* Johns Hopkins University Press, 1995.

Bruce, Alfred W. *The Steam Locomotive in America.* Norton, 1952.

Bryant, H. Stafford. "Ps-4." *Trains*, October 1950, pp. 20–26.

Carlson, Neil E. "Super Power, Part 1." *Trains*, May 2000, pp. 36–43.

———. "Super Power, Part 2." *Trains*, June 2000, pp. 64–71.

Dunn, Ralph G. "The Presidents—B&O's Super Pacifics." *Trains*, June 1951, pp. 45–48.

Dunscomb, Guy L. *A Century of Southern Pacific Steam Locomotives.* Author, 1963.

Edwards, Emory. *Modern American Locomotive Engines.* Baird, 1883.

Ellis, Hamilton. *Pictorial Cyclopedia of Railways.* Hamilton, 1968.

Hamilton, David S. *Pictorial History of Trains.* Chartwell, 1977.

Hirsimaki, Eric F. *Lima: The History.* Hundman, 1986.

Howell, J. R., and R. O. Buckius. *Engineering Thermodynamics.* 2d ed. McGraw-Hill, 1992.

Huddleston, Eugene L. *Uncle Sam's Locomotives: The USRA and the Nation's Railroads.* Indiana University Press, 2002.

Huddleston, Eugene L., and T. L. Dixon. *The Allegheny—Lima's Finest.* Hundman, 1984.

Hungerford, John B. *Cab in Front.* Hungerford Press, 1959.

Johnson, Ralph P. *The Steam Locomotive.* Simmons-Boardman, 1942.

Kiefer, Paul W. *A Practical Evaluation of Railroad Motive Power.* Simmons-Boardman, 1949.

King, Ed. "Big Bang, No Theory." *Trains*, April 1995, pp. 66–69.

Landmarks in Mechanical Engineering. Purdue University, 1997.

LeMassena, Robert A. "Beyond Super-Power." *Trains*, August 1987, pp. 36–42.

———. "Timken vs. Everyone Else." *Trains*, November 1997, pp. 60–63.

Middleton, William D. *When the Steam Railroads Electrified.* Kalmbach, 1974. Revised; 2d. ed., Indiana University Press, 2001.

Morgan, David P. "Big Boy." *Trains*, November 1958, pp. 40–51.

———. "Duplex-Drives." *Trains*, November 1959, pp. 16–25.

———. "Faith in Steam." *Trains*, November 1954, pp. 18–30.

———. "Hey, Horatio! What You Started—It's Stopped!" *Trains*, May 1954, pp. 48–53.

———. "The Ideal Steam Locomotive." *Trains*, August 1949, pp. 28–30.

———. "Loree's Locomotives." *Trains*, July 1952, pp. 20–25.

———. "Most Famous Hudson." *Trains*, January 1950, pp. 47–49.

———. "A Pacific Primer." *Trains*, September 1988, pp. 32–41.

———. "Poor Man's Mallets." *Trains*, November 1957, pp. 19–22.

———. "PRR Ventures in Locomotives." *Trains*, October 1949, pp. 14–19.

———. *Steam's Finest Hour.* Kalmbach, 1959.

———. "Super Power." *Trains*, January 1952, pp. 13–21.

Rankine, William J. M. *A Manual of the Steam Engine and Other Prime Movers*. Griffin, 1885.

Reid, H. *The Virginian Railway*. Kalmbach, 1961.

Shaughnessy, Jim. *Delaware & Hudson*. Syracuse University Press, 1997.

Shiplin, E. F. P. *The Norfolk & Western: A History*. Rev. ed. N&W Historical Society, 1977.

Weatherwax, David S. "She Has Whistled in Her Last Flag." *Trains*, November 1952, pp. 48–49.

Westcott, Linn H. *Model Railroader Cyclopedia*. Vol. 1, *Steam Locomotives*. Kalmbach, 1960.

Westing, Frederick. "An American Beauty." *Trains*, August 1954, pp. 24–26.

———. "Baldwin's Barnstorming Behemoth." *Trains*, April 1954, pp. 50–56.

———. "The Hudson." *Trains*, November 1957, pp. 44–59.

———. *The Locomotives That Baldwin Built*. Bonanza, 1966.

———. "Nomad of the Nineties." *Trains*, June 1957, pp. 36–42.

White, John H. *A Short History of American Locomotive Builders in the Steam Era*. Bass, 1982.

Wood, S. R., and D. P. Morgan. "The Thrifty Compound." *Trains*, September 1951, pp. 44–48.

Yoder, Jacob H., and George B. Warren. *Locomotive Valves and Valve Gears*. Van Nostrand, 1917.

INDEX

Page numbers in italics refer to illustrations or illustrations with accompanying text.

0-2-2 locomotives, 15
0-4-0 locomotives, 15
0-6-0 locomotives, 38
0-6-6-0 Mallet compound articulated locomotives, 24
0-8-8-0 Mallet compound articulated locomotives, 24
2-2-0 locomotives, 15
2-4-2 Columbia type locomotives, 47
2-6-0 Mogul type locomotives, 19, 39, 41
2-6-2 Prairie type locomotives, 79
2-8-0 Consolidation type locomotives, 41, 97, 98; examples, 22, 30, 40, 45, 74; introduction, 19; popularity of, 47, 94
2-8-2 Mikado type locomotives, 37, 47, 52, 58, 98, 178, 186, 187; class H10, 28, 82, 84–85, 84, 88, 174; performance, 97
2-8-4 Berkshire type locomotives, 85–88, 117, 119; examples, 87, 101, 102, 118, 188
2-10-0 locomotives, 40, 41, 49
2-10-2 Santa Fe type locomotives, 49, 50, 53
2-10-4 Texas type locomotives, 103, 151; class 5000, 120; class H1, 101; class I1, 89–91, 90; class J1, 123, 124, 159; class T1, 103, 120; oil-burning, 120, 122
2-6-6-2 locomotives, 51, 79, 135
2-6-6-4 locomotives, 106
2-6-6-6 locomotives, 141–45, 141, 143
2-6-8-0 locomotives, 79
2-8-8-0 locomotives, 24, 56, 57
2-8-8-2 locomotives, 135; class MC classes, 146, 148; class Y6, 136–38, 137
2-8-8-4 Yellowstone type locomotives, 104–106, 104, 105, 177
2-8-8-8-4 articulated locomotives, 79
4-2-0 locomotives, 9–10, 10, 15
4-4-0 American (Standard) type locomotives, 12, 15, 19, 21–23, 47; modernization of design, 24–27
4-4-2 Atlantic type locomotives, 47, 48
4-6-0 ten wheeler locomotives, 18, 19, 40
4-6-2 Pacific type locomotives, 47, 49, 60–68; dual-service Pacifics, 64–65; heavy Pacifics, 62, 65, 98; light Pacifics, 48, 61, 64, 128; super Pacifics, 154–55

4-6-4 Hudson type locomotive, 98–101, 99, 100, 101, 114, 115, 116, 128, 185
4-8-0 twelve wheeler locomotives, 75
4-8-2 Mountain type locomotives, 47, 49, 53, 54, 55, 59, 126, 140, 176; Mohawks class L4, 49, 149, 177
4-8-2 + 2-8-4 articulated locomotive, 23
4-8-4 Northern type locomotives, 92, 93–94, 93, 97, 98; alternative names for, 94; class J, 119, 133, 138–39, 139, 141, 162, 181; Niagara type, 94, 119, 155, 165; second-generation designs, 108–14, 109–13
4-10-2 Southern Pacific type locomotives, 76–79, 77
4-4-4-4 duplex locomotives, 155, 156
4-4-6-4 locomotives, 156, 158, 159
4-6-4-4 locomotives, 156, 157
4-6-6-2 locomotives, 148
4-6-6-4 Challenger type locomotives, 106–108, 107–108, 135
4-8-8-2 locomotives, 148
6-8-6 steam turbine locomotives, 159, 160–62
6-4-4-6 duplex locomotives, 156, 157

Advisory Mechanical Committee, 141–42
aerodynamics of blunt bodies, 124
Alco (American Locomotive Company), 10, 14, 72, 119; 2-8-8-4 locomotives, 104; 4-6-4 locomotives, 98–101, 116; 4-8-4 locomotives, 93, 94, 110, 114; 4-6-6-4 locomotives, 107; heavy Pacifics, 62, 65, 98; Schenectady shops, 14, 62, 119; summary of production, 149
Allegheny type class H8, 141–44, 141
Allen, Horatio, 7, 9, 75
Allen, Samuel G., 60
America, 7
American Arch Company, 60
American Locomotive Company. *See* Alco (American Locomotive Company)
American Railway Master Mechanics Association (ARMMA), 46
American Society of Mechanical Engineers (ASME), 31, 84, 151

American (Standard) type. *See* 4-4-0 American (Standard) type locomotives

American Steam Carriage Company, 10

articulated compound locomotives, 23–24, *23*, 69–81, 103, 106–108, 131

Atlanta, Birmingham & Coast Railroad, *18*

Atlantic & Western Railroad, *168*

Atlantic Coast Line, 18, 47

————locomotives: No. 1655 (4-6-2) P5b, 64; No. 1696, *xiv*; No. 1730 (4-6-2) class P5b, *65*; No. 7122 (4-6-0), *18*

Atlantic type. *See* 4-4-2 Atlantic type locomotives

atmospheric engine, 4–6

Atterbury, William W., 64

Austrian State Railways, 76

Babcock & Wilcox water tube fireboxes, 161

backheads, 178

backshops, 188

Baker valve gears, 21, 116, 181

balanced-compound locomotives, 71, 72

Baldwin, Matthias William, 9

Baldwin disk drivers, 180

Baldwin Works, 9, 14, 51, 72, 161; 4-6-4 locomotives, 116; 4-8-4 locomotives, 108, 110, 112; 2-6-6-4 locomotives, *106*; 2-8-8-4 locomotives, *104*; duplex locomotives, 156; No. 60000 (4-10-2), 76–79, *77*; promotion of compound designs, 69–73, 76; summary of production, 149

Baldwin-Lima-Hamilton Corporation, 161

Baltic type locomotives, 101

Baltimore & Ohio Railroad, 8, 67, 79; 4-6-2 locomotives, 49, 60, 61, 67–68; *George Emerson* (4-4-4-4), 155, 166; No. 5800 "constant torque" concept locomotive, 167

————locomotives: No. 4405 (2-8-2) class Q4, 59; No. 4604 (2-8-2), *178, 186, 187*; No. 5216 (4-6-2) class P5a, 61; No. 5301 (4-6-2) class P7d, 67; No. 5315 (4-6-2) P7e, 68; No. 7400 (4-4-6-2) class KK1, 69

Basford, George, 83, 85

bearing housings, 180

Belpaire, Alfred Jules, 19

Belpaire fireboxes, 17, 19–20, 27, 50, 176, 178; "double bubbles," 166

Berkshire type. *See* 2-8-4 Berkshire type locomotives

Besler steam motors, 167

Best Friend of Charleston, 9

Beyer-Garratt locomotives, 23, 24

Bicentennial Train, *109*

Big Boys 4-8-8-4 (UP), *130*, 131–35, *132*

Bilty, C. H., 47, 101

Blackett, Christopher, 6

Blue Ridge type 2-6-6-6 locomotives, 142–45, *143*

boiler horsepower, 43

boiler performance, 97, 98

boiler pressure: and performance of saturated and superheated steam, 36; thermal efficiencies and, 36, 38, 41. *See also* steam generation

boiler tubes, 2, 175

boilers, 2, 79, 86, 176; features, 37, 175–79, *176, 177, 178*; safety alarms, 28; safety regulations, 27–28. *See also* evaporators; fireboxes; smokeboxes

booster engines, 45, 51, 55, 75

Boston & Albany Railroad, 87, 100; No. 1 (2-8-4) Berkshire type, *87*

Boulton & Watt, 6

Boxpok disk drivers, 180

brake horsepower, 45

brake valves, 177

brakeman's shanty, *182*

brasses, 96

brick arch, 178

British locomotive designs, 31; exported to America, 7–10, 15, 16, 23–24, *23*; imported from America, 10

British railroads, 7, 10

The Broadway Limited (B&O), 62

Brooks Works, 14, 15, 60, 72–73

Brotan-design fireboxes, 76

Btu, 42

builders, 10, 12, 14, 31, 169; summary of production, 149

cab, engine, *2*, 20–21, 178

Calley, John, 5

Camden & Amboy Railroad and Transportation Company, 8, 9

camelback locomotives, 17, 20–21, 74

Campbell, Henry, 15

The Capital Limited (B&O), 61

capped stacks, *16, 19, 127*

Caprotti, John, 154

Caprotti valve gears, 68, 154–55

Carnot, Nicholas L. S., 33

Casanave, Frank D., 25

Cassatt, Alexander J., 64

cast-steel main frames, 136

cast-steel power cylinders, 86

Central of Georgia Railway locomotives, No. 454 (4-8-4) GS2, 112

Central Railroad of New Jersey, 21

Central Vermont Railroad, 103

Challenger type. *See* 4-6-6-4 Challenger type locomotives

Chesapeake & Ohio Railroad, 117; 2-10-4 locomotives, 102, 103; 4-6-2 locomotives, 49, 60; 4-6-4 locomotives, 116, 128; 4-8-4 locomotives, 119; 2-6-6-2 locomotives, 51; 2-6-6-6 locomotives, *140, 141*; 2-8-8-2 locomotives, 56; turbine locomotives, 161, 162

————locomotives: No. 500 (2-D+2-D-2), *162*; No. 500 (4-6-4), *128*; No. 1624 (2-6-6-6) class H8, *141*; No. 1625 (2-6-6-6) class H8, *140*; No. 3033 (2-10-4) class T1, *102*

Chicago, Burlington & Quincy Railroad, 108

Chicago & Illinois Midland Railroad locomotives, No. 502 (4-4-0), *25*

Chicago & North Western Railroad, 93

Chicago Great Western Railroad, 79, 103

civil engineers, 1, 13

Clement, Martin, 156

Clinchfield Railroad locomotives: No. 656 (4-6-6-4) class E1, *107*; No. 870 (4-6-6-4) class E3, *107*

coal, 20, 93, 178, 183; combustion process, 89; optimum burning rate per hour, 85–86

coaling towers, 183

coaling trestles, *107*, 183

coefficient of static friction, 42

Coffin, Joel, 60, 86

Coffin-Allen enterprises, 60, 83

Cole, Francis J., 10, 83, 86; *Table of Locomotive Ratios*, 46

Cole performance ratios, 46, 86, 88

Colorado type locomotives, 91

Columbia type. *See* 2-8-0 Consolidation type locomotives

combination links, *23*, 181

combustion chambers, 179
compound locomotives, 23–24, 56–57, 69–79
Consolidation type locomotives. *See* 2-8-0 Consolidation type
    locomotives
Cooke Works, 14, 145
Cooper, Peter, 8
Cooperstown & Charlotte Railroad locomotives, No. 4 (4-4-0),
    16
Cotton Belt Railroad locomotives, No. 812 (4-8-4), 110
counterweights, 3
cowcatchers, 10, 16, 181
crankpins, 2, 179–80
crew change points, 186
cross-compound locomotive, 70, 71
crosshead links, 23
crossheads, 2, 21, 179
crown sheets, 17, 27–28, 178
cutoff, 23
cycle power (equation), 43
cylinders. *See* power cylinders

Davis, Thomas, 21
Daylight color scheme, 108, *109*
de Glehn balanced-compound locomotives, 72
De Witt Clinton, 9
Delaware & Hudson Canal Company, 7, 8, *11*, 13, 20, 45, 73–
    76, *73–75*
————locomotives: No. 1 dynamometer, 45; No. 44 switcher,
    20; No. 237 (4-4-0) camelback, 20; No. 300 Transit (2-2-4),
    13; No. 901 (2-8-0), 45; No. 1400 *Horatio Allen* (2-8-0), 74;
    No. 1401 *John B. Jervis* (2-8-0), 74; No. 1403 *L. F. Loree*
    (4-8-0), 75; *Saratoga* inspection engine, 16; *Stourbridge
    Lion*, 11
diesel-electric locomotives, 104, 144, 156, 170, 173; compared to
    steam power, 164–65; roads resistant to change, 164
disk drivers, 17, 180
diverter valve, 56
Dixie type locomotive, 94
doghouses, 182
double-acting engine, 6
drawbar force, 35, 149, 150
drawbar horsepower, 45, 150
drawbars, 181
Dreyfuss cowling, 115, 116
driver tires, 180
drivers, 2, 42, 179–80; "constant torque," 167; summary of, 3.
    See also running gear; suspension
dry steam, 34, 35
Duluth, Missabe & Iran Range locomotives: No. 223 (2-8-8-4)
    class M3, *105*; No. 227 (2-8-8-4) class M3, *105*; No. 228
    (2-8-8-4) class M4, *104*, *184*
duplex locomotives, 155–60
D-valves. *See* slide valves
dynamometers, 45

E. L. Miller (4-2-0), 9, 15
eccentric crank, 21, 23, 181
eccentric rod, 21, 23, 181
Edwards, Emory, 31
ElectroMotive Division (GM), 155
elephant ears (smoke deflectors), *126*, *127*
Elesco feedwater heaters, 85, 86, 100
Ely, Theodore N., 25
emergency stops, 23

Emerson, George, 69
Emerson-type water tube fireboxes, 68, *69*
The Empire State Express, 116
engine cab, 2, 20–21, 178
engineering, 28, 30–31, 46; in diesel age, 173; educational op-
    portunity, 31; "main drawing" specs, 15, 19, 28, 30; metals
    available, 5, 19
engineering landmarks, 151
Ennis, J. B., 10
equalization rigging, *49*. *See also* suspension
equalizer bars, 181
erecting floor, 188
Erie Railroad, 51, 60, 62, 79, 101
————locomotives: No. 2509 (4-6-2) class K3, *62*; No. 3036
    (2-8-2), 51; No. 3325 (2-8-4) class S2, *101*
Eureka & Palisade Railroad locomotives, No. 4 *Eureka* (4-4-0),
    12
evaporators, 175. *See also* superheaters
exhaust nozzle, 175
exhaust steam, 2, 36, 37, 38
Experiment, 7
exported locomotives, 40, 49, 60, 72
external combustion steam engines, 41

factor of adhesion, 41
Farris, C. H., 135
feedwater heaters, 37, 38, 41, 175; Elesco type, 85, 86, 100; first
    simple design, 7; Worthington design, 37, 58, 85
firebox grates, 19, 43; design ratios, 46, 86
fireboxes, 2, 18, 19, 20, 176; common styles, 19–21; shape com-
    parison, 17, 176, 178; thermic syphons, 89, 179; water tube
    type, 68, 69, 75, 76, 78, 161; Wooten type results in camel-
    back, 20
The Firefly (Frisco), 61
firemen, 95, 177, 178, 184
first-generation diesel-electric locomotives, 170
first-generation steam locomotives, 36, 169
Fishwick, John, 164
Fisk, Pliny, 14
Florida East Coast, 53
flues, 37, 175
footboards, 181, 187
footplates, 181
Foster, Rastrick & Co., 8
Four Aces, 94–97
fourth-generation locomotives, 170
Franklin Institute of Philadelphia, 78, 79
Franklin poppet valve gear, 154, 159. *See also* valve gears
Franklin Railway Supply Company, 51, 60, 154
freight locomotives, 2, 41, 42, 45
friction bearings, 94, 180
Frisco Railroad locomotives: No. 216 (4-4-0), 17; No. 1026
    (4-6-2) light Pacific, 61, 128; No. 1057 (4-6-2) light Pacific, 48;
    No. 1517 (4-8-2), 59; No. 1522 (4-8-2), 59; No. 4137 (2-8-2), 58;
    No. 4306 (2-10-2), 53
front end. *See* smokeboxes
fuel consumption, and thermal efficiency, 35, 38
fuel economy: simple vs. compound articulated engines, 57;
    weighed against mechanical complexity, 78
furnaces. *See* fireboxes

Garratt type locomotives, 23, 24
General, 12

General Steel Castings, 136
GM ElectroMotive Division, 155
Golden State type locomotive, 94, 108, 109, 127
Goss, William F. M., 46
grades, 56; stalls on, 42, 148
Grant Works, 10
Great Eastern Railway locomotives, 4-4-0 Claude Hamilton
    class, 16
Great Northern Railroad, 50, 51; No. 3233 (2-8-2), 50
Greenbriar type locomotive, 94
gross ton-miles per train hour, 141
Gulf, Mobile & Northern Railroad locomotives, No. 263
    (2-10-0), 40

Hackworth, Timothy, 7
Hamilton, David S., 31
Hardin, F. H., 99
Harriman style, 26, 40, 52
Harrison, Fairfax, 67
Harrison, Joseph, Jr., 15
headers, 175
heat, mechanical equivalent of, 42–43
Hedley, William, 6
Heintzelman, Taylor, 146
Hiawatha types. See 4-4-2 Atlantic type locomotives
Hoadley, Joseph, 14
horsepower, 43–45, 141
Huddleston, E. L., 57
Hudson type. See 4-6-4 Hudson type locomotive
hydrodynamic lubrication, 95

ideal Carnot cycle, 33, 36, 38
Illinois Central Railroad, 39, 49, 50, 54; 2-8-0 locomotives, 30,
    40, 171; 2-8-2 locomotives, 52, 171
————locomotives: No. 742 (2-8-0), 30; No. 959 (2-8-0), 40;
    No. 1274 (2-8-2), 52; No. 1563 (2-8-2), 171; No. 2527 (4-8-2),
    54; No. 2713 (2-10-2), 50; No. 3543 switcher (0-8-0), 39
impulse turbines, 161
indicated horsepower, 43–44
indicator cards, 43
Industrial Revolution, 1, 5
Ingersoll, Howard L., 51
inspection engines, 16
Institution of Chartered Mechanical Engineers, 31, 164–65
International Holding Company, 14

Jabelmann, Otto, 106, 131
Jervis, John B., 9
John Bull, 9
Johnson, Birger J. O. (JOB), 29, 30
Johnson, Ralph P., 156
Johnson bars, 23
journal bearings, 95–96, 95, 180

Kansas City Southern Railroad, 122, 124; No. 901 (2-10-4), 122
Katy Railroad, 24, 29–30, 29, 39
————locomotives: No. 49 (0-8-0) C1a, 39; No. 309 (4-4-0), 24
Kiefer, Paul W., 98, 119, 149, 164
Kruttschnitt, Julius, 146
Kuhler, Otto, 156

Landmarks on the Iron Road (Middleton), 1
leading wheels (trucks), 3, 15, 19, 73, 179; wheel arrangements
    of, 182–83. See also tenders

Leiter, Joseph, 14
The Liberty Limited (PRR), 63
lighting, 2
lignite coal, 93
Lima Locomotive Corporation, 60
Lima Locomotive Works, 14, 118, 166; 2-8-2 designs, 84–85, 84,
    88; 2-8-4 Berkshire type, 85–88, 117, 119; 2-10-4 Texas type
    designs, 89–91, 90, 103, 124; 4-8-4 locomotives, 108, 112;
    2-6-6-6 design, 141–45, 143; 2-8-8-4 locomotives, 106; concept
    designs, 142, 165–66, 166; summary of production, 149;
    technical leadership, 60, 83, 166
Liverpool & Manchester Railway, 7
Locomotion, 7
locomotive design, British vs. American, 9–10. See also engi-
    neering
Loewy, Raymond, 156
Long, S. H., 10
Loree, Leonor Fresnel, 73
Louisville & Nashville Railroad, 25, 48, 60, 117, 118, 119
————locomotives: No. 172 light Pacific (4-4-2) class K2a, 48;
    No. 1960 (2-8-4) class M1, 118; No. 1963 (2-8-4) class M1, 118
lubrication, 95, 96, 185; mechanical, 21, 136, 181
"lubritorium" buildings (N&W), 140, 141

MacArthur types, 49
McGavock, G. P., 135
"main drawings." See engineering, "main drawing" specs
main frame, 179, 181
main rods, 2, 179
Mallet, Anatole, 23
Mallet compound articulated locomotives, 23–24
A Manual of the Steam Engine and other Prime Movers
    (Rankine), 31
Mason Machine Works, 21
mean effective pressure, 44–45
mechanical equivalent of heat, 42–43
mechanical work, 43
mechanics, skilled: as apprentices, 28; N&W training program,
    135
metals used in construction, 5, 19
Michigan Central Railroad locomotives: No. 132 (2-8-2) Mi-
    kado H10, 82; No. 8000 (2-8-2) Mikado H10, 84
Middleton, William D., 1
Mikado type. See 2-8-2 Mikado type locomotives
Miller, E. L., 9
Milwaukee Road, 47, 48, 92, 101, 116
————locomotives: Apex of the Atlantic 4-4-2 locomotive, 48;
    No. 100 (4-6-4) class F6, 101; No. 262 (4-8-4) class S3, 92
Missouri Pacific Railroad, 40, 47, 60, 88, 102, 110, 111
————locomotives: No. 384 (4-6-0) class TN63, 40; No. 1912
    (2-8-4), 102; No. 2201 (4-8-4) class N73, 111
Missouri-Kansas-Texas Railroad locomotives, No. 664 (2-8-0)
    (class K6c), 22. See also Katy Railroad, locomotives
Modern American Locomotive Engines; Their Design, Construc-
    tion, and Management (Edwards), 31
modularity of diesel engines, 170, 173
Mogul type locomotives. See 2-6-0 Mogul type locomotives
Mohawk & Hudson River Railroad locomotives, De Witt
    Clinton, 9
Mohawk type, 49, 149, 177
Morgan, David P., 73, 161
Mother Hubbards. See camelback locomotives
Mountain type. See 4-8-2 Mountain type locomotives
Muhfeld, John, 75

Nashville, Chattanooga & St. Louis Railroad locomotives: No. 357 (2-8-0), 19; No. 566 (4-8-4) class J2, 110

Nathan Company, 136

New Haven Railroad locomotives, 4-6-4 Hudson class I5, 114

New York Central Railroad, 51; 2-8-2 Mikado H10 locomotives, 28, 82, 84–85, 84, 174; 4-6-4 Hudson type locomotives, 98–100, 99, 100, 115, 116, 185; 4-8-2 Mohawk type locomotives, 49, 149, 177; 4-8-4 Niagara type locomotives, 94, 119, 155, 165; comparison study of diesel vs. steam, 164–65; drawbar force and horsepower comparisons, 150

————locomotives: No. 12 (2-8-2), 28; No. 132 (2-8-2) class H10, 174; No. 3113 (2-8-2) L4a, 88; No. 3127 (4-8-2), 126; No. 5344 (4-6-4) class I5, 115; No. 5363 (4-6-4) class J1d, 99; No. 5436 (4-6-4) class J3a, 100; No. 5452 (4-6-4) class J3A, 115; No. 5500 (4-8-4) Niagara, 155; No. 6000 (4-8-4) Niagara, 119; No. 7820 (0-8-0) U3a, 182

New Zealand Railways, 60

Newcomen, Thomas, 5

Niagara type locomotive, 94, 119, 155, 165

Nicholson thermic syphons, 89

Nickel Plate Road locomotives, No. 747 (2-8-4) class S2, 117, 188

Noll, F. C., 139

Norfolk & Western Railway: 4-8-4 J class, 133, 138–39, 139, 141, 162, 181; 2-6-6-4 Class A locomotives, 133, 135–36, 136, 144; 2-8-8-2 Y6 locomotives, 136–38, 176; "Big Three," 133, 135–41, 136–39; corporate reaction to abandoning steam power, 164; employee training program, 135; Jawn Henry No. 2300 class TE1, 161, 162, 163, 164; "lubritorium" buildings, 140, 141; No. 611 class J, 134, 151; Roanoke shops, 14, 95, 135, 141, 170, 172; turbine locomotives, 161, 162. See also Norfolk & Western Railway, locomotives

————locomotives: No. 72 Mallet compound, 70; No. 134 (4-8-2), 140; No. 600 (4-8-4) J class, 133; No. 607 (4-8-4) J class, 139, 181; No. 611 (4-8-4) J class, 134; No. 1203 (2-6-6-4) Class A, 133; No. 1208 (2-6-6-4) Class A, 138; No. 1218 (2-6-6-4) Class A, 134; No. 1221 Mallet compound, 56; No. 1242 (2-6-6-4) Class A, 136; No. 2123 (2-8-8-2) Y6 class, 133; No. 2136 (2-8-8-2) class Y6a, 137; No. 2176 Mallet compound, 57; No. 2183 (2-8-8-2) class Y6b, 137; No. 2300 Jawn Henry, 162, 163

Norris, William, 10

Northern Pacific Railroad, 49, 93, 94, 104; No. 2607 (4-8-4) class A, 93

Northern type. See 4-8-4 Northern type locomotives

official weight, 87

oil-burning locomotives, 148, 179

Old Ironsides, 9

Overland types. See 4-10-2 Southern Pacific type locomotives

Pacific type. See 4-6-2 Pacific type locomotives

passenger locomotives, 2, 41, 42, 59, 60; first in America, 8; maximum power speeds, 46

passenger miles, between 1900 and 1920, 60

pedestal tender, 182–83

Pennsylvania Railroad: 0-6-0 switchers, 38; 4-4-0 L, P, D, and DD1 class designations, 25, 26, 27; 2-8-8-0 locomotives, 56; 2-10-4 class J1 locomotives, 123, 124; "big engine" (6-4-4-6) class S1, 156, 157; corporate culture, 64, 155–56; duplex locomotives, 156–60; Juniata shops, 56, 70, 124, 156; K4 Pacifics, 62–64, 62, 63, 154–55; Mussolini (super Pacific), 154; steam turbine locomotives, 159, 160–61. See also Pennsylvania Railroad, locomotives

————locomotives: No. 2082 (4-4-0) D16sb, 26; No. 4306 (2-10-0) class I1, 40; No. 5352 (4-6-2) class K4s, 63; No. 5399 (4-6-2) class K4s, 152; No. 5421 (4-6-2) class K4s, 63; No. 5485 (4-6-2) class K4s, 62; No. 5500 (4-4-4-4) class T1, 157; No. 6110 (4-4-4-4) class T1, 157; No. 6130 (4-6-4-4) class Q1, 158; No. 6176 (4-4-6-4) class Q2, 158; No. 6200 (6-8-6) class S-2, 159; No. 6412 (2-10-4) class J1, 123; No. 6487 (2-10-4) class J1, 123; No. 6496 (2-10-4) class J1, 123; No. 6739 (4-8-2) class M1b, 55; No. 6796 (4-8-2) class M1b, 54; No. 8026 switcher (0-6-0), 38

Pere Marquette Road, 117

performance ratios: Cole, 46, 86; H10 and A1 compared, 88

period of transition, 5–14, 169

Philadelphia, Germantown & Norris Railroad, 9, 15

physical modeling, 46

Pictorial History of Trains (Hamilton), 31

Pilcher, J. A., 135

pilot beams, 181, 187

pilots, 10, 16, 181

piston rods, 2, 179

piston strokes, 2

piston valves, 21, 22

pistons, 2, 179; efficiency using superheated steam, 34–35; speed limit, 153; strokes not synchronized, 2

Pittsburgh & Lake Erie Railroad, 119

Pittsburgh & West Virginia Railroad, 106

Pittsburgh Works, 25

Planet, 8

Plant System, 72

Player, John, 72

Pocono type locomotive, 94

pony truck, 3

poppet valves, 116, 152, 153–55, 159, 181; rotary cams, 166

Portland Works, 10

Potomac type locomotive, 94

power cylinders, 2, 176, 179; cast-steel, 86, 136; cycle of stationary engine, 5–6; indicated steam pressure, 43–45, 44; mean effective pressure, 44–45; performance graph, 97, 98

power reverse, 23

Puffing Billy, 6–7

pulling force, 42

radius rods, 23, 181

rail mileage in 1840, 9

Railroad Age Gazette, 146

Rankine, William J. M., 31–32

Rankine cycle, 32, 34, 35, 38

rated tractive effort. See tractive effort

reaction type turbine, 161

reciprocating engines, 153

Reid, W. L., 10

Rensselaer Polytechnic Institute, 31

reverse link, 21, 23, 181

reversing direction, 23

reversing wheel, 177

Rhode Island Locomotive Works, 14

Richard Norris & Son, 10

rigid-frame locomotives, compound designs, 70–73, 131

road-built locomotives, 108, 149

Roanoke Machine Works, 14, 135

Robert Stephenson & Company, 7

Rock Island Railroad: 4-8-4 locomotives class R67b, 92, 93–94

————locomotives: No. 5109 (4-8-4) class R67b, 92; No. 5117 (4-8-4) class R67b, 92

Rocket, 7
Rogers, Thomas, 10
Rogers Locomotive & Machine Company, 10
Rogers Works, 14, 15, 19
roller bearings, 73, 94–97, 180, 181; rolling resistance per ton, 95; slow acceptance by roads, 68, 94, 96
rolling dynamometers, 45
roundhouse, 188
rules of thumb, 28, 46
running gear, 176, 179–81
Russell, Frank, 146

safety valve domes, 176
safety valves, 2
sand domes, 2, 175
Santa Fe Railroad: 2-10-0 locomotives, 49; 2-10-4 class 5011, 120, 121; 4-6-2 locomotives, 60, 73; 4-6-4 locomotives, 114, 116; 4-8-4 locomotives, 112, 113, 114, 129; experimental articulated engines, 79; final steam locomotive order, 120
————locomotives: No. 2903 (4-8-4) class 2900, 113; No. 5028 (2-10-4), 120; No. 5035 (2-10-4), 121
Santa Fe type. *See* 2-10-2 Santa Fe type locomotives
saturated steam: efficiency and boiler pressure, 36; thermal energy of, 35
Saunders, Stuart, 164
Schaefer, Hugo, 146
Schenectady Works, 14
Scott, W. R., 146
Scullin disk drivers, 115, 180
Seaboard Air Line, No. 2502 (2-6-6-4) R1, 106
second-generation locomotives, 169–70; design goals, 42, 98; rigid-frame, 47–49
Seguin, Marc, 7
service and repair facilities, 185–87; government regulations, 186
Shay engines, 14
side rods, 2; tandem, 86
simple articulated engines, 56–57, 104, 106–108
simple engines, 23
skyline casings, 127
slide valves, 18, 21, 22
Sloan, Matthew, 30
Smeaton, John, 6
Smith, Robert, 164
smoke ducts, 66
smoke lifters, 124, 127–29
smoke stacks, 124–25, 125, 175; capped, 16, 19, 127; cowling for, 116, 129; mechanical extensions, 113
smokebox doors, 175
smokeboxes, 2, 86, 124; features, 37, 174
Snyder, Herbert L., 83
South Carolina Railroad locomotives: *Best Friend of Charleston*, 9; *E. L. Miller*, 9; *West Point*, 9
Southern Pacific Railroad: 4-4-0 locomotives, 25, 26; 4-8-4 Golden State locomotives, 94, 108, 109, 127; 4-10-2 Southern Pacific types, 76; cab-forward locomotives, 145–48, 145, 147; *El Gobernador*, 145; No. 4294 cab-forward, 151. *See also* Southern Pacific Railroad, locomotives
————locomotives: No. 260 (4-4-0) E40, 26; No. 463 (2-6-0) M10, 39; No. 786 (2-8-2) Mikado Mk5, 37, 52; No. 2482 4-8-4 class P10, 127; No. 3500 (2-8-4), 102; No. 3906 (4-6-6-2) class AM2, 144; No. 4032 (2-8-8-2) class MC6, 144; No. 4133 (cab-forward) class AC6, 147; No. 4227 (cab-forward) class AC10,

147; No. 4253 (cab-forward) class AC11, 145; No. 4449 (4-8-4) class GS4, 109; No. 4458 (4-8-4) class GS5, 109
Southern Pacific type. *See* 4-10-2 Southern Pacific type locomotives
Southern Railway System: 4-6-2 passenger locomotives, 65–67, 65, 66; company culture, 67; No. 1401 (4-6-2) class Ps4, 67; tender-tractors, 80
————locomotives: No. 1380 (4-6-2) class Ps4, 66; No. 4537 (2-8-2) with tractor engine, 80; No. 4817 (2-8-2) heavy Mikado, 58; No. 6482 (4-6-2) class Ps4, 66; No. 6495 (4-8-4) class Ts1, 128; No. 6637 (2-8-2), 51; No. 6691 (4-6-2) class Ps4, 65
spark arresters, 175. *See also* smoke lifters
spool valves. *See* piston valves
stack extenders, 113, 129
Stanford, Leland, 145
stationary dynamometers, 45
stationary steam engines, 1, 4–6
staybolted type firebox, 75, 176
steam dome, 2, 175
steam epoch, periods of, 169–70
steam generation, 2, 33–38, 41; cycle power (equation), 43; at high speeds, 98; Rankine cycle, 32; thermodynamic process of, 32, 34
Steam Locomotive Boiler Regulations, 27
steam locomotives: engineering landmarks, 151; first American, 8; total number built, 169
steam turbine locomotives, 160–64, 162–63
steam turbines, 34, 36
Stephenson, George, 6, 7
Stephenson, Robert, 7
Stephenson valve gears, 21, 74, 181
Stevens, Andrew J., 145
Stevens, John, 8
Stillman, Howard, 146
Stockton & Darlington Railway, 7
Stoddard, George A., 145
stoker tunnel, 176, 177
stokers, mechanical, 178
stops, emergency, 23
Stourbridge Lion, 8, 11
super power locomotives, 93; design goals, 42, 98
superheated steam, 34–35; efficiency and boiler pressure, 36, 38, 41
superheater tubes, 175
superheaters, 34–35, 73, 174, 175–76; 4-4-0 modernization, 27
suspension, 49, 180–81; 4-4-0's three-point system, 15, 27; lever control, 133
sweating on driver tires, 180
switching engines, 187; driver diameter, 2; examples, 20, 38, 39, 70, 94

Table of Locomotive Ratios (Cole), 46
tallow pot, 95
tandem compound locomotives, 72–73
Taunton Works, 10
ten wheeler type. *See* 4-6-0 ten wheeler locomotives
tenders, 3, 182–84; booster engines, 45, 75; loading, 183–84; with tractor engines, 79, 80; Vanderbilt tenders, 40
Tennessee, Alabama & Georgia Railroad locomotives, No. 350 (2-8-2), 51
Tennessee Central Railroad locomotives, No. 501, 18
Texas & Pacific Railroad, 89–91, 90

————locomotives: No. 605 (2-10-4) class I1, 90; No. 610 (2-10-4) locomotive, 151; No. 630 (2-10-4) class I1b, 90

Texas type. *See* 2-10-4 Texas type locomotives

thermal diffusivity, 98

thermal efficiency (equation), 35. *See also* Rankine cycle; steam generation

thermic syphons, 89, 179

third-generation locomotives, 170

throttle lever, 177

throttle valves, 175

Timken Roller Bearing Company, 94–97

Tom Thumb, 8

tonnage capability, 97–98, 97

Townsend, Bert, 166

tracks, 6, 27, 41; wooden rails, 11

tractive effort, 41–42

tractive force, 97, 98

tractor engines, 79, 80

trailing trucks, 3, 19, 89

trailing wheels, 47, 179

Trains, 73, 161

transfer tables, 188

transits, 13

Trevithick, Richard, 6

triplex compound locomotives, 79

tube sheet, 175

turbine locomotives, 160–64

turntables, 188

The Twentieth Century Limited (NYC), 62

Uncle Sam's Locomotives (Huddleston), 57

Union Pacific Railroad: 4-4-0 design specs, 15, 19; 4-8-4 locomotives, 112, 113, 114; 4-10-2 Southern Pacific types, 76; 4-6-6-4 locomotives, 106–108, 108, 131–32; 4-8-8-4 Big Boys, 129, 130, 132–35, 132

————locomotives: No. 809 (4-8-4), 113; No. 841 (4-8-4), 113; No. 3902 (4-6-6-4), 108; No. 3949 (4-6-6-4), 108; No. 4017 (4-8-8-4) Big Boy, 130; No. 4021 (4-8-8-4) Big Boy, 130; No. 4023 (4-8-8-4) Big Boy, 132

Union Railroad locomotives, No. 300 switcher (0-10-2), 70

U.S. Military Academy, 31

U.S. Railroad Administration: 2-8-8-2 designs, 136; designs of USRA, 58, 59, 182; forced standardization, 57, 60, 135; Pacific designs, 64, 64, 65

valve gears, 2, 21–23, 181; Caprotti, 68, 154–55; Franklin, 154, 159; functional components, 21, 23; maximizing performance, 153–54; "monkey motion" of, 21; popular designs, 21; setting on rebuilt engines, 30–31; Walschaerts, 21, 159, 181

Van Sweringen–controlled roads, 117, 141–42

Vanderbilt tenders, 40, 182

Vauclain, Samuel M., 70, 79

Vauclain compound engines, 71, 72

Virginian Railway, 117; 2-6-6-6 Blue Ridge locomotives, 142, 143, 144; 2-8-8-8-4 articulated, 80

————locomotives: No. 700 (2-8-8-8-4) articulated, 79, 80; No. 906 (2-6-6-6) class BA, 143

Vogt, Axel S., 25

Wabash Railroad locomotives, No. 701 (4-6-4) class P1, 116

walking beam, 6

Wallis, J. T., 64

Walschaerts, Egide, 21

Walschaerts valve gear, 21, 159, 181

War Production Board, 112, 116, 124

war years: aftermath of, 164; increased rail traffic, 110; period features, 114

waste heat. *See* exhaust steam

water, loading of, 183

water tanks, auxiliary, 136, 141

water tube fireboxes, 75; Babcock & Wilcox design, 161; Brotan design, 76; Emerson type, 68, 69; slow acceptance by roads, 78

Watt, James, 6, 43

weight, official, 87

weight equalizers, 15. *See also* suspension

West Point Foundry, 9

Western & Atlantic Railroad locomotives, *General*, engine No. 3, 13

Western Maryland Railroad, 119

Western Pacific Railroad locomotives, No. 485 (4-8-4) GS2, 112

Western Railway of Alabama locomotives, No. 186 (4-8-2), 53, 176

Westinghouse Electric Corporation, 161

whale back tenders, 182

wheel arrangements, 2–3, 3

Wheeling & Lake Erie Railroad locomotives, No. 3968 switcher (0-6-0) class B5, 94

wheels. *See* drivers

Whyte, Frederic Methvane, 3

Whyte system, 3, 179

Willard, Daniel, 155

Winterrowd, W. H., 83

Woodard, William E., 154; death, 155; joins Lima Works, 83

Wooten firebox, 20, 73, 178

work: mechanical, 43; net, 35

working fluid, 33, 35, 43

Worthington feedwater heaters, 37, 58, 85

Wyoming type locomotive, 94

Yellowstone type. *See* 2-8-8-4 Yellowstone type locomotives

J. Parker Lamb has been photographing America's railroads since 1949 and writing about them since 1960. An early interest was the transition, during the 1950s, from steam to diesel power in the South, where he grew up. Since then his work has allowed him to travel extensively, recording the evolution of rail technology throughout the United States and Canada for a half-century. Lamb's photography has appeared in numerous magazines and scores of books. This is his fourth book. The previous three are *Classic Diesels of the South*; *Katy Diesels to the Gulf*; and *Steel Wheels Rolling*. After a 42-year career as a mechanical engineer, he is now retired in Austin, Texas.

CPSIA information can be obtained
at www.ICGtesting.com
Printed in the USA
LVOW05*2050080218
565807LV00029B/389/P

9 780253 342195

A Child's Book of Prayers

A Child's Book of Prayers

SELECTED BY LOUISE RAYMOND

ILLUSTRATED BY MASHA

RANDOM HOUSE · NEW YORK

Copyright, 1941, by Artists and Writers Guild, Inc.

Printed in the United States of America

Just for Today

Lord, for tomorrow and its needs,
    I do not pray:
Keep me, God, from stain of sin,
    Just for today;
Let me no wrong or idle word
    Unthinking say:
Set Thou a seal upon my lips,
    Just for today.

Let me both diligently work,
    And duly pray;
Let me be kind in word and deed,
    Just for today;
Let me in season, Lord, be grave,
    In season, gay;
Let me be faithful to Thy grace,
    Just for today.

In pain and sorrow's cleansing fires,
    Brief be my stay;
Oh bid me if today I die,
    Come home today;
So for tomorrow and its needs,
    I do not pray;
But keep me, guide me, love me, Lord,
    Just for today.

Sybil F. Partridge

The Lord's Prayer

Our Father, who art in heaven, Hallowed be thy Name, Thy kingdom come, Thy will be done, On earth as it is in heaven. Give us this day our daily bread, And forgive us our trespasses, As we forgive those who trespass against us. And lead us not into temptation, But deliver us from evil. For thine is the kingdom, and the power, and the glory, for ever and ever. Amen.

Here I Lay Me

Here I lay me down to sleep.
I pray the Lord my soul to keep;
And if I die before I wake,
I pray the Lord my soul to take.

There are four corners on my bed,
There are four angels at my head.
Matthew, Mark, Luke and John,
Bless the bed that I lie on.

Little Jesus

Ex ore infantium, Deus, et lactentium perfecisti laudem

Little Jesus, wast Thou shy
Once, and just so small as I?
And what did it feel like to be
Out of Heaven, and just like me?
Didst Thou sometimes think of *there,*
And ask where all the angels were?
I should think that I would cry
For my house all made of sky;
I would look about the air,
And wonder where my angels were;
And at waking 'twould distress me—
Not an angel there to dress me!
Hadst Thou ever any toys,
Like us little girls and boys?
And didst Thou play in Heaven with all
The angels that were not too tall,
With stars for marbles? Did the things
Play *Can you see me?* through their wings?
And did Thy Mother let Thee spoil
Thy robes, with playing on *our* soil?
How nice to have them always new
In Heaven, because 'twas quite clean blue!

Didst Thou kneel at night to pray,
And didst Thou join Thy hands, this way?
And did they tire sometimes, being young,
And make the prayer seem very long?

And dost Thou like it best, that we
Should join our hands to pray to Thee?
I used to think, before I knew,
The prayer not said unless we do.
And did Thy Mother at the night
Kiss Thee, and fold the clothes in right?
And didst Thou feel quite good in bed,
Kissed, and sweet, and Thy prayers said?

Thou canst not have forgotten all
That it feels like to be small:
And thou know'st I cannot pray
To Thee in my father's way—
When Thou wast so little, say,
Couldst Thou talk Thy Father's way?

So, a little Child, come down
And hear a child's tongue like Thy own;
Take me by the hand and walk,
And listen to my baby-talk.
To Thy Father show my prayer
(He will look, Thou art so fair),
And say: "O Father, I, Thy Son,
Bring the prayer of a little one."

And He will smile, that children's tongue
Has not changed since Thou wast young!

Francis Thompson

Cradle Hymn   Away in a manger, no crib for a bed,
The little Lord Jesus laid down his sweet head.

The stars in the bright sky looked down where he lay—
The little Lord Jesus asleep on the hay.

The cattle are lowing, the baby awakes,
But little Lord Jesus no crying he makes.
I love Thee, Lord Jesus! Look down from the sky,
And stay by my cradle till morning is nigh.

Be near me, Lord Jesus, I ask Thee to stay
Close by me forever, and love me, I pray.
Bless all the dear children, in Thy tender care,
And take us to heaven, to live with Thee there.

Martin Luther

A Prayer for a Birthday

O Jesus, shed Thy tender love
    Upon me, please, today.
On this my birthday give me grace
    My special prayer to say.

Few are my candles, few my years;
    So let my promise be
That all the years that I may live
    I'll love and worship Thee.

A Child's Grace

Thank you for the world so sweet,
Thank you for the food we eat,
Thank you for the birds that sing,
Thank you, God, for everything.

Mrs. E. R. Leatham

Father, We Thank Thee

For flowers that bloom about our feet,
    Father, we thank Thee,
For tender grass so fresh and sweet,
    Father, we thank Thee,
For song of bird and hum of bee,
For all things fair we hear or see,
Father in heaven, we thank Thee.

For blue of stream and blue of sky,
    Father, we thank Thee,
For pleasant shade of branches high,
    Father, we thank Thee,
For fragrant air and cooling breeze,
For beauty of the blooming trees,
Father in heaven, we thank Thee.

For this new morning with its light,
    Father, we thank Thee,
For rest and shelter of the night,
    Father, we thank Thee,
For health and food, for love and friends,
For everything thy goodness sends,
Father in heaven, we thank Thee.

Ralph Waldo Emerson

22

Now the Day Is Over

Now the day is over,
    Night is drawing nigh,
Shadows of the evening
    Steal across the sky;

Jesus, give the weary
    Calm and sweet repose;
With thy tenderest blessing
    May our eyelids close.

Grant to little children
    Visions bright of thee;
Guard the sailors tossing
    On the deep, blue sea.

Comfort every sufferer
    Watching late in pain;
Those who plan some evil
    From their sins restrain.

Through the long night watches,
    May thine angels spread
Their white wings above me,
    Watching round my bed.

When the morning wakens,
    Then may I arise
Pure, and fresh, and sinless
    In thy holy eyes.

                        Amen.

Sabine Baring-Gould

Jesus, Tender Shepherd

Jesus, tender Shepherd, hear me;
  Bless thy little lamb tonight;
Through the darkness be Thou near me,
  Keep me safe till morning light.

All this day thy hand has led me,
  And I thank thee for thy care;
Thou has warmed me, clothed and fed me;
  Listen to my evening prayer!

Let my sins be all forgiven;
  Bless the friends I love so well:
Take us all at last to heaven,
  Happy there with thee to dwell.

Mary Duncan

A Child's Grace

Here a little child I stand
Heaving up my either hand;
Cold as paddocks though they be,
Here I lift them up to Thee,
For a benison to fall
On our meat and on us all.
                    Amen.

Robert Herrick

The Infant's Grace Before and After Meat

Bless me, O Lord, and let my food strengthen me to serve Thee, for Jesus Christ's sake. Amen.

(From "The New England Primer," 1785-1790)

31

Prayer on Christmas

O gentle baby Jesus,
    In the manger lying,
Dost Thou know that round thy head
    The children's prayers are flying?

Come is the blessed season
    Everyone is keeping;
All the children north and south
    Pray to Jesus, sleeping.

O gentle baby Jesus,
    In the manger lying,
Dost thou know that round thy head
    The children's prayers are flying?

"Oh Jesus, let me follow
    Thy way of selfless giving;
Take my hand to lead me on
    Thy road of gentle living."

33

O gentle baby Jesus,
    In the manger lying,
Dost thou know that round thy head
    The children's prayers are flying?

Praise God, from whom all blessings flow,
Praise him, all creatures here below;
Praise him, all ye heavenly host,
Praise Father, Son, and Holy Ghost.
                                    Amen.

"*He prayeth well, who loveth well*
Both man and bird and beast.

"*He prayeth best, who loveth best*
All things both great and small;
For the dear God who loveth us,
He made and loveth all."

Samuel Taylor Coleridge

Grateful acknowledgment is made to Charles Scribner's Sons for permission to reprint in this book "Little Jesus," by Francis Thompson

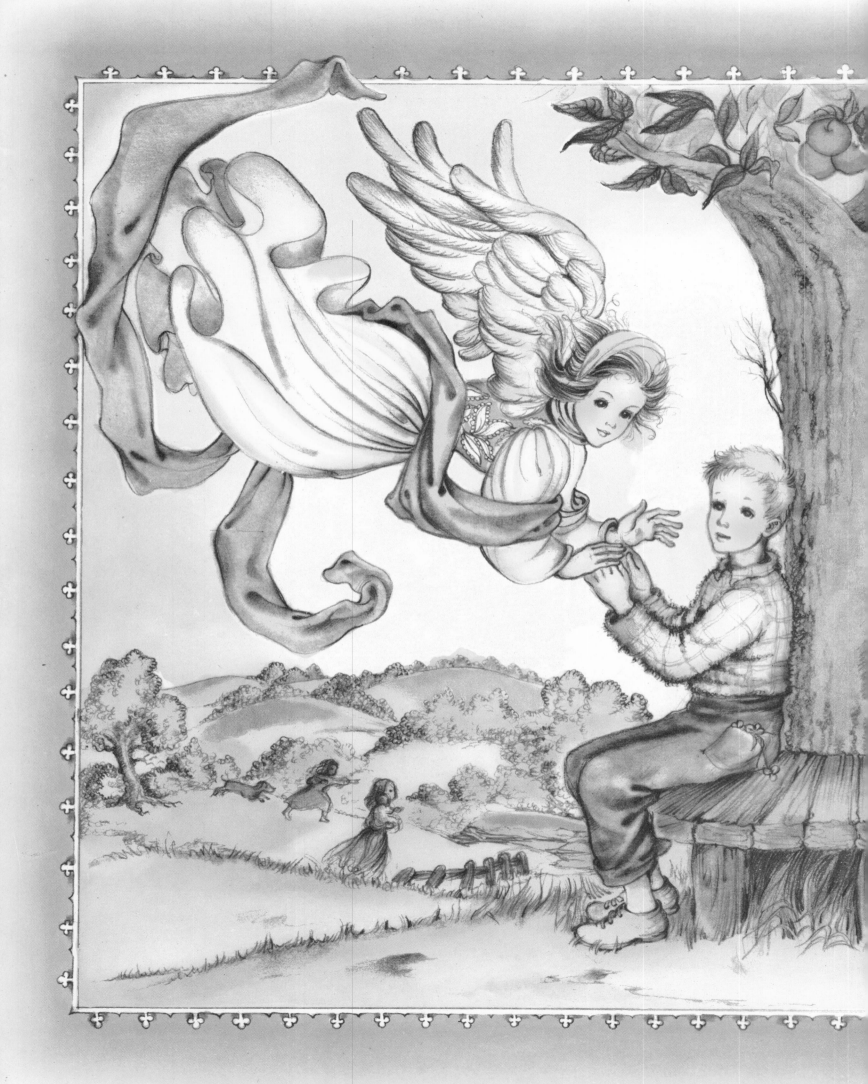